Publications of the John Gower Society

III

Gower's Confessio Amantis
A CRITICAL ANTHOLOGY

This collection gathers in one place the essays that have done most
to shape the modern critical discussion of the *Confessio Amantis*,
and illustrates, by the choice of the landmarks of Gower criticism,
how the study of the poem has evolved. It also provides representative examples of major approaches to the poem and selected
studies of its most important aspects, and it includes translations of
two essential essays available hitherto only in German.

The essays span nearly three-quarters of a century, and offer a
diversity of views on both major and minor aspects of Gower's
poem. Together, however, they provide a valuable indication of
precisely what kinds of challenges the *Confessio Amantis* has posed
for modern readers: defining the basis for its coherence, identifying
its doctrine, relating its doctrine to its design, and assessing both its
moral and its literary qualities. They will provide the groundwork
for all future study of the *Confessio*.

Publications of the John Gower Society

General editors   R. F. Yeager and A. J. Minnis
ISSN 0954–2817

I

A Concordance to John Gower's *Confessio Amantis*
edited by J. D. Pickles and J. L. Dawson

II

John Gower's Poetic: The Search for a New Arion
R. F. Yeager

GOWER'S CONFESSIO AMANTIS

A CRITICAL ANTHOLOGY

EDITED BY

PETER NICHOLSON

D. S. BREWER

This collection first published 1991 by D. S. Brewer, Cambridge

D. S. Brewer is an imprint of Boydell & Brewer Ltd
PO Box 9, Woodbridge, Suffolk IP12 3DF
and of Boydell & Brewer Inc.
PO Box 41026, Rochester, NY 14604, USA

ISBN 0 85991 318 X

British Library Cataloguing-in-Publication Data
Gower's 'Confessio Amantis': A critical anthology.
– (Publications of the John Gower Society)
I. Nicholson, Peter II. Series
821
ISBN 0–85991–318–X

Library of Congress Cataloging-in-Publication Data
Gower's Confessio amantis : a critical anthology / edited by Peter
Nicholson.
      p.   cm. – (Publications of the John Gower Society ; 3)
Includes bibliographical references.
ISBN 0–85991–318–X (alk. paper)
  1. Gower, John, 1325?–1408. Confessio amantis. I. Nicholson,
Peter, 1948– . II. Series.
PR1984.C63G58   1991
821'.1–dc20   91–15424

The paper used in this publication meets the minimum requirements
of American National Standard for Information Sciences –
Permanence of Paper for Printed Library Materials, ANSI Z39.48–1984

Printed in Great Britain by
St Edmundsbury Press Ltd, Bury St Edmunds, Suffolk

ACKNOWLEDGEMENTS

The *Confessio Amantis* G. C. *Macaulay*

From *The Cambridge History of English Literature*, vol. II, *The End of the Middle Ages*, ed. A. W. Ward and A. R. Waller (Cambridge: University Press, 1908), pp. 166–76. Reprinted with permission.

Gower C. S. *Lewis*

Reprinted from *The Allegory of Love* by C. S. Lewis (1936), pp. 198–222, by permission of Oxford University Press.

John Gower in His Most Significant Role George R. *Coffman*

From *Elizabethan Studies in Honor of George F. Reynolds*, University of Colorado Studies, Series B, vol. 2, no. 4 (Boulder, Colorado, 1945), pp. 52–61. Reprinted by permission of the University Press of Colorado.

Gower's 'Honeste Love' J. A. W. *Bennett*

From *Patterns of Love and Courtesy: Essays in Memory of C. S. Lewis*, ed. John Lawlor (London: Edward Arnold, 1966), pp. 107–21. Used with permission.

Gower's Narrative Art Derek *Pearsall*

Reprinted by permission of the Modern Language Association of America from *PMLA*, 81 (1966), 475–84.

John Gower's Narrative Art Arno *Esch*

A translation of 'John Gowers Erzählkunst,' from *Chaucer und seine Zeit: Symposion für Walter F. Schirmer*, ed. Arno Esch (Tübingen: Niemeyer, 1968), pp. 207–39. Translated with permission of Max Niemeyer Verlag.

The Character Genius in Alan de Lille, Jean de Meun, and John Gower George D. *Economou*

Chaucer Review, 4 (1970), 203–10. Copyright 1970 by the Pennsylvania State University. Reproduced by permission of The Pennsylvania State University Press.

Rhetoric and Fiction: Gower's Comments on Eloquence and Courtly Poetry Götz *Schmitz*

Revised and translated by the author from chapter three, 'Rhetorik und Poetik: Gowers Äusserungen zur Rede- und Dichtkunst,' of *The Middel Weie: Stil- und Aufbauformen in John Gowers "Confessio Amantis"*, Studien zur Englischen Literatur, Band 11 (Bonn: Bouvier, 1974), pp. 27–54. Used with permission of Bouvier Verlag.

The Priesthood of Genius: A Study of the Medieval Tradition
  Denise N. Baker

Speculum, 51 (1976), 277–91. Reprinted by permission of the Medieval Academy of America.

John Gower, *Sapiens* in Ethics and Politics   *A. J. Minnis*

Medium Ævum, 49 (1980), 207–29. Reprinted by permission of the Society for the Study of Mediaeval Languages and Literature.

Natural Law and John Gower's *Confessio Amantis*   *Kurt Olsson*

Medievalia et Humanistica: Studies in Medieval and Renaissance Culture, New Series, 11 (1982), 229–61. Reprinted with permission.

CONTENTS

INTRODUCTION

There are several reasons for offering a collection of this sort: to gather in one place the essays that have done most to shape the modern critical discussion of the *Confessio Amantis*; to illustrate, by the choice of the landmarks of Gower criticism, how the study of the poem has evolved; and to provide representative examples of major approaches to the poem and selected studies of its most important aspects. These goals are not necessarily compatible in each case, but all have been present in some degree during the compilation of this volume. Thus some of the earlier selections are of more historical interest, while some of the later are offered more as samples of the different types of work on the poem that have occurred in the last twenty-five years. If this volume has any coherency, it is as a record of our attempt better to understand Gower's poem, and it is hoped that as such, it will provide an introduction both to the *Confessio Amantis* and to its most important criticism.

The essays that have been chosen all bear on the interpretation of the *Confessio* in the most general sense; thus a great many excellent but more specialized studies have been excluded. The cut-off date was 1983: the appearance in that year of another collection entitled *Gower's Confessio Amantis: Responses and Reassessments*, edited by A.J. Minnis, marked the beginning of an important new phase in the study of the poem, and if there were no restriction of time virtually all of the essays included there would qualify for reprinting here. Obviously not everything of importance from before 1983 could be included. Except for the selection by Götz Schmitz, for instance, which was chosen because of the opportunity to make available in English an important but neglected work, none of the major book-length studies of the poem is represented, in part because of the difficulty of excerpt, in part because it was felt that they would already be sufficiently accessible to most readers. These are listed in the "Suggestions for Further Reading" at the end of this volume, along with some other important essays (some of them later than 1983) that either complement or extend the studies that are included here or that might have been selected for inclusion in their own right.

The first selection is an excerpt from the chapter on Gower in the *Cambridge History of English Literature* by G. C. Macaulay, the editor of the collected edition of Gower's works which has remained the basis for all study of the *Confessio* since its appearance in 1899–1902. Macaulay offers here a view of the *Confessio* which he also expressed, somewhat more warmly, in the introductory remarks in his edition, and which thus provided several generations of readers with their first critical orientation to the poem. For Macaulay, the work is most important as a collection of tales. He has little good to say about its other contents: he dismisses the Prologue, for instance, and is impatient with the poem's many "digressions" and with the difficulties posed by the role of Genius. But he praises Gower highly

1

as a storyteller, and his most important critical legacy is his account of the clarity, the correctness, the graciousness, and the occasional picturesqueness of a poet who is perhaps best appreciated in excerpt.

Macaulay's view provides the context for C. S. Lewis' remarks in *The Allegory of Love*. Lewis begins with an attempt to view the poem as a whole. Using the *Romance of the Rose* rather than other tale collections as a model, he defends the attempt to treat love and morality together and praises Gower for the success with which he has made the diversity of his material cohere. Though he insists that the tales are not the "sole end and aim of the poem," he is as appreciative as Macaulay of the qualities that make them worth rereading. The sensitivity of his judgment extends to other parts of the poem as well, and is perhaps best revealed in his discussion of the conclusion. Dismissed by earlier readers as the worst product of Gower's attempt to impose a moral framework on his treatment of love, for Lewis it is the moving culmination of the plot concerning the aging and coming to reason of the lover.

A radically different view of the poem is offered in the essay that follows. For Coffman, Gower's "most significant role" is neither as a storyteller nor as a poet of love but as an advocate of reason and moral responsibility. His is very close to the view of the poem that was later adopted by John Hurt Fisher, in his landmark work on *John Gower: Moral Philosopher and Friend of Chaucer* (1964). Coffman describes the *Confessio Amantis* as Gower's *summa moralis*, the culmination of his attempt to preach to his countrymen on their moral and social duties, the unity of which derives entirely from the coherence of its ethical scheme. The treatment of love, in this view, is entirely subordinate to Gower's broader ethical plan, and Gower's poetry is less significant than his philosophy.

Bennett's essay takes a different approach to the combination of love and morality in the poem. In response to Fisher, Bennett reestablishes love as its central subject, but in response to Lewis, he gives a very different assessment of its doctrine, and he offers a new attempt to embrace all of the elements of the *Confessio* within a single harmonious vision. Bennett touches lightly on a great many aspects of the poem in his essay, but his central argument is of great importance to all later discussions of the *Confessio*. He demonstrates that the Christian and "courtly" elements of the poem are thoroughly interfused, that Gower's highest ideal of love, both as a moralist and as a poet of *courtoisie*, has its proper culmination in a chaste marriage, and that such a love is compatible both with *caritas* and with the social ideals that Gower expresses in his Prologue and epilogue, and thus serves to bind the *Confessio* into a whole.

The next two essays return us to the study of the tales, but from a rather different perspective, and offer varying but complementary views of Gower's "narrative art." Pearsall emphasizes the importance of the tales as the most complete realization of the central values of the poem. The poet's "doctrine," he asserts, goes beyond what could be expressed in mere expository fashion; and it is in fiction, particularly in tales about love, that Gower's moral preoccupations find their most effective expression. Focusing on Gower's alterations of his sources, particularly of Ovid, Pearsall identifies Gower's humane and sentimental response to the moral and emotional predicaments of his characters as the most characteristic aspect of his storytelling. Esch echoes Pearsall both on Gower's moral insight and on the persuasiveness of his treatment of motive and character, but he directs attention to Gower's "art" in another sense. Offering a very close reading of three different tales, he credits the poet with a skillful and subtle use of imagery and gesture, of point of view, of suspense, and of parallelism; and he emphasizes the restraint and economy of means with which Gower creates his effects, attributing to him a preciseness of purpose which allows us to value his tales even when his purposes are very different from Chaucer's.

Economou and Baker approach the *Confessio* by way of the allegorical figures of the frame. Gower's use of Genius, Venus, and Cupid and his repeated allusions to Nature and to Reason are indications of his debt to the tradition of writers that includes Bernardus Silvestris, Alain de Lille, and Jean de Meun. Economou's essay is a particularly clear statement of the relations among these poets. By placing Gower within this tradition, he establishes that Gower's praise of marriage is by no means exceptional, and that his allegorical apparatus is an important guide to his attitude towards love. He concludes that in advocating "honeste love," Gower restored the harmony among Venus, Nature, and Reason that had been established by Alain de Lille but broken, in adopting the figures for a different purpose, by Jean de Meun. Baker offers some important modifications of Economou's view. She sees Gower's Venus as an embodiment of "natural sexuality divorced from Reason," not as a disciple of Nature and Reason as Economou does. She thus defines Genius' role in more traditional terms, serving two masters with incompatible aims, and she returns to the sources for an explanation of his "dual ministry." Her argument takes her by a circuitous route: she describes the sources for Alain de Lille's Genius; she notes how Jean de Meun transformed Alain's true priest into a false one; and she describes how Gower abandoned Genius' procreative function to focus entirely on the problem of a true or false priesthood that he found in his sources, thus accounting for Genius' dual role. Baker concludes with a reading of Book III of the *Confessio* as an illustration of how Gower uses Genius to develop his argument on the relation between natural law and reason.

The three remaining essays all, like Baker's, confront directly the seriousness of moral purpose of the poem, and offer new perspectives on both its design and its meaning. Schmitz studies Gower's use of language in relation to the moral purpose of his work as a whole. He demonstrates that Gower's "plain" style, so highly praised by Lewis and others, was not only consciously chosen but a reflection of a novel view of rhetoric which defines the use of language as a moral issue. Studying the comments on language that Gower intersperses throughout his poem, he finds that the poet consistently emphasizes the need for a correspondence between word and truth and between word and deed. Gower thus exhalts clarity and simplicity over eloquence and ornateness, reversing the traditional values of medieval rhetoric, and he repeatedly associates manipulation of language with guile, deceit, and fraud. Schmitz concludes by describing how this attitude towards language is related to the broader moral themes of the poem, and how it is manifested in such things as the relation between Amans and his confessor.

3

Minnis revives the picture of Gower as a learned moralist: identifying him as a *sapiens*, a "wise man" or "sage," a term he derives from medieval scholastic writing, he investigates the background of medieval literary theory that would have provided Gower with his conception of the structure of his poem, and suggests a number of important new models for Gower's design. Instead of collections of exempla, for instance, he offers medieval versions of Ovid's works with their extensive commentaries as a better model for Gower's handling of his tales. In other scholastic sources, he finds precedents for the two different "prologues" with which Gower begins his work, and for his inclusion of a discussion of politics within his general treatment of ethics, in Book 7. By demonstrating Gower's familiarity with this material, he also proves his main point, that from a medieval perspective the diverse materials of the *Confessio* are all of a piece and are all directed towards a single goal.

Olsson, finally, offers a comprehensive study of the question of nature and natural law in the poem, looking not merely at the allegorical figures but also at the many references to "kynde" in the tales and in Genius' lessons. He first distinguishes five different senses of "natural law," providing the background in medieval Latin writing and discussing some of the problems that arise in applying the various senses to human conduct. He then examines the development of the poem as a whole in order to demonstrate his proposition that the *Confessio* is conceived as a sustained argument on the meaning of "natural law," proceeding from the lowest sense, the "animalic" law of nature, to the highest sense, the law of "natural reason," or in Olsson's words, from what binds man to what frees.

These essays span nearly three-quarters of a century, and they obviously offer a diversity of views on both major and minor aspects of Gower's poem. Together, however, they provide a valuable indication of precisely what kinds of challenges the *Confessio Amantis* has posed for modern readers: defining the basis for its coherency, identifying its doctrine, relating its doctrine to its design, and assessing both its moral and its literary qualities together. For all their disagreement, they reflect a consistency of approach in their attempt both to understand the poem on its own terms and to find the proper models by which Gower's accomplishment is to be measured, and they provide the groundwork for all future study of the *Confessio*.

Except, of course, for the translations that have been specially commissioned for this volume, these essays are reprinted as they originally appeared; in some cases we have even reproduced the original typography. Macaulay's essay is an excerpt from a longer chapter, and Schmitz has taken the liberty of revising and expanding his essay is the course of translating it into English. In the rest, the only changes are the correction of some obvious errors, and no attempt has been made to regularize such things as the way in which quotations from the poem are presented and cited.

I wish to express my gratitude to the authors, editors, and publishers who have given their permission to use these essays here. Special thanks go to George Economou, Denise Baker, and Kurt Olsson for their help in obtaining permission to reprint their work; to Linda Barney Burke, who volunteered to do the translation of the essay by Arno Esch; and to Götz Schmitz, who secured permission both for his essay and for Esch's, who did the translation of his own essay for this volume, and who reviewed the translation of Esch's piece. I also wish to thank Alastair Minnis, Derek Pearsall, Linda Burke, Russell Peck and others who were present at the meeting of the John Gower Society at Kalamazoo on May 4, 1989, when the idea for this collection was hatched, and who offered their suggestions on its contents, and Robert F. Yeager, who gave helpful advice at an early stage of planning. Finally, I must thank Richard W. Barber of Boydell & Brewer, whose willingness to help and to deal with the dozens of details involved in the production of a book of this sort made the appearance of this volume possible.

Peter Nicholson
Honolulu
August, 1990

THE *CONFESSIO AMANTIS*

G. C. MACAULAY

As regards the motives which determined Gower to the composition of a book in English, we have his own statement in the first edition of the book itself, that, on a certain occasion, when he was in a boat upon the Thames near London, he met the royal barge, and was invited by the king to enter it ; that, in the conversation which ensued, it was suggested to him that he should write some new book, to be presented to the king ; and that he thereupon adopted the resolution of composing a poem in English, which should combine pleasure and instruction, upon the subject of love.

It is not necessary, however, to assume that this incident, which was put forward by the author as a reason for the presentation of his book to Richard, was actually the determining factor of his decision to write in English. The years which followed the composition of *Vox Clamantis*, assuming it to have been produced about 1382, were a period of hitherto unexampled productiveness in English poetry. Chaucer, at this time, had attained almost to the full measure of his powers, and the successive production of *Troilus and Criseyde*, partly addressed to Gower himself, about 1383, and of *The Legend of Good Women*, about 1386, must have supplied a stimulus of the very strongest kind, not only by way of recommending the use of the English language, but also in suggesting some modification of the strictly didactic tone which Gower had hitherto taken in his larger works. The statement that to Gower's *Confessio Amantis* Chaucer owed the idea of a connected series of tales is quite without foundation. *The Legend of Good Women* certainly preceded *Confessio Amantis*, which bears distinct marks of its influence, and in *The Legend of Good Women* we have already a series of tales set in a certain framework, though the framework is slight, and no conversation connects the tales. Even if we suppose Chaucer to have been unacquainted with Boccaccio's prose, a supposition for which there is certainly some ground, he was fully capable of evolving the scheme of *The Canterbury Tales* without the assistance of Gower. On the other hand the influence of Chaucer must certainly have been very strong in regard to Gower's English work, which was probably composed in the years between 1386 and 1390, the latter year being the date of the completion of the first edition of the poem.

6

The most noteworthy point of *Confessio Amantis*, as compared with Gower's former works, is the partial renunciation by the author of his didactic purpose. He does, indeed, indulge himself in a prologue, in which he reviews the condition of the human race; but, at the beginning of the first book, he announces the discovery that his powers are not equal to the task of setting the world to rights:

> It stant noght in my sufficance
> So grete thinges to compasse,
> Bot I mot lete it overpasse
> And treten upon other thinges.

He avows, therefore, that, from this day forth, he intends to change the style of his writings, and to deal with a subject which is of universal interest, namely love. At the same time, he will not wholly renounce his function of teaching, for love is a matter in which men need very much guidance, but, at least, he will treat of the subject in such a way as to entertain as well as instruct: the book is to be

> betwen the tweie,
> Somwhat of lust, somwhat of lore.

Hence, though the form may suggest instruction, yet the mode of treatment is to be popular, that is to say, the work is to consist largely of stories. Accordingly, we have in *Confessio Amantis* more than a hundred stories of varying length and of every kind of origin, told in a simple and pleasing style by one who clearly had a gift for story-telling, though without the dramatic humour which makes Chaucer's stories unique in the literature of his time. The framework, too, in which these stories are set, is pleasing.

The Lover, that is to say the author himself, is one who has been long in the service of love, but without reward, and is now of years which almost unfit him for such service. Wandering forth into a wood in the month of May he feels despair and wishes for death. The god and the goddess of love appear to him; but the god passes him by with an angry look, casting, at the same time, a fiery lance which pierces his heart. The goddess remains, and to her he makes his complaint that he has served long and received no wages. She frowns upon him, and desires to know what service it is that he has done, and what malady oppresses him. He professes readiness to reply, but she enjoins upon him first a confession to be made to her priest Genius, who, if he is satisfied, will give him absolution, and she will then consider his case. Accordingly, Genius is summoned and Venus disappears. The Lover, after some preliminary conversation, is examined with regard to his sins against love, the examination being arranged under the usual heading of the seven deadly sins and their subordinate vices. The subdivision which we find in the earlier books of *Confessio Amantis* is the same as that which we have already encountered in Gower's *Mirour*: each sin is regarded as having five principal offshoots; but, in the latter half of the work, this regularity of subdivision is, to a great extent, abandoned. In the case of each of the subordinate vices the confessor sets forth the nature of the fault, and, at the request of the Lover, illustrates his meaning by a story or by a series of stories. In each case, after explanation of the nature of the vice, a special application is made to the case of love, and the stories illustrate either the general definition or this special application, or both, no very clear line being drawn in many cases between the two. The Lover, meanwhile, when he has at last been made to understand the nature of the fault generally and also its particular application to love, makes his confession or denial as regards his love, and is further instructed or rebuked by the confessor. By the general plan, one book should have been devoted to each of the seven principal sins, Pride, Envy, Anger, Sloth, Avarice, Gluttony and Lechery; but an additional book is interpolated between the last two, dealing with quite irrelevant matters, and, in general, there is much irregularity of plan in the last four books, by which the unity of construction is seriously marred. The ordinary conduct of the work may be illustrated by a short summary of the second book, the subject of which is Envy.

The first of the brood of Envy is Sorrow for another's joy. The Lover confesses that he is often guilty of this in regard to his rivals, and he is reproved by the tale of Acis and Galatea. He accepts the rebuke and promises to offend no more. The second vice under this head is Joy for another's grief. To this, too, the Lover pleads guilty, and the odious character of the vice is illustrated by the story of the traveller and the angel, in which one man preferred to lose an eye in order that his fellow might lose both. The third is Detraction, and here, too, the Lover admits that he has been in some measure guilty. When he sees lovers come about his mistress with false tales, he is sometimes moved to tell her the worst that he knows of them. The confessor reproves him. By the Lover's own account, his lady is wise and wary, and there is no need to tell her these tales: moreover, she will like him the less for being envious. The vice of Detraction is then illustrated by the tale of Constance, who long suffered from envious backbiting, but whose love at length prevailed. Then, again, there is the story of Demetrius and Perseus, in which Perseus brought his brother to death by false accusations, but suffered punishment himself at last. The confessor passes then to the fourth vice, named False Semblant. When Envy desires to deceive, she employs False Semblant as her messenger. The Lover admits here, too, that he is guilty, but only in matters which concern his mistress. He thinks himself justified in gaining the confidence of her other lovers by an appearance of friendship, and using the knowledge which he thus obtains to hinder their designs. The confessor reproves him, and cites the case of the Lombards in the city, who feign that which is not, and take from Englishmen the profit of their own land. He then relates the tale of Hercules and Deianira, and how Nessus deceived her and destroyed him at last by False Semblant. Yet there is a fifth vice born of Envy, and that is Supplantation. The Lover declares that here he is guiltless in act, though guilty in his thought and desire. If he had the power, he would supplant others in the love of his lady. The confessor warns him that thought as well as act is sin, and convinces him of the heinousness of this particular crime by a series of short examples, Agamemnon and Achilles, Diomede and Troilus, Amphitryon and Geta, and also by the longer tale of the False Bachelor. This evil is worst when Pride and Envy are joined together, as when pope Celestine was supplanted by Boniface; and this tale also is told at length. The Lover, convinced of the evil of Envy, desires a remedy, and the confessor reminds him that vices are destroyed by their contraries, and the contrary to Envy is Charity. To illustrate this virtue the tale is told of Constantine, who, by showing mercy, obtained mercy. The Lover vows to eschew Envy, and asks that penance may be inflicted for that which he has done amiss.

In the other books, the scheme is somewhat similar, and, at length, in the eighth the confession is brought to a close, and the Lover demands his absolution. The confessor advises him to abandon love and to set himself under the rule of reason. He, strongly protesting, presents a petition to Venus, who, in answer, consents to relieve him, though perhaps not in the way that he desires. She speaks of his age and counsels him to make a *beau retret*, and he grows cold for sorrow of heart and lies swooning on the ground. Then he sees the god of love, and, with him, a great company of former lovers arrayed in sundry bands under the guidance of Youth and Eld. Youth takes no heed of him; but those who follow Eld entreat for him with Venus, and all the lovers press round to see. At length Cupid comes towards him and draws forth the fiery lance with which he had formerly pierced the Lover's heart; and Venus anoints the wound with a cooling ointment and gives him a mirror in which his features are reflected. Reason returns to him, and he becomes sober and sound. Venus, laughing, asks him what love is, and he replies with confusion that he knows not, and prays to be excused from attendance upon her. He obtains his absolution, and Venus bids him stay no more in her court, but go 'wher moral vertu dwelleth,' where the books are which men say that he has written; and so she bids him adieu and departs. He stands for a while amazed, and then takes his way softly homewards.

The plan of the work is not ill conceived; but, unfortunately, it is carried out without a due regard to proportion in its parts, and its unity is very seriously impaired by digressions which have nothing to do with the subject of the book. After the prologue, the first four books are conducted in a comparatively orderly manner, though the discussion on the lawfulness of war in the third can hardly be regarded as necessary, and the account of the discovery of useful arts in the fourth is too slightly connected with the subject. In the fifth book, however, a casual reference to Greek mythology is made the peg on which to hang a dissertation of twelve hundred lines on the religions of the world, while, in the sixth book, the discussion of Sorcery, with the stories first of Ulysses and Telegonus and then of Nectanabus, can hardly be regarded as a justifiable extension of the subject of Gluttony. Worse than this, the tale of Nectanabus is used as a pretext for bringing in as a diversion a summary of all earthly learning, the supposed instructions of Aristotle to Alexander, which fills up the whole of the seventh book[1]. The most important part of this is the treatise on Politics, under five heads, illustrated by many interesting stories, which occupies nearly four thousand lines. To this part of his work, which is absolutely irrelevant to the main subject, the author evidently attached great importance; and it is, in fact, another lecture aimed at the king, at whose suggestion the book was written, the author being unable to keep himself from improving the occasion. This proceeding, together with the great extension which has been given to Avarice in the fifth book, has the effect of almost entirely anticipating the proper contents of the eighth book. Nothing remains to be spoken of there except Incest, with reference to which the tale of Apollonius of Tyre is told, and this, after all, has no sufficient bearing upon the subject to

---

[1] The statement, often repeated, that Gower is largely indebted to the *Secretum Secretorum* in this seventh book is quite inaccurate; very little is, in fact, drawn from this source. The *Trésor* of Brunetto Latini is a much more important authority.

justify its inordinate length. It may justly be remarked, also, that the representation of the priest of Venus is full of absurd incongruities, which reach their climax, perhaps, when he is made to denounce Venus herself as a false goddess. In general, the characters of the moralist and of the high-priest of love are very awkwardly combined in his person, and of this fact the author shows himself conscious in several passages, as I, 237 ff. and VI, 2421 ff. The quasi-religious treatment of the subject was, no doubt, in accordance with the taste of the age, and there is a certain charm of quaintness both in this and in the gravity with which morality is applied to the case of love, though this application is often very forced. It must be admitted, also, that the general plan of the poem shows distinct originality, and, apart from the digressions and irrelevancies which have been noted, it is carried through with some success. The idea of combining a variety of stories in a single framework, with the object of illustrating moral truths, had become familiar in the literature of western Europe chiefly through a series of books which were all more or less of Oriental origin. Of these, the most important were the legend of Barlaam and Josaphat, the romance of the Seven Sages in its various forms and *Disciplina Clericalis*. With these, Gower, as we know, was acquainted, and also, doubtless, with various examples of the attempt to utilise such stories for definitely religious purposes in such edifying compositions as those of William of Wadington and Robert of Brunne. Moreover, Chaucer, in his *Legend of Good Women*, had already produced a series of stories in an allegorical framework, though the setting was rather slight and the work was left unfinished. The influence of Chaucer's work is apparent in the opening and concluding scenes of *Confessio Amantis*, and some suggestions were also derived from the *Roman de la Rose*, in which Genius is the priest of Nature, who makes her confession to him. But no previous writer, either in English or in any other modern language, had versified so large and various a collection of stories, or had devised so ingenious and elaborate a scheme of combination.

As regards the stories themselves, there is, of course, no pretence of originality in substance. They are taken from very various places, from Ovid (much the most frequent source), from the Bible, from Valerius Maximus, Statius, Benoit de Sainte More, Guido delle Colonne, Godfrey of Viterbo, Brunetto Latini, Nicholas Trivet, the *Roman des Sept Sages, Vita Barlaam et Josaphat, Historia Alexandri* and so on[1]. Gower's style of narration is

---

[1] Gower does not seem in any instance to have been indebted to *Gesta Romanorum*.

simple and clear; in telling a story he is neither tedious nor apt to digress. To find fault with him because he is lacking in humorous appreciation of character is to judge him by altogether too high a standard. He is not on a level with Chaucer, but he is distinctly above the level of most of the other story-tellers of his time, and it may even be said that he is sometimes superior to Chaucer himself in the arrangement of his incidents and in the steadiness with which he pursues the plot of his story. Gower is by no means a slavish follower of his authorities, the proportions and arrangement of his stories are usually his own, and they often show good judgment. Moreover, he not seldom gives a fresh turn to a well-known story, as in the Bible instances of Jephthah and Saul, or makes a pretty addition to it, as in the case of the tales from Ovid of Narcissus or of Acis and Galatea. His gift of clear and interesting narrative was, undoubtedly, the merit which most appealed to the popular taste of the day, and the plainness of the style was rather an advantage than a drawback.

The stories, however, have also poetical qualities. Force and picturesqueness cannot be denied to the story of Medea, with its description of the summer sun blazing down upon the glistening sea and upon the returning hero, and flashing from the golden fleece at his side a signal of success to Medea in her watch-tower, as she prays for her chosen knight. Still less can we refuse to recognise the poetical power of the later phases of the same story —first, the midnight rovings of Medea in search of enchantments (v, 3962 ff.), and again later, when the charms are set in action (4059 ff.), a passage of extraordinary picturesqueness. The tales of Mundus and Paulina and of Alboin and Rosemund, in the first book, are excellently told; and, in the second, the story of the False Bachelor and the legend of Constantine, in the latter of which the author has greatly improved upon his materials; while, in the third book, the tale of Canace is most pathetically rendered, far better than by Ovid. The fourth, which is altogether of special excellence, gives us Rosiphelee, Phyllis and the very poetically told tale of Ceix and Alceone; the fifth has Jason and Medea, a most admirable example of sustained narrative, the oriental story of Adrian and Bardus and the well-told romance of Tereus and Philomela. In the seventh, we find the Biblical story of Gideon well rendered, the rape of Lucrece and the tale of Virginia. The long story of Apollonius, in the eighth book, is not one of Gower's happiest efforts, though it is often taken as a sample of his style owing to the connection with Shakespeare's *Pericles*. His natural taste for simplicity sometimes stands him in good stead, as in the description of the tears of Lucrece for her husband, and the reviving beauty of her face when he appears (VII, 4830 ff.), a passage in which he may safely challenge comparison with Chaucer. The ease of his more colloquial utterances, and the finished style of some of the more formal passages, are equally remarkable. As examples of the second quality we may cite the reflections of the emperor Constantine (II, 3243 ff.), the letters of Canace (III, 279 ff.) and of Penelope (IV, 157 ff.), the prayer of Cephalus (IV, 3197 ff.) and the epitaphs of Iphis (IV, 3674) and of Thaise (VIII, 1533 ff.).

In addition to the merits of the stories we must acknowledge a certain attractiveness in the setting of them. The conversation which connects the stories is distinguished by colloquial ease, and is frequently of an interesting kind. The Lover often engages the sympathy of the reader, and there is another character always in the background in whom we may reasonably be interested, that of the lady whom he serves. Gower, who was quite capable of appreciating the delicacy and refinement which ideal love requires, has here set before us a figure which is both attractive and human, a charming embodiment of womanly grace and refinement.

Passing from the substance of the poem to the language and versification, we remark, first, that the language used is, practically, the same as that of Chaucer, and that there is every reason to attribute this identity to the development, apart from the individual influence of either poet, of a cultured form of English speech which, in the higher ranks of society, took the place of the French that had so long been used as the language of literature and of polite society. This is not the place to discuss the development of modern English literary speech ; what we have to say in relation to Gower is that, by the purity and simplicity of his style, he earned the right to stand beside Chaucer as a standard authority for this language. *Sui temporis lucerna habebatur ad docte scribendum in lingua vulgari*, as Bale remarks; and it is worth noting that, in the syntax of Ben Jonson's *English Grammar*, Gower is cited as an authority more often than any other writer. It may be observed that, by Morsbach's test of a comparison with contemporary London documents, both Chaucer and Gower are shown to be more conservative of the full forms of inflection than the popular speech, and Gower is, in this respect, apparently less modern than Chaucer. He adopted a system of spelling which is more careful and consistent than that of most other Middle English authors, and, in general, he seems to have been something of a purist in matters of language.

With regard to versification, the most marked feature of Gower's verse is its great regularity and the extent to which inflectional endings are utilised for metrical purposes. We have here what we might have expected from the author's French verse, very great syllabic accuracy and a very regular beat, an almost complete combination of the accentual with the syllabic principle. As an indication of the extent of this regularity, it may be mentioned that in the whole of *Confessio Amantis*, which contains more than thirty-three thousand four-accent lines, there are no examples of the omission, so frequent in Chaucer, of the first unaccented syllable. Displacement of the natural accent of words and the slurring over of light syllables are far less frequent with Gower than with Chaucer, and in purity of rime, also, he is somewhat more strict. The result of Gower's syllabic accuracy is, no doubt, a certain monotony of rhythm in his verse; but, on the other hand, the author is careful so to distribute his pauses as not to emphasise the rime unduly. He runs on freely from one couplet to another, breaking the couplet more often than not in places where a distinct pause occurs, and especially at the end of a paragraph, so that the couplet arrangement is subordinated distinctly, as it is also by Chaucer, to the continuity of the narrative. The five-accent line is written by Gower in stanzas only, as in the *Supplication* of the eighth book and in the English poem addressed to Henry IV. In these it is a marked success, showing the same technical skill that we note elsewhere, with more variety of rhythm and a certain stately dignity which can hardly appear in the short couplet.

GOWER

C. S. LEWIS

THE artistry of the *Confessio Amantis* has not always been recognized. Gower has told us that his design was to

> go the middel weie
> And wryte a bok betwen the tweie,
> Somewhat of lust, somewhat of lore,[1]

—that is, in more familiar critical language, to combine 'profit with delight'. Delight, for a fourteenth-century poet, almost inevitably meant courtly love, and 'lore' would naturally include both ethical diatribe and information, both wisdom and knowledge. The work is to be moral, yet also encyclopedic, and the whole is somehow or other to be given a courtly and amatory colouring. In other words, Gower is proposing to do for his countrymen what Guillaume de Lorris and Jean de Meun had already done in France, and the impulse behind his work is the same which drove Chaucer to undertake a translation of the *Roman* itself. It is by considering the *Romance of the Rose* as Gower's original that we first become conscious of the technical problem involved in the *Confessio Amantis* and of the success—imperfect indeed but none the less astonishing—with which Gower has solved it. For in his original all was in confusion. The design of the first writer was incomplete; and, in the continuation, the amatory, satiric, pedagogic, and religious interests jostled with one another untidily and unprofitably. If Gower had been nothing more than the mere man of his own age with a talent for verse which he is sometimes supposed to have been, he would have been content to reproduce this confusion; for architectonics were not the strong point of the Middle Ages. But Gower everywhere shows a concern for form and unity which is rare at any time and which, in

[1] *Confessio Amantis*, Prol. 17.

the fourteenth century in England, entitles him to all but the highest praise. He is determined to get in all the diversity of interests which he found in his model, and even to add to them his own new interest of tale-telling; but he is also determined to knit all these together into some semblance of a whole. And he almost succeeds.

The key to Gower's solution of the problem is to be found in Andreas. It will be remembered that Andreas had extended the erotic code so that it almost coincided with the real ethical code. Except on certain obviously untractable points, the virtues of a good lover were indistinguishable from those of a good man; the commandments of the god of Love for the most part were mere repetitions of the commandments of the Church. The special courtly and amatory ethic—whose exposition forms a natural part of a medieval love poem—was not so very 'special' after all. If the exposition of this code, from being an episode, were enlarged to become the framework of the whole book, then you would in effect have something which was always ostensibly (and sometimes actually) a treatment of courtly love, but which could at any moment pass into serious moralizing with no excessive strain on the fabric of the poem. Sloth in love is a vice by Cupid's law; but Sloth *simpliciter* is a vice by the moral law. But it is permissible—nay, it is logical—to precede your account of the *species* 'Sloth in Love' by an account of the *genus* 'Sloth'. Thus at one stroke the main problem is solved, and all the serious 'sentence' can be dovetailed into a poem on love without discrepancy. Furthermore, an old and reasonable homiletic tradition,. exemplified in such a work as *Handling Synne,* justified the illustration of the virtues and vices by exemplary tales. Thus Gower can bring in his stories, and another problem is solved. It still remains to find some plausible reason for tabulating the virtues and vices. A sermon, or a confession, naturally suggests itself; and the confession is clearly the better device of the two. A sermon would leave Love, or his representative, the sole speaker: in a confession the Lover can speak as well, and tell his own love story. The choice of Genius as the confessor is obvious, for Genius has already been made a priest by Alanus and Jean de Meun. The scheme in its essentials is now complete. It only remains to variegate it with a few episodes or digressions—in which some 'lore' hitherto unused can be accommodated—and to add a prologue at the beginning, and a recantation or palinode at the end. Both these are to serve as transitions between the world of courtly love and that ordinary world which the reader is living in before he begins to read and to which he returns again when he has finished the book. In the prologue, therefore, we are introduced to Love, but not yet to Love in its sexual sense. Gower traces the condition of the world to the fact that Division has ousted Love.[1] In the epilogue he effects his withdrawal from the court of love, as we shall see, in a very charming and original manner.

It will be obvious that the device of the lover's con- fession is the master-stroke which organizes the whole of Gower's material. It is, as far as I know, entirely Gower's own,[2] and he has seldom received full credit for it. It may be urged that the unity which he gains by it is, after all, an external and mechanical unity: that the poem shows rather the cleverness of a Chinese puzzle than the organic life of a work of art. I might grant both points and yet claim for Gower a higher place than has usually been ac- corded him. After being so long the 'moral' Gower, to be even the 'clever' Gower, would be no bad exchange; and if we thought him artificial we should at least have outgrown the misunderstanding which represents him as naïve. But I am far from granting so much. The unity of Gower's poem is not dramatic, for he was not writing drama. But it is not merely external—not merely one of those abstract excellences which critics can detect while readers

[1] *Confessio Amantis*, Prol. 881 et seq. Empedocles' Love and Strife were known to the Middle Ages from Aristotle, *Met.* 1. iv and elsewhere: cf. Dante, *Inf.* xii. 42.

[2] The confession in the *Roman de la Rose* taught Gower nothing except, possibly, the name and office of Genius.

fail to feel them. His work is more *pleasurable* because he has laboured to arrange it well; that is, to arrange it plausibly and with variety. It has, in places, merits of an even higher order; but the beauty of the architectonics is constant.

One can say almost as much of the style—almost, but not quite, for Gower can be prosaic. He is our first considerable master of the plain style in poetry, and he has the qualities and defects that go with such a style. He can be dull: he can never be strident, affected, or ridiculous. He stands almost alone in the centuries before our Augustans in being a poet perfectly well bred. When I read Chaucer I am tossed to and fro between rich and racy imitations of the speech of taverns on the one hand, and, on the other, the heights of a newly discovered poetic diction. Often a single line such as

> Singest with vois memorial in the shade

seems to contain within itself the germ of the whole central tradition of high poetical language in England. It is not so much poetical, as 'English poetry' itself—or what Englishmen most easily recognize as poetry; and the diction of the Chaucerians in the century that followed is a blundering witness to the fact. There is nothing of this in Gower. In him we seem rather to be listening to the speech of 'ladies dead'—the language of our ancestors not as they spoke in the street or in the field, but as they spoke in polite and easy society. The politeness, to be sure, is that of the Middle Ages, not of the eighteenth century: it is noble rather than urbane, of the castle not of the town: the speech of a society in which courtiers still 'went upon the carole', and rode hawking along the river banks. It thus has a sweetness and freshness which we do not find in the 'polite' style at later periods. Often a couplet in Gower sounds like a snatch of song—

> The daies gon, the yeres pass,
> The hertes waxen lasse and lasse.[1]

---

[1] *Confessio Amantis*, ii. 2259.

Fy on the bagges in the kiste!
I hadde ynogh, if I hire kiste.[1]

Who dar do thing which Love ne dar?[2]

These effects are not striven for. They are the natural
reward of a direct and genuine language and a metre well
controlled. They rise only by the smallest perceptible
eminence above the verse that surrounds them, and yet
they rise. When something songful is to be said, Gower
finds himself singing. Nor is it only in such hints of song
that the unexpected powers of his simple diction reveal
themselves. Again and again, in gnomic or pathetic passages, he astonishes us by the memorable precision and
weight of his lines. As in this—

> The hevene wot what is to done,
> Bot we that duelle under the mone
> Stonde in this world upon a weer.[3]

Or in this complaint to heaven, spoken by a girl over the
body of her lover:

> For he your heste hath kept and served,
> And was yong and I bothe also:
> Helas, why do ye with ous so?[4]

Of a country laid waste he writes:

> To se the wilde beste wone
> Wher whilom duelte a mannes sone.[5]

A princess sees her knight going into danger:

> Sche preide, and seide 'O God him spede
> The kniht which hath mi maidenhiede?'[6]

In all these—and there are many more—the poetry is so
pure in its own kind that no analysis can resolve it into
elements. They seem, to the inexperienced, to be what
any one would, and could, have said; yet to have said more
would be to have marred all. Sometimes this art of omission becomes more explicit, and even the dullest reader

[1] *Confessio Amantis*, v. 83.   [2] Ibid. vi. 1261.   [3] Ibid. Prol. 141.
[4] Ibid. iii. 1470.   [5] Ibid. iii. 1829.   [6] Ibid. v. 3739.

can see what Gower is leaving out. It is almost a rule with him not to tell us what his people thought—and a very good rule for certain kinds of poetry. Alcestis, after her great decision, returns to the husband for whom she is to die:

> Into the chambre and whan sche cam
> Hire housebonde anon sche nam
> In bothe hire armes and him kiste,
> And spak unto him *what hire liste*.[1]

Lucrece lies sleeping as Tarquin approaches her bed, 'but what sche mette, God wot.'[2] Of the princess who has fallen in love with Apollonius we are told that

> *forto thenken al hir fille*
> Sche hield hire ofte times stille
> Withinne her chambre.[3]

Who wishes to know, or to know further, *what* she thought when she had closed the door? So in the story of Rosiphilee we are content to learn that when she came to the forest-clearing,

> It thoghte hir fair, and seide, 'Here
> I wole abide under the schawe',
> And bad hire wommen to withdrawe,
> And ther sche stod *al one stille*
> *To thenke what was in hir wille*.[4]

The silence of the poet enables us to hear the silence of that wood; for we have all done what Rosiphilee was doing.

All plain styles, except the very greatest, raise a troublesome problem for the critic. Are they the result of art or of accident? If we were sure that Gower was himself unconscious of the beauties I have quoted, that he said so little only because he had little in his mind, our enjoyment of his poetry would not be impaired, but our judgement of the poet would be different. The question is perhaps ill put. Not all that is unconscious in art is therefore accidental. If seemingly plain statements rise to poetry, where the subject is imaginary, this shows at least that the writer

[1] Ibid. vii. 1937.   [2] Ibid. vii. 4967.   [3] Ibid. viii. 861.   [4] Ibid. iv. 1292.

had his eye on the object; that he was thinking not of himself but of his tale, and that he saw this latter clearly and profoundly; and such vision is a poetical, as well as a moral, excellence. That Gower always, or often, calculated—as Stevenson might have calculated—those reticences which delight us in his poetry, is very unlikely. But there is evidence that he knew, in his own way, what he was about. The famous line

> The beaute faye upon her face[1]

attained its present form only by successive revisions—revisions which demonstrate, so far as such things can be demonstrated, the working of a fine, and finely self-critical, poetic impulse. The first version—

> The beaute of hire face schon
> Wel bryhtere than the cristall ston,

—is just what would have contented the ordinary 'unconscious' spinner of yarns in rhyme; but it did not content Gower. Nor am I persuaded that the plain style of the *Confessio Amantis* was the only style he could compass. An element of choice came to aid his natural propensity. There are indications that he could have assumed a different manner if he had so desired.

> Ferst to Nature if that I me compleigne,
> Ther finde I hou that every creature
> Som time ayer hath love in his demeine,
> So that the litel wrenne in his mesure
> Hath yit of kinde a love under his cure;
> And I bot on desire, of which I misse:
> And thus, bot I, hath every kinde his blisse.[2]

I do not think it would be easy, at sight, to attribute this to Gower. No doubt, the different quality of these lines is largely due to the different metre; but if Gower can thus adapt himself with equal felicity to the two metres, and use two differing styles, then the style of his octosyllabics is art, not nature—or is nature in such a way as

---

[1] *Confessio Amantis*, iv. 1321.   [2] Ibid. viii. 2224.

not to be the less art. The movement of the stanza I have quoted, and the rhetorical building of the clauses, are as perfect in their own way as anything in Gower's narratives: more perfect than some of Chaucer's stanza work. Elsewhere in the *Confessio*, and this time in octosyllabics, Gower writes successfully in a manner slightly different from his wont. The beautiful *alba* put into the mouth of Cephalus[1] is too long to quote in full; but a few selections will show the heightening that I refer to:

> And thus whan that thi liht is faded
> And Vesper scheweth him alofte,
> And that the nyht is long and softe,
> Under the cloudes derke and stille
> Thanne hath this thing most of his wille . . .
>
> Withdrawgh the banere of thin armes,
> And let thi lyhtes ben unborn,
> And in the signe of Capricorn,
> The hous appropred to Satorne,
> I preie that thou wolt sojorne,
> Where ben the nihtes derke and longe . . .
>
> That thou thi swifte hors restreigne
> Lowe under erthe in Occident,
> That thei towardes Orient
> Be cercle go the longe weie.

The whole passage is interesting, for it seems to have been a sort of holiday for Gower. The whole 'tale of Cephalus' is nothing but Cephalus' *alba*, and is all, apparently, original.

To some, Gower's poetry seems lacking in imagery. The glittering of the golden fleece 'bright and hot' as Jason rows back with it from the dangerous island, or the beards of the three beggars which were white 'as a bush that is besnewed', may serve to show that he is not wholly lacking in this respect. But they are admittedly not typical of Gower. The pictorial imagination finds little to feed on in the *Confessio Amantis*; but often this is because imagina-

[1] Ibid. iv. 3208 et seq.

tion of another kind, and a kind perhaps more proper to narrative, is brought into play. Gower does not dwell on shapes and colours; but this does not mean that he keeps his eyes shut. What he sees is movement, not groups and scenes, but actions and events. In so far as he approximates to the visible arts at all, it is a cinematograph rather than a painting that he suggests. When Elda returns to the room where his wife lies murdered, we are not told what the scene looked like; but we are told that

> stille with a prive lyht
> As he that wolde noght awake
> His wif, he hath his weie take
> Into the chambre.[1]

King Philip, at the wars, is informed in a dream of the love which the god Amos has cast upon the queen. Here again there is no attempt to build up a picture; what is added is significant action and event:

> And tho began the king awake
> And sigheth for his wyves sake
> Wher as he lay . . .[2]

Medea sends her maid to Jason in secret, and the maid returns to tell her how she sped.[3] We can all imagine how Spenser or Keats would have dealt with the blushes and beauty of Medea. Gower, on the other hand, has nothing to say of how she looked. But he knows what she did— 'sche for joie hire maide kiste'—and the whole scene is alive in six words. When Apollonius embarks to take vengeance upon the land of Tharse,[4] the pageantry of the embarkation—which Chaucer or Marlowe might so happily have dwelled on—is passed over with the bald statement that the king took 'a strong pouer'. Then follows the couplet that Chaucer perhaps would scarcely have thought of:

> Up to the sky he caste his lok
> And syh the wind was covenable.

[1] *Confessio Amantis*, ii. 836. [2] Ibid. vi. 2153.
[3] Ibid. v. 3800. [4] Ibid. viii. 1928.

That first line is businesslike, but it is poetry. It might come from a traveller who wrote thinking of anything rather than literature: it might also come from a ballad: it might come from Homer. Ships and the sea, indeed, are always good in Gower; not only in such full-length passages as the storm (in the story of King Namplus),[1] but also in the two lines that make the vision of Alceone as vivid as a remembered dream of our own ('The tempeste of the blake cloude, The wode see, the wyndes loude'),[2] and even in such a brisk bit of ordinary connecting narrative as

> The wynd was good, the schip was yare,
> Thei tok here leve, and forth thei fare . . .[3]

—which looks easier to do than it is. This excellence in Gower's sea-pieces has led some to suppose that he was familiar with sea travel—as he may well have been; but it is, in fact, only one manifestation of his devotion to movement and progression, his preoccupation with things that change as you watch them. If he is to speak of knight errantry, he imagines his knight 'somtime in Prus, somtime in Rodes', and the heralds cry out,

> Vailant, vailant, lo, *wher he goth*![4]

The appearance of Nebuchadnezzar, transformed into a beast, is passed over; but we hear how he beheld himself and sighed.[5] The death of Ulysses is not described—but 'every man The King! The King! Began to crie'.[6] In the story of the Courtiers and the Fool Gower paints no interior, but the King and the two lords

> stoden be the cheminee
> Togedre spekende alle three,

while the fool sat by the fire 'as he that with his babil pleide'.[7] When Progne receives the fatal sampler on which her sister has woven the story of their common ruin, she faints: but afterwards 'Eft aros and gan to stonde And

---

[1] Ibid. iii. 981 et seq. [2] Ibid. iv. 3063. [3] Ibid. v. 3299.
[4] Ibid. iv. 1633. [5] Ibid. i. 2992. [6] Ibid. vi. 1711.
[7] Ibid. vii. 3951 et seq.

eft she takth the cloth on honde'.[1] When the Lover
dances with his mistress—

> Me thenkth I touche noght the flor;
> The Ro which renneth on the mor
> Is thanne noght so lyht as I.[2]

If we have few set pictures in Gower it is sometimes
because the poet nods; more often it is because he is wide
awake and on the move.

This ever-present movement is the strength of Gower
as a narrative poet. It is in this capacity alone that he
is usually praised, and deservedly; but in speaking of his
Tales we must beware of some false opinions. They are
not, as has been supposed, the only part of the *Confessio
Amantis* which deserves reading. They are not the sole
end and aim of the poem, for which all the rest exists.
The love allegory in which they are set, the moral, and
even the scientific, digressions by which they are inter-
rupted, are just as interesting to Gower as the tales themselves, and often just as capable of giving pleasure to the
reader. To read the tales alone, or the framework alone,
is to miss the variety which the poet has taken pains to
provide for us; and then 'it dulleth ofte a mannes wit'.
Nor is it by any means certain that the Tales, as a whole,
constitute Gower's best work. They contain, perhaps,
his best work; but certainly they also contain his worst;
for story-telling is a function which brings out the defects
as well as the qualities of the plain style. It does not follow
that a tale which avoids all the characteristic faults of
Chaucer—the rhetoric, the digression, and the occasional
rigmarole—is therefore a good tale. Perhaps it makes no
faults because it makes nothing; certainly there are tales
in Gower so concise that they read not like narrative
poems but like metrical arguments for narrative poems
still to be written. Such are the *Sirens*, *Capaneus*, the
Beggars and the Pasties, and many others. Even where
this fault is avoided Gower can still fail. The humorous

[1] *Confessio Amantis*, v. 5789.   [2] Ibid. iv. 2785.

tale of *Hercules and Faunus* is flat; and possibly no other narrator ever allowed a story to get under weigh, as Gower does in *Acis and Galatea*, before telling us—and then in a most casual parenthesis—that one of the three characters involved, and already set in action, is a Giant.

Even when we have ruled out the failures—which are, after all, in the minority—it remains, from the very nature of the case, a difficult matter to assess Gower's skill. In this kind of narrative, so spare, so direct, and so concentrated on the event, it is not easy to distinguish the merit of the telling from the intrinsic merit of the story. We sometimes suspect that Gower succeeds only when he has a good story to tell, and fails only when he has a bad one. This does not, of course, detract from his value; but it modifies the critic's judgement. Stories, or stories of this kind, are not matter but already form: Gower's art is rather to liberate the beauty of this form, to find this Hercules in the marble, than to add it. And of his art, so conceived, we may say, I think, that it is nearly always on the same level of achievement—always somewhere beneath the highest, yet very high. What changes is his discretion in selecting the tales. The stories of *Constance* or of the *Education of Achilles* are not worse told than those of *Florent* or *Apollonius*: Gower's error lay in telling them at all. Here, as everywhere in medieval literature, we must try to repress our modern conception of the poet as the sole source of his poetry: we must think more of the intrinsic and impersonal beauty or ugliness of matters, plots, and sentiments which retain their own living continuity as they pass from writer to writer. *Trouvere* as well as *maker* is the name for a poet.

If we are speaking of the art of narration in its strictest sense, this is as far as we can go. But of course there are qualities not strictly narrative, though properly manifested in narrations, which are really characteristic of Gower. The account of Medea's sorceries (*Thus it befell upon a nyht*, &c.)[1] seems to have stuck in the mind of

---

[1] Ibid. v. 3957 et seq.

every reader from Shakespeare down; and the *beaute faye*[1]
upon the faces of the dead in *Rosiphilee*, which I have
already referred to, is quoted as often as any line in the
whole poem. Both passages have a common quality, and
it is this quality, perhaps, which marks Gower's point of
maximum differentiation as a poet. For Gower is 'romantic' in the nineteenth-century meaning of the word. He
excels in strange adventure, in the remote and the mysterious: like his own Jason, him

> sore alongeth
> To se the strange regiouns
> And knowe the condiciuns
> Of othre marches.[2]

He loves to tell us, in the story of Nectanabus,

> Hou fro the hevene cam a lyht
> Which al hir chambre made lyht.[3]

His strangely vivid, because strangely ambiguous, description of the dream[4] in *Ulysses and Telegonus* is almost
among the great dreams of English poetry. And this
quality in Gower is worth noticing because it is rare in
the Middle Ages. It is indeed what many expect to find
in medieval literature, but we do not often find it. It is
not in the *Romance of the Rose*; it is not in Chrétien, nor
in Langland, nor Alanus; it is rare in the metrical romance;
and it is, in places, even painfully lacking in Chaucer.
Gower's use of this neglected, yet characteristically English, vein of poetry, entitles him to the praise of independence. No doubt it is possible to overrate—as perhaps
the present writer does—'the fairy way of writing'. But
it has its own function. In this dim medium the shocking
tale of *Tereus* acquires a bittersweet beauty not otherwise
attainable. Like all romantics Gower builds a bridge
between the conscious and the unconscious mind.

A consideration of the *Confessio Amantis* falls naturally

---

[1] *Confessio Amantis*, iv. 1321. [2] Ibid. v. 3282.
[3] Ibid. vi. 1981. Spenser (cf. *F.Q.* v. vii. 13 et seq.) possibly owes something
to this passage. [4] Ibid. vi. 1519–63.

into three divisions—the tales (of which I shall say no more), the didactic passages (religious, moral, and scientific), and the love allegory in which all the rest are set. As a didactic poet in general Gower does not stand very high. I do not mean by this that accidents of time have rendered his alchemy, astronomy, and anthropology uninteresting; that is the sort of thing which the good reader can overcome by an effort of historical imagination. I mean that we find in Gower no such real grasp of conceptual thought, and no such power of felicitous popularization, as we find in Jean de Meun. Contemporary readers could, I fancy, have got all that Gower has to tell them, and got it better, elsewhere. His euhemeristic account of the pagan deities descends to mere abuse. The following description of Apollo, with its flat and grumbling expostulation, seems to me irresistibly funny:

> He was an hunte upon the helles;
> Ther was in him no vertue elles
> Wherof that enye bokes karpe
> Bot only that he kouthe harpe . . .[1]

Sometimes he falls into mere absurdity, as where he tells of a certain star:

> Nature on him his name caste
> And clepeth him Botercadent;[2]

yet time, which obliterates so many beauties, creates some, and if much of Gower's 'doctrine' has lost whatever merits it once had, parts of it have acquired a quaintness which only very sophisticated readers can fail to enjoy. It must be a hard heart that can resist geography of this kind:

> Fro that unto the worldes ende
> Estward, Asie it is algates
> Til that men come unto the gates
> Of Paradis, and there Ho![3]

As a moral and religious poet, on the other hand, Gower is often excellent, and that not only in explicitly didactic

---

[1] Ibid. v. 919.   [2] Ibid. vii. 1419.   [3] Ibid. vii. 568.

passages. His ethics and his piety, now stern, now tender, and now again satiric, colour the whole work, and always for the better. Sometimes they colour it without the author's knowledge. The heathen theogamies which form the pivot of *Mundus and Paulina* and *Nectanabus* are conceived in the light of the Christian sentiment that surrounds the story of the Annunciation:

> Glad was hir innocence tho
> Of suche wordes as sche herde,
> With humble chere and thus answerde . . .[1]

This is not art, for doubtless Gower never dreamed of envisaging the story otherwise; but it makes the story better. At the opposite end of the scale we have those passages where Gower shows, unexpectedly, his powers as a humorist—the picture of the drunkard who wakes next morning (unlike his weak successors in our own day) with the stirring cry, 'O whiche a sorwe it is a man be drinkeles'[2]—or the longer, and even funnier, passage in which the faithless husband gives his wife an account of his day's sport.[3] But neither tenderness nor satire is Gower's highest reach as a moralist. His true quality comes out rather in the ring of such a line as

> The newe schame of sennes olde,[4]

where we are surprised at this element of iron in a poet elsewhere so gentle, so fanciful, and so at peace. Yet we find it again and again. The noble description of the Last Judgement in Book II:[5]

> That dai mai no consail availe,
> The pledour and the plee schal faile;

the lines on the insight of God into 'the privites of mannes herte', which

> speke and sounen His ere
> As thogh thei lowde wyndes were;[6]

[1] *Confessio Amantis*, i. 852. Cf. vi. 1918.   [2] Ibid. vi. 55.
[3] Ibid. v. 6123 et seq.   [4] Ibid. vii. 5116.   [5] Ibid. ii. 3406–30.
[6] Ibid. i. 2807.

and the paragraph in Book V[1] which begins 'Whan Peter, fader of the feith'—all these serve to remind us in how worthy a sense (and how unlike the sneering modern interpretation) he deserves the name of 'moral' Gower. Above all, the vision of the elements sickening with the Fall of Man, in the Prologue, which is not the offspring of platitude and conformity, but of a stern, and passionate, and highly imaginative impulse, rises to a climax that is nothing short of the sublime—

> The Lond, the See, the firmament,
> Thei axen alle jugement
> Ayein the man and make him werre[2]—

—lines which are as far outside Chaucer's range as the *Milleres Tale* is outside Gower's.

But it is time to turn to the Love Allegory itself, which forms the framework of the whole *Confessio*, and which concerns the present study most nearly. I have already protested against the view which treats Gower's allegory as nothing more than the thread on which his stories are strung. Gower comes before us as a poet of courtly love; and I think he makes good his claim. He has not indeed written a love poem comparable to *Troilus* or to the first part of the *Romance of the Rose*. But he has his own contribution to make. In his own way he works side by side with Chaucer to realize what Guillaume de Lorris had rendered possible.

The story is simple. The poet, 'Wisshinge and wepinge al min one', and wandering in the usual May morning, meets Venus and is handed over by her to the priest Genius, to confess himself as regards the code of love. The confessor—availing himself, as I said above, of the parallelism between the erotic and the moral law—goes through six of the seven deadly sins, illustrating them with stories, and eliciting replies from his penitent. He digresses twice on a large scale, once to give an account of the religions of the world, and once to give a general scheme of

---

[1] Ibid. v. 1904.   [2] Ibid. Prol. 959.

education: minor digressions deal with Crusading and with Great Inventors. The seventh deadly sin, in a moral work, ought to have been Luxury, which naturally cannot be a sin against Venus; its place is taken by Incest, agreeably with the doctrine of Andreas.

It is at once apparent that we have here no allegorical conduct of a complex love story, as we had in Guillaume de Lorris. But this does not mean that we have no presentation of love; on the contrary, in the replies of the poet to the questions put by Genius, we have his life as a lover presented directly and without allegory. These replies make no inconsiderable part of the poem; for the historian, even if they had no intrinsic beauty, they would have great importance; for in them Gower is doing, after his own fashion, what Chaucer did in *Troilus*—presenting directly, in terms of tolerably realistic fiction, what he has learned from the allegory of the *Roman*. Guillaume de Lorris has taught Gower, as well as Chaucer, to look within; and now that the lesson has been learned it is possible to look outwards again. Hence it comes that the lover's speeches are full of the movement of the actual world. We see the 'yonge lusty route' of his rivals surrounding his mistress: we see Gower himself bowing and proffering his service, conducting her to church, playing with her dog, and riding beside her chariot: we see the lady at her needlework, or at the dice, dancing, or listening to the story of Troilus as he reads aloud. We see Gower postponing the moment of leave-taking, and, after he has gone, rising at night to look across the housetops to his lady's window.

To those who find allegory difficult this direct method will doubtless come as a relief; but it is not only the method that deserves attention. The content may claim to be a 'just representation of general nature'—and therefore, as seldom fails, of individual nature too. The experience of the lover is presented with a truth that convinces us, and with much mingling of humour and pathos. Gower is not the slave of any *mere* convention. When he conforms,

his heart goes with it. When he writes a full-length paean
in the praise of Love—

> It makth curteis of the vilein &c[1]—

he repeats what his predecessors have said. But he wishes
to repeat it, and is not the less a poet because he agrees
with the common experience of gentle hearts. His humility, perhaps, smacks more of that age, and less of all time;
though it may be argued that his cowering like 'the yonge
whelp' at his mistress's rebuke is rather disagreeable than
incredible. But we forgive even this when he pierces to
the spiritual reality behind all this tradition of humility
and thus reminds us of the sense in which courtly love is
no convention and cannot die:

> So lowe couthe I nevere bowe
> To feigne humilite withoute,
> That me ne leste betre loute
> With alle the thoghtes of myn herte.[2]

In the light of such a passage we can understand and
approve the remark of Genius:

> Sche mai be such, that hire o lok
> Is worth thin herte manyfold—[3]

and while we read we feel that this is but reason. We feel
it the more easily because such devoutnesses exist in Gower
side by side with much shrewdness and realism. He explicitly rejects that part of the code which demands that
a lover should be a knight-errant.

> Forto slen the hethen alle
> I not what good ther mihte falle . . .
> What scholde I winne over the see
> If I mi ladi loste at hom ?[4]

He is too good a moralist to have any delusions about
himself. Gower the poet handles Gower the lover with
a somewhat sour, half-smiling, detachment. He knows
that he does not offer his mistress a virgin heart, or body.

[1] *Confessio Amantis*, iv. 2300. [2] Ibid. i. 718.
[3] Ibid. v. 4542. [4] Ibid. iv. 1659, 1664.

He 'has tasted in many a place', with no higher purpose than 'forto drive forth the dai'.[1] He can claim that he has been always sincere towards his lady; but 'as touchende othre' he cannot say so much.[2] The *lover* confesses with naïveté—which assuredly argues no naïveté in the *poet*—that he is spiteful and a backbiter. He cannot help telling the lady discreditable stories about the young men who visit her, and his excuse for doing so is delicious:

> So fayne I wolde that sche wiste.[3]

Equally true, and equally comic, is the confusion of mind which enables him to feel a moral indignation against his rivals who busy themselves

> Al to deceive an innocent.[4]

We have the picture of a very ordinary kind of human heart—'A nothing that would be something if it could'. It is only in his love that the Lover is transfigured. This can cast him into a waking trance, in which

> Me thenkth as thogh I were aslepe
> And that I were in Goddes barm.[5]

This can make him lighter than the roe when his lady dances; and her words are 'as the wyndes of the South'. It is this which has penetrated him so deeply that its eradication, if ever it were eradicated, would leave but little of the man to survive,

> For liche unto the greene tree
> If that men toke his rote aweie
> Richt so myn herte scholde deie.[6]

It is this love which teaches him, though simple, to surprise his Confessor with an answer of unerring and subtle truth. Genius has been speaking of the sin of Ravine, whose counterpart in the code of love is Rape. Is the penitent guilty in this matter? The question is shocking in this context of courtly love. We wonder what indignation,

---

[1] *Confessio Amantis*, v. 7792. [2] Ibid. i. 742. [3] Ibid. ii. 491.
[4] Ibid. ii. 465. [5] Ibid. vi. 226. [6] Ibid. iv. 2680.

what protests of courtesy and humility, what rhetoric or what exaggeration will be sufficient to meet it. But there is that in the poet's heart which enables him to neglect all these, and to make a reply that exhausts the subject for good and all. It is in nine short words—

> Certes, fader, no:
> For I mi ladi love so.[1]

If Gower's heroine is but a pale shadow beside Cryseide, his hero is at times a worthy rival to Troilus.

There is some danger of monotony in the continued failure of this lover's suit; and though the tales and other digressions relieve this, the poem would be unsatisfactory if it left the lover's history where it found it. But Gower has a story to tell. He has, perhaps, no very striking beginning; but he has a middle and an end—one of the best ends, indeed, in medieval poetry. For the *Confessio Amantis* tells the story of the death of love. The lines about the green tree which must die without its root are beautiful in themselves; but they gain incalculably when we discover that the green tree actually is to lose its root, and that this indeed is the primary subject of the poem. At the beginning we may suspect that the ill success of the lover is merely conventional, that the 'cruelty' of the lady serves only to delay a happy ending. But even from the first there are indications that this is not what Gower intends to do. The words of Venus, at her first appearing, strike cold:

> With that hir lok on me sche caste,
> And seide, 'In aunter if thou live!
> Mi will is ferst that thou be shrive'.[2]

Long afterwards we learn the reason. This lover is separated by a fatal barrier from the 'yonge lusti route' of his rivals. He is old. The *Confessio Amantis*, written by an old poet, in failing health, appropriately tells the story of an old man's unsuccessful love for a young girl. It is a subject that lends itself with equal ease to a rather brutal

[1] Ibid. v. 5532. [2] Ibid. i. 188.

kind of comedy or a sentimental kind of tragedy: finer and truer than either of these is Gower's conception in which the aged lover at last reconciles himself to the reality of the situation and wakes from his long illusion, 'in calm of mind, all passion spent'. The handling of this quiet close is so beautiful, and the thing itself so wisely and beautifully imagined that it constitutes Gower's highest claim as a poet; and that not only for its content, but for its artistry.

It is worth our while here to pause and consider Gower's ending simply as the solution of a technical problem. I have tried to show how the very nature of courtly love demanded that the perfect love poem should end with a recantation. The claims of the objective moral law—of *Resoun* as the Middle Ages said—must, in the end, be faced. Hence the last Book of Andreas, and the conclusion of *Troilus and Cryseide*. Gower, as well as another, is faced with this necessity. For him, as for Chaucer, the love which he celebrates is a sin, and in the lover *Will* has usurped dominion over *Resoun*.[1] Gower is not enough of a philosopher to achieve, like Dante, or even to attempt, like Alanus, any reconciliation between the claims of his two worlds: but he is much too careful and sincere an artist to be content with some formal palinode which would stultify the whole of the rest of his poem. He solves the problem by keeping his eye on the object. He finds in his own experience—the experience of an old man —how Life itself manages the necessary palinode; and then manages his in the same way. It is Old Age which draws the sting of love, and his poem describes the process of this disappointing mercy. Venus promises the lover that he will find peace

> Noght al per chance as ye it wolden,
> Bot so as ye be reson scholden.[2]

—lines which describe, perhaps unconsciously, the very nature of life's discipline in this, as in a thousand other matters, and which might even express the promise kept

[1] *Confessio Amantis*, viii. 2135.   [2] Ibid. viii. 2369.

by Venus to successful lovers. This is the deepest note in
Gower; but though it is heard distinctly only at the end,
its influence is over the whole poem. For when once he
has hit upon the theme 'Love cured by Age', he has no
more need for the clumsy device of a separate palinode:
the whole story becomes a palinode, and yet remains a love
story—a pathetic, yet not dismaying, picture of Passion at
war with Time, while more than half aware that Reason
sides with Time against it. It is this latter, this half-
awareness, that saves the *Confessio Amantis* from the
spiritual shallowness of a mere lament over the vanished
pleasures of youth. It also explains certain places in the
poem which are commonly misunderstood. Critics smile
when Genius, priest of Venus, denounces Venus herself as
one of the false deities; and if we insist on the original
significance of Genius (the god of reproduction) there may
be some absurdity. But it is not quite the kind of absurdity
that we are tempted to suppose. Gower has not blundered
into it by an oversight. He knows very well what he is
doing, and goes out of his way to underline what we consider the inconsistency. Genius himself is well aware of it.
He is forced against his will to pass sentence on the very
powers that he serves. His penitent presses the question
on him, demanding

> The godd and the goddesse of love
> *Of whom ye nothing hier above*
> *Have told*, ne spoken of her fare,
> That ye me wolden now declare
> Hou thei ferst comen to that name,

and the Priest replies

> Mi sone, I have it left for schame.[1]

He would have kept silence if he could: but if you press
him, he must confess that the whole world which he
represents, Venus and Cupid and the court of Love, are
but idle dreams and feigned consecrations of human in-
firmities. In all this there is some clumsiness: but there is

[1] Ibid. v. 1374–83.

also something very far from absurdity. Genius here stands
for Love—for that whole complex in the lover's mind
which he calls his 'love', and of which he has made his
deity and his father confessor: and in these lines we have
the poetic history of that strange moment—familiar in the
history of other passions as well as of love—wherein a man,
laying his ear close to his own heart, first hears the master
passion itself there speaking with a doubtful voice, and
presently hinting that it knows (the conscious will shouting
it down in vain)—that it knows itself to be all other than
the tongue claims for it—that its foundations are crumbling—that its superstructure is but a tissue of illusions and
decaying habits, soon to dissolve and leave us face to face
with inner emptiness. In the curious tergiversations of
Genius we see love itself betraying the Lover, though for
a long time yet he cannot—lest his Green Tree lose its
root—cease, in some sense, to love. I do not say that all
this was present in Gower's mind in the same conceptual
form which I have been compelled to give it. But some
such significance is implicit in these lines, and becomes
almost explicit in the eighth Book. By then the game is
almost played out. Genius has ceased to speak for the
Love-deities who were originally his patrons. He is simply
the lover's deepest 'heart', telling him bitter truths, now
no longer avoidable; and the change is marked by the
words,

> Mi sone, unto the trouthe wende
> Now wol I for the love of thee,
> And lete all other trufles be,[1]

and the passage ends with the grave lines

> For I can do to thee nomore
> Bot teche thee the rihte weie:
> Now ches if thou wolt live or deie.[2]

It is difficult to speak of what follows without seeming
to over-praise a poet so neglected, and in some respects
so negligible, as Gower. We have here one of those rare

---

[1] *Confessio Amantis*, viii. 2060.   [2] Ibid. viii. 2146.

passages in which medieval allegory rises to myth, in which the symbols, though fashioned to represent mere single concepts, take on new life and represent rather the principles—not otherwise accessible--which unite whole classes of concepts. All is shot through with meanings which the author may never have been aware of; and, on this level, it does not matter whether he was or not. The two-edged promise of Venus I have already quoted. Is this an allegorical presentation of the death of love—or of love only? Or is it the voice of Life itself? The answer is that it is both: for doubtless it is a rule in poetry that if you do your own work well, you will find you have done also work you never dreamed of. And so with all the other elements in Gower's closing scene; the deadly cold that quenches the lover's heart, the companies of singing Youth and singing Age whom he sees in his trance, the figure of Cupid as he stoops over his body to pull out the long-embedded dart, the ointment 'mor cold than eny keie' with which the wound is healed, and the beads, given him by Venus, which bear the inscription *Por reposer*. All these images tell the story of this particular lover, and this death of love, to admiration; but it is of death in many other senses that our minds are full while we read, and we rise from the book, as the Lover rose from his trance, 'thenkende thoghtes fele'. But not of death as evil; rather of death as new life, with a clarity which this conception rarely attains in profane writings. 'Foryet it thou, and so wol I', says Genius when all the ritual has been undergone; and Venus bids the poet 'go where vertu moral duelleth'. The words strike ghost-like on some modern ears. But no one can miss the heartfelt peace of the line— so simple in itself, so perfect in its context—

Homward a softe pas I went.

If Gower had known to stop here he would have made an ending worthy to stand beside that of the *Iliad* or of *Samson Agonistes*.

Unfortunately he did not. He adds a long and

unsuccessful coda; and I am half glad to close on a note of censure, lest the beauties I have described should carry our critical judgement too far captive. Gower has risen to great poetry, but he is not a great poet. The restraint which is visible in single lines and short passages innumerable deserts him in the conduct of the poem as a whole. He says too much, not at this point or that, but too much *simpliciter*. Often the plain style sinks to prose. He has told, along with his good stories, many bad ones. But he has merits which render all his faults forgivable. Inferior to Chaucer in the range, and sometimes (not always) in the power, of his genius, he is almost Chaucer's equal as a craftsman. In the content of his work it is interesting to notice that he is profoundly English. His romanticism, and his choice of the theme of Time and Age—both these look back to the Anglo-Saxons and forward to the nineteenth century. Yet his form is French. The heart is insular and romantic, the head cool and continental: it is a good combination.

JOHN GOWER IN HIS MOST SIGNIFICANT ROLE

GEORGE R. COFFMAN

No major figure in the range of English literary history has suffered more from the "slings and arrows of outrageous fortune" than John Gower. Thanks in no small part to Lowell and Jusserand, during the past century he became almost a popular legend as a "monument of dulness and pedantry."[1] Adjudged a great medieval encyclopedist, he has been held superficial and unspeculative in the fields of scientific and philosophic thought.[2] During the eighteenth and nineteenth centuries especially, he came to be widely regarded as an "ingrate and a sychophant" in his personal and political relationships.[3] It is not the purpose of this paper to attempt an assessment of these critical dicta and indictments. It is rather to suggest that the social instead of the literary aspects of Gower's writings may form the basis for an interpretation of him in his most significant role.

The age in which he lived, frustrated in its onward march just a few years before his death, is a tremendously exciting one. And more than any other single writer he mirrors directly the whole social range of that cosmic and chaotic period —albeit with a somewhat myopic vision. In a large and significant sense it may be more important to study him as a recipient of the heritage of certain ideas which he adapts to a functional end than as a writer who assimilates his materials for the purposes of literary art. And possibly even his poetry may assume greater validity and vitality if we consider his work as a whole rather than as fragmentary bits. Two more statements must suffice before I turn directly to the subject of this paper. A survey of his writings, with the little that we know about his life, will, I believe, confirm in the reader's mind G. C. Macaulay's cautious judgment against charges of political timidity and obsequiousness on Gower's part. And a survey of his writings, with their clear and repeated personal references, gives one the opinion that through them he comes to know Gower's spiritual and social biography.

* * *

---

[1] E.g., James Russell Lowell, "Chaucer," in *My Study Windows* (Boston, 1871), pp. 258–60, and J. J. Jusserand, *A Literary History of the English People* (London, 1925), I, 264–72. The unwritten chapters on Gower's literary reputation would include a long roll of those who have been uncritical in both their praise and their depreciation of him. That chapter is no part of this brief paper, which constitutes prolegomena to a larger and more comprehensive study.

[2] E.g., George H. Fox, *The Mediaeval Sciences in the Work of John Gower* (Princeton, 1931), Princeton University Studies in English. No. 6. *Passim.*

[3] All of this, again, is part of a long, involved, and incomplete chapter in Gower's biography. Obviously there is space here to give the curious and interested reader only a few notable references: *e.g.*, John Urry, *Works of Geoffrey Chaucer* (London, 1721), Introduction, d, (4); Joseph Ritson, *Bibliographica Poetica* A Catalogue of the Engliesh Poets of the Twelfth, Thirteenth, Fourteenth, Fifteenth, and Sixteenth Centurys (London, 1802), pp. 24–25; Karl Meyer, *John Gower's Beziehungen zu Chaucer und König Richard II* (Bonn, 1889), *passim.* William Godwin, *Life of Geoffrey Chaucer* (London, 1803), I. 240–46, presents a spirited defense of Gower in his relations with Richard II. G. C. Macaulay, *The Works of John Gower* (Oxford, 1899–1902), I–IV, gives a brief, judicial review of the matter (II, xxi–xxvi). Incidentally, all quotations in this paper are from this, the standard edition of Gower's works.

As I follow through Gower's French, Latin, and English works I find something akin to a guiding principle. This in totality indicates that he was rightly called the moral Gower. He is an advocate of a moral order. By this he means God's order for the universe and the established order for human society. This moral order is preserved by reason, a divine gift which is added to the four elements constituting man's physical being. In practical application a man of reason is characterized by wisdom and virtue. Since Gower's writings show that he has no faith in the common people, his social gospel presupposes no social equality but is limited to fostering honesty and integrity within established society by all members of it. This social aspect of Gower is stressed by G. R. Owst, *Literature and the Pulpit in Medieval England*, albeit he implies a more democratic spirit than Gower possesses:

> In all the literature that has been published (in medieval England), it would be difficult to find a more perfect mirror of the social gospel as presented by the pulpit, in its artistry as well as its doctrine, within a single frame, than his *Mirour de l'Omme*, or *Speculum Meditantis*.[4]

His literary pattern for his social cause is the *Speculum* of the medieval encyclopedist or the *Manual* of the homilist; or it may be the direct verbal scourge or whiplash of the reformer. In the sweep of his materials Gower ranges over the whole world and includes all classes of society but always with particular reference to contemporary England. In sum, as represented by the *Mirour, Vox Clamantis*, and *Confessio Amantis*, and his lesser poems, he progresses with consistency and growing clarity toward his central thesis. The rule of reason, to repeat, is the basic element in his conception of an ordered universe. The use of this God-given intellectual power will, he is convinced, result in a world of peace and harmony, in proper human relations, in worthy rulers, and in a prosperous England.

But Gower makes clear that this program here outlined is man's responsibility. He maintains that God in endowing man with reason charged him, the microcosm, with complete control of the material universe, the macrocosm. In fact, he made him through the elements so essentially a part of the universe that failure to act in accordance with wisdom and virtue adversely affects all nature. This is the place to call attention to a long passage in the *Mirour* (ll. 26605–27240), which lays the basis for his whole doctrine of individual responsibility.[5] All classes of society have become corrupted. The blame is laid on the age. After having questioned the elements, the planets, and the stars, the author returns and makes man the cause. The logic of the manner in which this reacts on nature follows. Gower accepts the authority of books as to the creation,[6] and as to the promises of God for the prosperity of the good. Furthermore, through the addition of evidence of plagues, pestilences, tempests, and other unfavorable manifestations

---

[4] (Cambridge University Press, 1933), pp. 230–231.

[5] This idea is repeated with variations or modifications in *Vox Clamantis* (VII, esp. vii), and in the Prologue to *Confessio Amantis* (ll. 905 ff.).

[6] Macaulay in his notes refers especially to Gregory's *Hom. in Evang.*, ii, 39: "omnis autem creaturae aliquid habet homo. Habet namque commune esse cum lapidibus, vivere cum arboribus, sentire cum animalibus, intelligere cum angelis."

of nature he accepts the word that God through creating man a microcosm and endowing him with the divine power of reason has established an unbreakable pantheistic and sympathetic relationship with the macrocosm.   Through failure to observe the precepts of wisdom and virtue, the component elements of God-given reason, and through the consequent corruption of church and court, dishonesty in professional and business life, and discontent and rebellion among the farmers and artisans, the destructive forces of nature are unleashed against the human race.   Here he goes a step beyond the preacher or homilist to make clear that this is not merely an immediate and possibly capricious act of an angry God to punish man.   It is rather that the cosmic relationship of all created things with man, their ruler, inevitably makes this come to pass in the scheme of the universe.   This idea is reflected through medieval theology in the immediate effect of Adam's sin on external nature.   In other words, Gower believes the evidence of books and *thinks* that God's plan really works.   The thing for man is not merely to do wishful thinking and feeling even through prayer, but to use his divine wisdom to study and reflect, and to develop proper human relations through a change of heart.   Thus he would recreate a paradise on earth.[7]

In kinship with Thomas Aquinas before him and Milton afterwards Gower affirms that if reason be the guide for the human race all will go well.   The difference is that Gower is not interested in the abstract theological, philosophic, or scientific aspects of this.   He is concerned with its relation to man in contemporary society.

All this is the groundwork for convincing man of his freedom and fixing his responsibility.   To this end he attacks the exponents of astrology and the supporters of a fatalistic attitude represented by the word *fortune* or *fate*.   Since the

---

[7] Two modern instances, *mutatis mutandis*, may not be impertinent here.   The first is from R. E. Sherwood's preface to *There Shall Be No Night* (Scribner's, 1940).   He is justifying the theme of this play—that man is insane—as a thesis which he has been developing through twenty years.   The essence of this he expresses in the words of Squier, the representative of the modern human beast in *The Petrified Forest*.   After having talked of the monstrosities of the perverted intellectual of today he asks Gabby, one of the other characters, if she knows what is causing the present world chaos.   This is his answer to her negative reply: "It's nature hitting back.   Not with the old weapons—floods, plagues, holocausts.   We can neutralize them.   She's fighting back with strange instruments called neuroses.   She's deliberately inflicting mankind with the jitters.   Nature is proving that she can't be beaten by the likes of us.   She's taking the world away from the intellectuals and giving it back to the apes" (p. xxi).   One will recall that Sherwood expressed this same idea through Dr. Valkonen in *There Shall Be No Night*.   The second instance is from Arthur H. Compton's *Freedom of Man* (Yale University Press, 1935).   He, too, is talking about man's relation to nature: " 'Is nature friendly to us?'   Assuredly if we will learn her laws and adapt our lives accordingly.   If we do not, she may become our merciless enemy.   Such is the stern yet kindly dictum which science has to offer. . . . Two Old Testament statements embody the same idea in deistic terms: 'All things work together for him who serves the Lord,' is the exact parallel of nature's laws that are friendly to the well-adapted organism.   On the other hand, nature's ruthless attitude toward the man who will not adapt himself is accurately caught in the proverb 'The wages of sin is death.'. . . Coming back then to the view that the laws of nature are the method in which our intelligent God works, we must believe that His attitude toward us is revealed by the way nature treats us.   Is He friendly?   Yes, if we obey His laws" (pp. 113–114).

It is pertinent also here by way of corrective to call attention to a failure to interpret this passage in the *Mirour*, in relation to its context [T. O. Wedel, *The Medieval Attitude Toward Astrology* (Yale, 1920), pp. 134–41].   Here quoting from *Mirour*, *Vox Clamantis*, and *Confessio Amantis*, Wedel concludes that "It is not so much the man of character as the man of prayer who rules the stars" (p. 141).   In the implications of this statement Dr. Wedel ignores one aspect of Gower's most significant role.   God *will* aid man in answer to his prayers but only if his character and his actions accord with reason.   George G. Fox, *op. cit.* pp. 92–93, referring to the same passage says, "When Gower attempts to vindicate free will . . . he does it by arguments that are anti-astrological and non-scientific.   That is, he insists on the purely obvious influence of celestial bodies, and tacitly denies the occult emanation upon which all astrology is based.   He is more pious than the theologians."   The cogent refutation of Fox is that Gower bases his statement on the logic of the argument that reason has power over the stars.

wise man with God aiding will rule the stars,[8] man simply confesses his failure to use his reason if he blames astrological influences for his lot. Fortune also is the subject of repeated attacks by Gower.[9] The reason is that although it and fate were by his and Chaucer's day principally decorative literary terms, survivals of a functional element in an earlier civilization, they still remained symbols for an attitude which shifted the blame for one's own weakness.

Gower's ethical basis for an ordered universe through the responsibility imposed on the individual by the divine gift of reason finds expression in his reaction to Richard II and Henry IV. Specifically, it represents the application of his rationale to the practice of kingship. The ruler, whether by appointment or line of descent, is a responsible agent and is subject to indictment by his fellow countrymen. Space does not permit even the briefest survey of the heritage from Thomas Aquinas, Dante, Marsiglio of Padua, William of Ockham, and Wycliffe. It must suffice for the present to give an epitome of the system of Aquinas by a distinguished medievalist:[10]

The world of Thomas Aquinas was dominated by a few great simple universal ideas, of which the life of man, both individual and associated was the reflex. At the heart of things was God, revealed in the uniformity and harmony of nature. The center and crown of creation was man, to whom was given the rule over the earth, which again was the center of the material universe, served by the obedient sun and accompanied by the planetary and starry host in tributary homage. Corresponding to this manifest order of nature, the associated life of man was also an image of ordered unity. It had, to be sure, its varieties of race, nation and social class, but these varieties were only the differentiations of an essentially unified system. The one and only God had made one sole and sufficient revelation of himself and his revelation had included a scheme of social order.

This I quote *in extenso* because it might well be an epitome of Gower's entire rationale. In Gower's indictment or approval of government he may seem to the casual reader to be choosing from Aquinas, Dante, Marsiglio of Padua, William of Ockham, and Wycliffe in an eclectic manner. Actually he selects with discrimination those elements of government which seem best adapted to his general principles for responsible human beings and for an ordered universe. In brief, a king's acts should be dictated by reason—*i.e.* wisdom and virtue.

Gower was the monitor for Richard II through *Vox Clamantis* and *Confessio Amantis*; and he made him the object of a moralist's denunciation in the *Cronica Tripertita*. And in the poem *To Henry IV in Praise of Peace* he was the herald of what he hoped would be a new day under Henry IV. Here the only important

[8] See *Confessio Amantis*, VII, 633 ff., esp. 651–4. The astronomer has just been quoted as saying that the stars rule man's destiny. Gower adds:

> But the divin seith otherwise,
> That if man weren goode and wise
> And plesant unto the godhede,
> Thei scholden noght the sterres drede.

See also the Latin stanza preceding line 633, and *Vox Clamantis*, II, 239, which embodies the well-known proverb: In virtute dei sapiens dominabitur astra. Cf. Wedel, *op. cit.*, pp. 134–135.

[9] One illustration must suffice here. In his review of man's attempt to shift the responsibility for his evil state to fortune and the stars (Prologue to *Confessio Amantis*, ll. 529–47), Gower anticipated Shakespeare in his attribution to Edmund of a cynical negation of the power of fortune and the stars and his declaration of immediate parental responsibility for his present bastard state.

[10] Ephriam Emerton, "The Defensor Pacis of Marsiglio of Padua," *Harvard Theological Studies*, VIII, (1920), p. 2.

thing to stress is that his ambitions and his hopes were all a part of his ethical system. As is well known, in *Vox Clamantis*, he first defends the boy king because unwise councillors are responsible. Later he blames Richard himself as a heedless and undisciplined youth. Similarly in *Confessio Amantis*, written at the king's request and at first expressing confidence in him, he later deletes all favorable references to him, holds him primarily responsible for the evil state of affairs, affirms that the book was written for England's sake, and presents it to the future Henry IV. Even in the *Mirour*, citing Siriach (ll. 22801 ff.), he admonishes Edward III in his dotage and under the domination of Alice Perrers—a king ought to cherish truth and to obey in everything. After a reference to Edward III's weakness he prays God to bring discord to all laws when a woman reigns in the land and the king is subject to her. Entirely to the point for Gower's significant role is his indictment in *Vox Clamantis* (VII, xvii) of all individuals who are victims of their passions, which closes with the assertion that a king ruled by his vices rather than by reason is only a slave to his body. An indictment in the *Cronica Tripertita*, directly condemnatory, echoes Wycliffe's doctrine that no man in mortal sin can hold dominion or lordship.[11] The passage from the *Cronica Tripertita* reads:

> Est qui peccator, non est dominator
> Ricardo teste, finis probat hoc manifeste.   (III, ll. 486–87).

Again in Book VII of *Confessio Amantis*, which is devoted entirely to instructing a king in proper conduct, Gower repeats this idea in phrasing which might well have come from English puritans when they indicted Charles I over two centuries later:

> For thing which is of kinges set,
> With kinges oghte it noght be let.
> What king of lawe takth no kepe,
> Be lawe he mai no regne kepe.
> Do lawe awey what is a king?
> Wher is the riht of eny thing,
> If that ther be no lawe in londe?
> This oghte a king wel understonde,
> As he which is to lawe swore,
> That if the lawe be forbore
> Withouten execucioun,
> It makth a lond torne up so doun,
> Which is unto the king a sclandre.
>
> (ll. 3071–3083)

All this is of fundamental importance. A king who does not govern himself and does not use good judgment in ruling his people violates the law of reason and thus is in the category Gower established in the *Mirour*.

The constructive teaching of his ethical system is to be found in the poem entitled by Macaulay *To King Henry IV in Praise of Peace*. This eulogy is an

---

11 See especially *De Officio Regis* (Wyclif Society, London, 1887) (ed. by A. W. Pollard and Charles Sayle), *passim*. For concise summary, see editors' introduction, pp. xxvi ff.

epitome of the central theme of Marsiglio of Padua's *Defensor Pacis*: the end of government is peace. After justifying Henry IV's claim to his title, as does Chaucer, through line of descent and election by Parliament, he returns to his constant theme that reason (good judgment) above all things is to be praised in a king:

> Aboute a kyng good counseil is to preise
> Above alle othre thinges most vailable;
> Bot yit a kyng withinne himself shal peise,
> And se the thinges that ben reasonable,
> And ther uppon he shal his wittes stable
> Among the men to set pes in evene,
> For love of him which is the kyng of hevene.
>
> (ll. 141–147)

Incidentally, his repeated concern for the welfare of England and his love for the home of his birth provide an immediate motive for illustrating through these English rulers the basis of his ethical standards. Its high point comes in a well-known lyric passage in Book VII of *Vox Clamantis*.

> Singula, que dominus statuit sibi regna per orbem,
> Que magis in Christi nomine signa gerunt,
> Diligo, set propriam super omnia diligo terram.
> In qua principium dixit origio meum.
> Quicquid agant alie terre, non subruor inde,
> Dum tamen ipse foris sisto remotus eis;
> Patria set iuvenem que me suscepit alumpnum,
> Partibus in cuius semper adhero manens,
> Hec si quic patitur, mea viscera compaciuntur,
> Nec sine me dampna ferre valebit ea:
> Eius in adversis do pondere sum quasi versus;
> Si perstet, persto, si cadat illa, cado.[12]
>
> (ll. 1289–1300)

The climax in the last ringing line recalls the height of Churchill's great argument in England's darkest hour four years ago:

> Si perstet, persto, si cadat illa, cado.

Another aspect of this whole matter of kingship sets Gower in artistic integrity over one hundred years beyond Boccaccio, Chaucer, and Lydgate, and allies him with the Elizabethan *Mirror for Magistrates* and Tudor tragedy. In the Latin summary of his three major works appearing at the close of *Confessio Amantis*, both the version concerning *Vox Clamantis* which fixes the responsibility on the nobles and the one which fixes it on the king, specifically place Richard's fate in the category of cause and effect and *not* as a result of capricious fortune. The

---

[12] The following is an attempted paraphrase of this fine passage: I love the separate Christian kingdoms the Lord has established throughout the world; but above all I love the land in which I was born. Whatever other lands may do, I am not shaken if I am outside their portals. But if my native land, which bred and reared me, suffers injuries, I too must suffer. Without me she cannot be strong to bear these ills. I bend under the weight of her adversities. If she stands firm, I stand firm. If she falls, I fall.

earlier version, which absolves the boy king, states clearly (evidencius declarat) that such calamities (the peasants' rebellion) happened among men from certain causes and not from fortune:

> Secundus enim liber, sermone latino versibus exametri et pentametri compositus, tractat super illo mirabili euentu qui in Anglia tempore domini. Regis Ricardi secundi anno regni sui quarto contigit, quando seruiles rustici impetuose contra nobiles et ingenuos regni insurrexerunt. Innocenciam tamen dicti domini Regis tunc minoris etatis causa inde excusabilem pronuncians, culpas aliunde, ex quibus et non a fortuna talia inter homines contigunt enormia, euidencius declarat. . . .[13]

The later version states that "the cruel king himself falling down from on high by his own evil doings, was at length hurled into the pit which he dug himself."

> Secundus enim liber sermono latino metrice compositus tractat de variis infortuniis tempore Regis Ricardi Secundi in Anglia contingentibus. Unde non solum regni proceres et communes tormenta passi sunt, set et ipse crudelissimus rex suis ex demeritis ab alto corruens in foveam quam fecit finaliter proiectus est. Nomenque voluminis huius Vox Clamantis intitulatur.[14]

In a word he accepts the essence of the definition of Chaucer's Monk preceding his tale but rejects pointedly any attribution to the Chaucerian "capricious fortune." He makes this a consistent example of man's responsibility, cause and effect, reason versus passion.

Here then is the word of a middle-class Englishman. He did not see the revolt as "a popular front." He saw it only as an uprising that was destroying the established order, the only one he could imagine. In this respect he was a spiritual brother of the author of *Piers Plowman*: both wanted merely spiritual conversion of individuals, with no social upheavals.

Gower's *Confessio Amantis* might well be called his *summa moralis*. In its totality it records this principle of man's responsibility resulting from the gift of reason. The author has suffered from piecemeal interpretation of this work to a greater extent than any other writer to my knowledge. The work has a large integrity and unity based on a defense of his ethical scheme for the universe. Read in the light of his *moral system* it transcends any mechanical pattern. Gower tells in the Prologue exactly what he is going to do. He does it well. It is worth doing. And he recapitulates in the Epilogue. In a major respect, *Confessio Amantis* is a King's Courtesy Book. In his earlier version he states this specifically. Also he states definitely in the Prologue that he is going to write of love, which subdues many a wise man, and is going to consider those in high office with relation to the virtues and vices of their offices.

> Whan the prologe is so despended,
> This bok schal afterward ben ended
> Of love, which doth many a wonder
> And many a wys man hath put under.

[13] Macaulay, *op. cit.*, III, 479–80, fn.

[14] *Ibid*. See Macaulay's translation *CHEL* (Cambridge, 1908), II, 158–9. "The second book, metrically composed in the Latin language, treats of the various misfortunes which happened in England in the time of king Richard II, whence not only the nobles and commons of the realm suffered great evils, but the cruel king himself, falling from on high by his own evil doings, was at length hurled into the pit which he dug himself. And the name of this volume is *Vox Clamantis*."

And in this wyse I thenke trete
Towardes hem that now be grete,
Betwen the vertu and the vice
Which longeth unto this office.

(ll. 73–80)

In the second place he treats of reason versus passion as relating to love between the sexes. In the third place he makes personal application of this to his own life— an old man in love with a young girl, with reason reasserting itself in the end. Furthermore, his approach and his return in the poem to England and its welfare are consistent with this dominant note in all three of his major works. Gower's complete works are as much a justification of the ways of God to man as are Milton's. His most significant role is his explanation and illustration of the ethical basis of God's universe for this little world of man.

This brings us to a brief comment on the question of courtly love, the theme of an able chapter by C. S. Lewis, in defense of Gower as a literary artist.[15] Gower recognizes in connection with love and reason that there is the law of kind. As far as possible within the established order he would have all relationships between sexes culminate in marriage. In the same mood that fortune and fate evoked his indictment, he has no time for courtly love because even though it may be no more than a literary convention or a decorative pattern for fiction, it is a symbol which might encourage those who wish through their passions to violate the laws of nature and of established society. His common-sense recognition of the "law of kind" and the self-willed corrupt nature of man justifies his writing of the perversities of sexual passion but does not permit him in his stories to sanction the vices as codified in the rules of Andreas Capellaneus. The important thing here is that this becomes a program for action as first based on his *apologia* for reason in the *Mirour*. His *Traitié* and his *Balades* represent again the constructive side of his theme. Both "are made especially for those who expect their love affairs to be perfected in marriage." The former sets forth also "the evils springing from adultery and incontinence." Lewis with all his excellent appreciation of the literary values in the stories told by the Confessor misses the largest informing element in failing to observe that the outer circle of the story carries his constant theme of England, that he makes clear his theme of reason versus passion in his love stories, and that the immediate pattern was in part at least a King's Courtesy Book. Lewis speaks of Book VII as a "general digression on education." It is not a "general digression." It is a body of specific instructions as to the education and behavior of a king. Lines 73–80 of the Prologue, quoted above, have prepared us for it.

Space does not permit even reference to the detailed evidence which would prove to the hilt that *Confessio Amantis* is Gower's *summa* and can be justly interpreted only as such. The palinode beginning with Book VIII, line 2009, and closing with line 2970 stresses for Gower himself the place of reason in his life. The Confessor says (2023), renounce love unless you can keep the proper

15 *The Allegory of Love A Study in Medieval Tradition* (Oxford, 1936), pp. 198–222.

balance between love and reason; and Venus in her final words (2925–27) tells him, after Cupid has withdrawn the dart of love and restored his reason, to return where *moral virtue* dwells—that about which he has been writing through almost twenty years.

We shall have to wait until we come to Milton before we find another English writer who, to paraphrase Macaulay, treats "the whole field of man's religious and moral nature, . . . the purposes of Providence in dealing with him" and "the method which should be followed by man in order to reconcile himself to God." Like Milton also he seems to record his spiritual biography in his works. Gower did "bolt to the bran" for his contemporaries problems of man's responsibility, the place of a ruler in a kingdom, and the whole question of courtly love in literature and life. This is because he was interested, not in philosophic thought or an abstract philosophy of life, but in a philosophy of living. There is no reason to doubt that in the well-known phrase "the moral Gower" Chaucer meant to express high regard for his fellow poet. An attempt at a modern phrasing of his most significant role is that he is an exponent of the practice of wisdom and virtue and of the gospel of individual responsibility, both directed toward "a good life" for contemporary society and the welfare of England, his own dear land. A study to which this is not even an adequate introduction may reveal, I am convinced, that as a practical conservative-liberal he was one of "the most thoughtful and intelligent" men of his age.

GOWER'S 'HONESTE LOVE'

J. A. W. BENNETT

Of all the revaluations forced upon us by the *Allegory of Love*, none was so unexpected as that suggested by the pages devoted to Gower. Here Lewis's descriptive criticism is at its genial best. Yet some of his warmest admirers have hinted that his judgement of the *Confessio* was partial, or even deliberately provocative. Those who feel that they are being provoked will doubtless class the half-chapter on Gower with the essays, printed elsewhere, on Morris, Kipling, and Rider Haggard. But there is good evidence that Lewis was captivated by the sheer craft and artistry of this little-read poet. How otherwise explain why he gave so much space to praise of the poem that he left himself almost no room for comment on the very features of its ethical scheme that should have earned it a special place in the history of Love-Allegory? Curiously enough, later critics of the work (almost all transatlantic) have continued to ignore its doctrine and, perhaps because of this, perhaps because of their surprising preoccupation with the massive French and Latin writers, have for the most part continued to damn or dismiss the *Confessio* as dull. J. H. Fisher's recent study even goes so far as to assert that 'the dullness cannot be palliated but must be recognised for what it is—success in its intended genre'. Dull the poem will doubtless seem if we take its genre to be social or political philosophy. But so to cabin it alongside the *Vox Clamantis* or *Speculum Meditantis* is to ignore the plain implications of its title. W. G. Dodd, writing on *Courtly Love in Chaucer and Gower*, did not ignore them. Unfortunately his method of proceeding produced its own kind of dullness. It was from the thraldom of such mechanical analysis that *The Allegory* rescued us. But to accept as definitive all the judgements of that masterpiece is to fall into another servitude.

I

The purely historical and verbal connexions between the *Confessio* and the *Roman de la Rose* Dodd and Lewis between them have adequately indicated. Each work may be described as an *Ars Amatoria*, so long as such a description is not taken to imply an identity of tone or an Ovidian flavour. So deep and pervasive was the influence of the *Roman* that Gower would not have had to read that rambling cyclopedia to learn of Malebouche (*C.A.* ii, 390), Danger (i, 2443; iii, 1538; viii, 2256; Balade x), Jalousie (v, 511–34). And long before the *Roman* was begun the roles of Venus and Cupid as King and Queen of Love had been firmly established; in presenting them Gower differs from his predecessors (and Chaucer) chiefly by eschewing any physical description of either—and he is almost equally reticent about Amans and his mistress. The blind-

ness of the love they enkindle is the theme of a passionate lament that
—without any warrant from Ovid—he puts into the mouth of Thisbe:

> O thou which cleped art Venus,
> Goddesse of love, and thou, Cupide,
> Which loves cause hast forto guide,
> I wot now wel that ye be blinde,
> Of thilke unhapp which I now finde
> Only betwen my love and me . . .
>
> (iii, 1462)

It is concordant with this piteous complaint (in its language so similar to
Crisseid's fatal outcry in Henryson's *Testament*) that Amans should
describe suitors in the court of love as for ever climbing a wheel of fortune
that lifts them only to hurl them down (iv, 2279). The Confessor himself,
telling the tale of Canace and Machaire, represents Cupid not only as
blind but as making his 'clients' blind (iii, 158–60); and he goes on to
depict the ill-fated pair as further blinded by Nature:

> . . . sche which is Maistresse
> In kinde and techeth every lif
> Withoute law positif,
> Of which sche takth nomaner charge,
> Bot kepth hire lawes al at large,
> Nature, tok hem into lore
> And tawht hem so, that overmore
> Sche hath hem in such wise daunted,
> That thei were, as who seith, enchaunted.
>
> (iii, 170)

Repeatedly the priest's *exempla* differ from their originals by such asser-
tions of the power of 'Kinde', or natural law (it distinguishes his tale of
Constance, for example, from the Man of Law's).[1] It is as if Gower had
combined the two characters of Genius and Nature in the *Roman*, where
Genius is Nature's priest, spokesman, and confessor. And the constant
awareness of the force of instinctive drives, of passion as a kind of
enchantment that casts a spell on Reason, gives to Gower's priest a rare
breath of sympathy and compassion that has its affinities with the specifically Christian *caritas* which is threaded through the whole system.

To the general tone of tenderness *courtoisie* has contributed as well as
Christianity—if indeed it is possible in this respect to distinguish them.
No one familiar with the literature of *courtoisie* will fall into the error of
reading the Venus who controls the action of the poem as identical with
the goddess of pagan worship. As Lewis noted, Gower faced some of the
difficulties inherent in this personification when he came to consider

---

[1] Genius also goes out of his way to maintain that Venus herself came forth
'by way of Kinde' (v, 800).

heathen mythology in Book V; and really they are no greater than those arising from the ambiguities attaching to the word *love* itself (exemplified in the distinction Genius has to draw between the love he countenances and 'loves court nowaday', iv, 2279). Significantly, it is Amans himself who prompts Genius to the discourse on mythology. After hearing the story of Venus and Mars, he is moved to inquire (it is an attractive feature of the machinery that he is always depicted as having a mind of his own),

> Hou such thing to the heveneward
> Among the goddes myhte falle:
> For ther is bot *o* god of alle.
>
> (v, 730)

The Book shows the priest at his most orthodox, outlining the Christian faith and deploring the falling away of modern prelates whcse avarice— he appeals to Colossians iii 5—was hardly different from the old idolatry. In this context *all* the heathen deities must be presented as 'fantasies'. But Amans rightly remarks that the god and goddess of love still 'stand in all men's speech' and wonders 'how thei ferst comen to that name'.

The question surely embarrasses Genius, not—as Lewis might seem to imply—because he can find no place for human love in his Christian apologetics, but because the Venus and Cupid of the pagan stories signify lust, lechery, promiscuity and even (v, 1426) prostitution. Genius is understandably ashamed that the deity he serves should figure in these stories; but he tells them

> for thei stonden nyh thi brest
> Upon the schrifte of thi matiere
>
> (v, 1384)

—in other words, so that Amans may avoid or clear himself of such sins, not so that he may abjure love. Admittedly there is a certain awkwardness here, but it hardly disturbs us as we read.

In making appropriate *exempla* out of other classical stories Genius does nothing more, and certain nothing more far-fetched, than had been done in the highly respectable *Ovide moralisé*, on which Gower doubtless drew; even the surprising interpretation of the tale of Mars and Venus has precedent in that popular work. And from the story of Pygmalion he extracts the unexceptionable moral (not to be found in Jean de Meun's version, where, as Gunn says, it represents 'the entelechy of feminine nature') that

> The god of love is favorable
> To hem that ben of love stable.
>
> (iv, 443)

If Genius's prime concern seems to be with a lover's faults and failings, we are never allowed to forget that these reflect vices common to
all mankind. Though the discourse on Surquiderie (Presumpcio) is
headed by elegiacs alluding to Cupid and the *laqueos Veneris*, in fact it
touches on love only in so far as it portrays the self-love of Narcissus—
presented, as always when reprehensible passion is involved, as a kind
of madness or enchantment:[1]

> He sih the like of his visage,
> And wende ther were an ymage
> Of such a Nimphe as tho was *faie*,
> Whereof that love his herte assaie
> Began, as it was after sene,
> Of his sotie and made him wene
> It were a womman that he syh.
>
> (i, 2315)

But the main drift of the preachment is against the presumptuous man
who

> . . . seith nought ones 'grant mercy'
> To godd, which alle grace sendeth,
> So that his wittes he despendeth
> Upon himself . . .;
>
> (i, 1902)

whilst the description of the vainglorious lover (i, 2681–2717) who
mistakes his own high spirits for lasting joys has moral and religious
overtones that remove it far from the world of the *Roman*, and verbal
anticipations of the fervent prayer with which the whole poem is to
close. Judged by the standards Genius here sets up, Chaucer's Squire
(and many another 'lovyere and lusty bacheler') would fall sadly short.
When priest turns to penitent and bids him

> Now scrif thee, Sone, *in Godes pes*,
> And of thi love tell me plein
> If that thi gloire hath be so vein,

we are within a Christian confessional. And when later he cites scripture
to his purpose it is not in parody:

---

[1] *cf.*, for example, Amphitryon's enchantment of Alcmena (ii, 2490). The
spell that Estella throws over Pip, in *Great Expectations*, has something of the
same sinister, magical power.

> After the vertu moral eke
> To speke of love if I schal seke,
> Among the holi bokes wise
> I finde write in such a wise,
> Who loveth noght is hier as ded.
>
> (iv, 2321)

That this is a conscious attempt to relate the doctrine of courteous love to Christian teaching is indicated by the marginal direction, which runs: *Nota de amore caritatis*. The association reminds us that lack of *caritas*, in people and priest alike, is the main theme of the Prologue to the whole work; that at the beginning of Book I we turn from scenes of strife and discord to consider *naturatus amor*; and that at the end of Book VIII we come back to

> thilke love which that is
> Withinne a mannes herte affermed,
> And stant of charite confermed.
>
> (viii, 3162)

'The hyhe God'—so prays the poet—'such love ous sende'; of the same 'hyhe God' Genius had said that He

> Yaf to the men in Erthe hiere
> Upon the forme and the matiere
> Of that he wolde make hem wise.
>
> (iv, 2363)

The creed of Genius, then, is the poet's creed; and Amans accepts the ethics that Genius affirms. The one point on which the priest cannot move him is his refusal to win favour by fighting for his mistress abroad; it is the least logical and least defensible point of 'þe lel layk of luf', and Amans' appeal is to the Gospels:

> A Sarazin if I sle schal,
> I sle the Soule forth withal,
> And that was nevere Christes lore.
>
> (iv, 1679)

But he admits that his own desperate thoughts of self-slaughter were equally culpable as sins of intention (iii, 1513) and duly begs for and receives absolution from them; nothing brings out more sharply the difference between the *mores* Gower is depicting and those of Troilus (see *TC* iv, 1231–41). And when Amans calls his mistress 'vertuous' and 'devout' (iv, 1136) we should take these words at their face value. Nowhere is there any hint that she is married, still less is there any suggestion that Amans is: he is as 'innocent' as his antecedent in the *Roman*,

53

and she, like the *amie* in the *Roman*, is a *damoisele* and a *pucele*. The adultery of an Iseult or a Guinevere has no place in Amans' thought.[1] Critics have argued that Gower substituted incest for *Luxuria* as a capital vice because 'Luxury naturally cannot be a sin against Venus'. It is at least as probable that Gower preferred to treat this perversion of love because it illustrates the strange workings of 'Kind' (by the same token, it is the mystery of transmutation as much as 'love-interest' that fascinated him in the *Metamorphoses*). *Luxuria* in its chief manifestation of adultery is, in fact, condemned wherever it appears, just as it had been in the *Vox Clamantis*. There (vii, 157 ff.) it figures as one of the *gallica peccata*, vices new come in from France: a false kind of love, 'Sic sub mendaci specie grossantur amoris'. Genius himself, on the other hand, sets forth at length the rationale of chaste marriage (employing a plain, earthy image which assures us that he speaks with Gower's voice):

> The Madle is made for the femele,
> Bot where as on desireth fele,
> That nedeth noght be weie of kinde:
> For whan a man mai redy finde
> His oghne wif, what scholde he seche
> In strange places to beseche
> To borwe an other mannes plouh,
> Whan he hath geere good ynouh
> Affaited at his oghne heste,
> And is to him wel more honeste
> Than other thing which is unknowe?
> Forthi scholde every good man knowe
> And thenke, hou that in mariage
> His trouthe plight lith in morgage,
> Which if he breke, it is falshode,
> And that descordeth to manhode . . .
>
> (vii, 4215)

'Corporis et mentis regem decet omnis honestas', says the Latin head-piece; and the margin directs us to his unimpeachable philosophical authority for this conception of 'honesty': Aristotle's 'de quinta principum regiminis Policia, que Castitatem concernit, cuius *honestas* impudicicie motus obtemperans tam corporis quam anime mundiciam specialius preseruat' [? = *Pol.* vii, 16]

---

[1] In the *Traitié* it is condemned as a *sotie*.

II

To 'les amantz marietz' Gower had devoted the whole of his *Traitié*; its theme and argument are consistent with the attitude described above:

> Et puis dieus qui la loi ordina
> En un char ad deux personnes mis,
> Droitz est qe l'omme et femme pour cela
> Tout un soul coer eront par tiel devis,
> Loiale amie avoec loials amis:
> Cest en amour trop belle retenue
> Selonc la loi de seinte eglise due.
> Ovesque amour quant loialte s'aqueinte,
> Lors sont les noeces bones et joiouses.
>
> (iii, 3—iv, 1)

And on this the marginal gloss runs:

> Qualiter *honestas conjugii* non ex libidinis aut avaricie causa, set tantummodo quod sub lege generacio ad cultum dei fiat, primordia sua suscepit.

But it is the presence, indeed the pre-eminence, of Penelope, Lucrece, Alceste, Alcyone in Venus's own court (in the *Confessio*) that underlines most firmly his view of chaste marriage:

> Bot above alle that ther were
> Of wommen I sih foure there,
> Whos name I herd most comended:
> Be hem the Court stod al amended;
> For where thei comen in presence,
> Men deden hem the reverence,
> As thogh they hadden be goddesses,
> Of al this world or Emperesses.
>
> (viii, 2605)

This outdoes Chaucer, of whom the Man of Law—in the very act, it seems, of censuring Gower—had said

> O Ypermystra, Penelopee, Alceste,
> Youre wifhod he comendeth with the beste!

And, in fact, Chaucer's commendation of Alcione (in the *Book of the Duchess*) is far less moving than Gower's depiction of her as

> Sche fondeth in hire briddes forme,
> If that sche mihte hirself conforme
> To do the plesance of a wif,
> As sche dede in that other lif:
> For thogh sche hadde hir pouer lore,
> Hir will stod as it was tofore,
> And serveth him so as sche mai.

(iv, 3109)

It is in key with this presentation that Genius should regard the love that 'upgroweth with your age' as not only a sign of 'gentilesse' and, if properly directed, a school of virtue, but also as finding its proper consummation in marriage. Ironically enough, the sheer beauty of the tale of Rosiphilee, in which this doctrine is most firmly embodied, has diverted attention from its sentence. The very fact that here for the first time Genius implies that 'mi ladi Venus' should not necessarily have the last word ought to alert us:[1]

> Mi ladi Venus, whom I serve,
> What womman wole hire thonk deserve,
> Sche mai noght thilke love eschuie
> Of paramours, bot sche mot suie
> Cupides lawe; and natheles
> Men sen such love sielde in pes,
> That it nys evere upon aspie
> Of janglinge and of fals Envie,
> Fulofte medlid with disese:
> Bot thilke love is wel at ese,
> Which set is upon mariage;
> For that dar schewen the visage
> In alle places openly.
> A great mervaile it is forthi,
> How that a Maiden wolde lette,
> That sche hir time ne besette
> To haste unto that ilke feste,
> Whereof the love is al honeste.
> Men mai recovere lost of good,
> Bot so wys man yit nevere stod,
> Which mai recovere time lore:
> So mai a Maiden wel thefore
> Ensample take, of that sche strangeth
> Hir love, and longe er that sche changeth

---

[1] *cf.* his later touch of independence (viii, 2079), preparing us for Amans's reservation in viii, 2392 ('sche which *seid* is the goddesse').

> Hir herte upon hir lustes greene
> To mariage, as it is seene.
> For thus a yer or tuo or thre
> Sche lest, er that sche wedded be,
> Whyl sche the charge myhte bere
> Of children, whiche the world forbere
> Ne mai, bot if it scholde faile.
>
> (iv, 1467)

This same 'love honeste' is again commended later:

> for it doth aweie
> The vice, and as the bokes sein,
> It maketh curteis of the vilein:
>
> (iv, 2298)

lines which make clear the sense of Genius's dictum that

> Love is an occupacion,
> Which forto kepe hise lustes save
> Scholde every gentil herte have.
>
> (iv, 1455)

This is 'courtois' sentiment at its highest, and deserves to be set beside Malory's famous but confused chapter on 'trewe love' (Caxton xviii, 25). It might be read as a 'courtois' adaptation of the Pauline view that it is better to marry than to burn.[1] But Genius's praise of 'honeste love' reminds us of the nobler and more positive view that marriage is *honorabile connubium* (Heb. xiii 14).

Indeed, it comes close to what Chaucer's Parson saw as 'the cause finale of matrimoigne': 'engendrure of children to the service of God' (*C.T.* x, 935). Gower's broader view, that society must be continuated 'lest the world should fail', is consistent with that abiding concern for the commonweal which modern critics, from Dr. Wickert to A. B. Ferguson, have discovered in all of his works.[2] Equally characteristic is the equation of secret love *paramours* with 'disese' and of honourable love with peace. As an English comment on the subterfuges of a Jason, a Lancelot, or a Troilus it sorts well with the response that Chaucer anticipated as he told the story of how Troilus gained his Criseyde—'so nold I nat love purchace!' (*TC* ii, 33). But to Gower 'pes' meant more than the absence of difficulty or embarrassment. It is the keyword of all

---

[1] A marginal note in some MSS. runs: *Non quia sic se habet veritas sed opinio amantium.* But it is hard to believe that this is authorial comment, or even an expression of second thoughts. It probably represents a gloss by a literal-minded copyist who misunderstood part or all of the passage.

[2] *Studien zu John Gower*, by Maria Wickert (1953); *The Articulate Citizen and the English Renaissance*, by Arthur B. Ferguson (1965) (see ch. ii and iii).

his poetry, the highest good that man may seek; and when he comes to describe heavenly felicity in his closing couplet it is to point us to that place 'wher resteth love and alle pes'.

III

Lewis, who so memorably described the closing scenes of the poem, thought this coda was a failure; 'Gower is not enough of a philosopher . . . even to attempt . . . any reconciliation between the claims of his two worlds'.[1] But is not the poet quietly adjusting these claims throughout the whole work? It is not only at the end that he goes 'a softe pas'; and the quiet unobtrusive manner may blind us to the nature of his achievement. But there is no mistaking the drift of the *moralitas* that crowns the end of his last and longest story:

> Lo, what it is to be wel grounded:
> For he hath ferst his love founded
> Honesteliche as forto wedde,
> Honesteliche his love he spedde
> And hadde children with his wif,
> And as him liste he ladde his lif;
> And in ensample his lif was write,
> That alle lovers myhten wite
> How ate laste it schal be sene
> Of love what thei wolden mene.
>
> (viii, 1993)

The doctrine illustrated by the tale of Rosiphilee at the centre of the poem and reaffirmed so emphatically near the end must surely remain valid, however irrelevant it may seem to Amans's plight as shortly revealed. And it surely forces us to give to the *Confessio* some of the historical importance that Lewis read into the *Kingis Quair*, a poem that perhaps does not praise Gower gratuitously. In King James's poem, says Lewis, 'the poetry of marriage at last emerges from the traditional poetry of adultery; and the literal narrative of a contemporary wooing emerges from romance and allegory'.[2] One can hardly assert that Amans's confessions give us a literal narrative of a contemporary wooing (or indeed be so sure that James gives us that), though in verisimilitude they surpass the later poem. One may, however, claim that the prose, if not the poetry, of fecund marriage is already emerging from the traditional poetry of *courtoisie*. And that Genius should link 'honest' marriage with child-bearing is not surprising if we recall his original role, in the *Roman*, as sponsor of reproduction. Gower's 'toning down'

[1] *The Allegory of Love*, p. 218.
[2] *ibid.*, p. 237.

of this aspect is all of a piece with his other modifications of the spirit and structure of the *Roman*; but he would hardly ignore the significance of Genius's name.

To recognize the meaning of that name, and to remember its history, is to see why the priest's attitude towards Amans's chances of personal success in his love-affair is throughout so non-committal. Being face to face with his penitent he knows from the outset what we as readers sense but slowly and do not clearly learn until the *dénouement*— that Amans is being shadowed by Elde. His persistence in unrequited love comes to have the quality of an obsession; and he himself admits that in this regard he is 'assoted': the word is used throughout the poem, as Malory was to use it throughout the *Morte*, of infatuation or ungovernable passion. This lovers' malady destroys Reason (which in Gower always connotes 'measure' and restraint). To persist in it, says Genius, is a sin (viii, 2098); and in so saying he first reminds us that his own priestly office makes it incumbent on him to instruct in virtue; then proceeds:

> Forthi to speken overmore
> Of love, which thee mai availe,
> Tak love where it mai noght faile.
>
> (viii, 2084)

As it stands, the advice is cryptic—the decorum of the poem forbids an explicit identification of this love with the Christian *caritas* that never faileth. But that we are moving out of the religion of love is clear a few lines later:

> For love, which that blind was evere,
> Makth alle his servantz blinde also.
> My Sone, and if thou have be so,
> Yit is it time to withdrawe,
> And set thin herte under that lawe,
> The which of reson is governed
> And noght of will
>
> (viii, 2130)

(though again the full implications are left to be drawn out by the poet himself, at viii, 3143 ff.) Amans, however, persists in presenting his appeal to the deities of love, and in it, for the first time, and almost by accident, he discloses his real plight. The ninth verse of his 'lettre' runs

> Ovide ek seith that love to parforne
> Stant in the hond of Venus the goddesse,
> Bot whan sche takth hir conseil with Satorne,
> Ther is no grace, and in that time, I gesse,
> Began mi love—
>
> (viii, 2273)

59

It began, that is, in the age assigned to malevolent Saturn, that last stage of life in which, as Raleigh was to record, 'We find by dear and lamentable experience, and by the loss which can never be repaired, that of all our vain passions and affections past, the sorrow only abideth.' And the plea in the next verse but one that Cupid if he cannot give a 'salve' will withdraw his dart is another preparative for the final farewell to love. Venus takes him at his word, and as she promises to make him heart-whole again reveals that though he has feigned 'a yong corage' his locks are grey:

> Mi medicine is noght to sieke
> For thee and for suche old sieke,
> Noght al per chance as ye it wolden,
> Bot so as ye be reson scholden,
> Acordant unto loves kinde.
>
> (viii, 2367)

Only Gower would make Venus, like a very schoolmistress, speak the language of reason; and she is to resort to it again (2919). But it has always been the language of her priest.

So the Senex comes to his senses, cured of love, conscious at last that it may be just another name for desire. Gower's delicate art shines through the little scene that follows:

> Venus behield me than and lowh,
> And axeth, as it were in game,
> What love was. And I for schame
> Ne wiste what I scholde ansuere . . .
>
> (viii, 2870)

'What is love?' is indeed the question that many of the *exempla* have raised, though never so directly; and most of them, following the best medieval pattern, have raised also the question of its relation to Reason.

As she dismisses Amans, Venus enjoins

> That thou nomore of love sieche.
> Bot my will is that thou besieche
> And preie hierafter for the pes.
>
> (viii, 2911)

This is doubly appropriate, for Venus herself espouses peace and tranquillity (*Venus otia amat*); and throughout his confessions Amans has shown something of the fervour for peace that informs the Prologue (in which war figures as destroying *charite*, 903–4). But, like the earlier reference to unfailing love, 'the pes' is a phrase with spiritual overtones (Amans himself has used 'werre, contek, strife' to signify inner discord, iii, 1132); and the prayer that duly follows in the second recension strengthens this impression. In it, returning to the theme of the Prologue, where priests are censured for neglecting the duty of 'charite' (110), he enjoins the clergy

> forto praie and to procure
> Oure pes toward the hevene above,
> And ek to sette reste and love
> Among ous on this erthe hiere.
> For if they wroughte in this manere
> Aftir the reule of charite,
> I hope that men schuldyn se
> This lond amende . . .
>
> (viii, 2998)

Thus there is no abrupt disjunction, but a gradually dawning sense that in the last stage of life, when man no longer has dues to pay to 'Kinde' (*cf.* viii, 2348), he must put by amorous concerns and both seek and practise *caritas*. Macaulay labelled the closing passage of the whole work a 'Farewell to Earthly Love'; but if these immediately preceding scenes mean anything

> . . . thilke love which that is
> Withinne a mannes herte affermed
> And stant of charite confermed—

this love, though certainly contrasted with the worship of Venus, is not wholly removed from secular concerns. Far from being asked, as Chaucer asks us, to think 'al nys but a faire This world' (*TC* v, 1840), we are to remember that God

> This large world forth with the hevene
> Of his eternal providence
> Hath mad,
>
> (viii, 2972)

and to pray for peace, unity and good governance,

> With outen which, it is no les,
> To seche and loke into the laste,
> Ther may no worldes joye laste.
>
> (viii, 2992)

The world will fail, Genius had argued, unless folk marry and bring forth children. It will come to ruin, says the poet, here (as in the Prologue) *in propria persona*, unless men seek peace and practise charity and kings seek 'Love and acord' (viii, 3018*). 'Honeste love' in wedlock, *caritas* in the commonwealth, are wholly compatible ideals, and it is Gower's distinctive achievement to have harmonized them in a single poem, whilst still setting forth the graces and 'gentilesse' of *courtoisie*.

GOWER'S NARRATIVE ART

DEREK PEARSALL

Recent books and articles on John Gower have laid stress on his role as a moralist and as keeper of the king's conscience during a particularly brilliant and bloody era.[1] He has been presented to us as a fearless critic of the corruption of his time and as the exponent of a moral philosophy which remains consistent throughout his three major works, the *Mirour de l'Omme*, the *Vox Clamantis*, and the *Confessio Amantis*. Gower himself would not have quarrelled with this image; indeed it is one that he tried to cultivate, as we see from some Latin verses which prefix the *Vox Clamantis* in certain manuscripts:

> Ad mundum mitto mea iacula, dumque sagitto;
> At ubi iustus erit, nulla sagitta ferit.
> Sed male viventes hos vulnero transgredientes;
> Conscius ergo sibi se speculetur ibi.[2]

Accompanying these lines is a picture, presumably representing Gower, of an old man dressed in a long gown. He is stern of countenance, has a bow, and is in the act of shooting an arrow at the round earth, which is shown divided into one half and two quadrants, as if to symbolise the three estates of society. Certainly the picture is not a false one. Gower had much to say about English politics and English society which was apt and true, even if he did say it in a generalised way which lacked the moving power of Chaucer's and Langland's graphic individuation. It was also a rare political acumen – a good deal rarer than the thunderous outrage of the professional apocalypticist – which enabled Gower to pick out Henry, earl of Derby, as the cynosure of English hopes as early as 1393.[3] It would clearly be quite wrong to see the *Confessio Amantis* against anything but the background of the whole man, but it is important that the background remain in the background. The current reappraisal of Gower is doing loyal service to Gower

---

[1]   In particular John H. Fisher, *John Gower: Moral Philosopher and Friend of Chaucer* (New York, 1964), which is likely to remain the standard work on Gower for many years; also *The Major Latin Works of John Gower*, translated (with introduction and notes) by E. W. Stockton (Seattle, Wash., 1962). Both writers owe a debt to earlier articles by George R. Coffman: "John Gower in his Most Significant Role," *Elizabethan Studies and Other Essays in Honor of George F. Reynolds* (Univ. of Colorado Studies in the Humanities, Vol. II, No. 4, (1945), pp. 52–61, and "John Gower, Mentor for Royalty: Richard II," *PMLA*, LXIX (1954), 953–964; also to Maria Wickert, *Studien zu John Gower* (Köln, 1953).

[2]   *The Complete Works of John Gower*, ed. G. C. Macaulay in 4 vols: Vol. I, French works; Vols II and III, English works; Vol. IV, Latin works (Oxford, 1899–1902), IV, 19. This edition is used throughout. The picture accompanying the verses is reproduced (from Cotton Tiberius A.iv) as the frontispiece to Vol. IV. See Stockton, *Latin Works*, p. 342.

[3]   The evidence for this prescience is in the revised Prologue to the *Confessio*, dated "the yer sextenthe of kyng Richard" (viz. 1392–93), where the story of Richard's commissioning "som newe thing" is suppressed, and the name of Henry of Lancaster introduced as dedicatee (Prologue, l. 87). See Fisher, *John Gower*, pp. 121–124.

the man, but may be doing less service to Gower the English poet. For the *Confessio* has an importance to the reader of poetry which is different in kind, not merely in degree, from that of the *Mirour* and the *Vox*. It is not simply that the poem is in English (though of course to the English reader this is a point in its favour), for Gower could write excellent poetry in French. It is not to be found in the *Mirour* but in the *Cinkante Balades*, which are as fine and artful a product of the fine art of loving as the fourteenth century produced, either in France or England.[4] The difference between the *Confessio* and the other two major poems is that the English poem finally "realizes" what Gower had always been trying to say: the meaning *is* the sense. In it, Gower's potential imaginative power is released fully for the first time, just as Chaucer's was released by the scheme of the *Canterbury Tales*, and his fine moral discrimination, his fine sentiment, and his central good sense at last find their true embodiment and expression.

Three factors contribute to the success of the *Confessio*: the verse, the narrative frame, and the stories. Of the first it would be impudent to speak, if by so doing one thought to add anything to the deeply sensitive appreciation of C. S. Lewis,[5] but some comments may be made on the overall structure of the poem before we move to discussion of the stories.

The dramatic fiction of the lover's confession is framed between a Prologue and Epilogue which reflect the author's enduring political and moral concerns. The Prologue is like a recapitulation of themes from the *Mirour* and the *Vox* – the moral corruption of man through the conflict of Will and Reason, the corruption of the three estates of society arising from strife and division, the corruption of the natural world arising from the microcosmic combat within fallen man – even to the extent of using again the historical allegory of the statue of Nebuchadnezzar's dream from Book VII of the *Vox Clamantis*. The recapitulation is perfectly deliberate:

> Whan the prologe is so despended,
> This bok schal afterward ben ended
> Of love, which doth many a wonder
> And many a wys man hath put under.
> (Prologue, ll. 73–76)

After the Prologue, Gower makes a confession of inadequacy to the task of reforming the world:

> I may noght strecche up to the hevene
> Min hand, ne setten al in evene
> This world, which evere is in balance . . .
> Forthi the Stile of my writinges

---

4 The *Balades* are due for appraisal. A start is made in M. Dominica Legge, *Anglo-Norman Literature and its Background* (Oxford, 1963), pp. 357–361.

5 *The Allegory of Love* (Oxford, 1936), pp. 201–208.

Fro this day forth I thenke change
And speke of thing is noght so strange.
(I.1–10)

So he turns to talk of love, which is not "strange" and which interests and concerns everyone. It sounds like a retreat, but this poem is subtler than it seems, for in fact the Prologue functions in the whole structure in two ways. In the first place, by developing as its principal theme the idea that division is the source of all evil,[6] it prepares the way for the transition to love, which is, for all its blind instinctual nature, a unitive and not a divisive principle and in which therefore the reconciliation of division may be found. In the second place, the Prologue provides the basic moral frame in which the picture of "love" is to be held steady. It thus works in the same way as the dream of Scipio in the *Parlement of Foules*: everything that Scipio Africanus says is true, but its truth has no pressure, no compelling relevance, and Chaucer has to move on from barren prescriptive moralising into the inner tangled mystery of "love" in order to find the answer to his question. Piers' rejection of the Pardon in Passus VII of *Piers Plowman* represents a similar moment, the shift from stated truth to the search for embodied truth.

Gower's concern with love, it soon becomes clear, is not that of the lover. The Priest of Love tells him,

I wol thi schrifte so enforme,
That ate leste thou schalt hiere
The vices, and to thi matiere
Of love I shal hem so remene,
That thou schalt knowe what thei mene.
(I.276–280)

He is, in fact, making a new approach to his old theme, using love as the focus of his attention not only because of its audience appeal but also because it is the most powerful and most enigmatic focus of human experience, and therefore reveals man's moral nature under its greatest stress, just as the flaws in a machine can be detected by subjecting it to abnormal strain. Gower, despite the fiction of the lover's confession, is not providing instruction in the art of love, but using love as the bait for instruction in the art of living. It says something for the medieval conception of "fine loving" that the two are so rarely at odds. Genius, therefore, though he is called the Priest of Venus – indeed he repudiates her on at least one occasion (V.1382) – and he becomes something akin to Conscience. From his discourse there emerges a pattern by which restraint, discrimination, and "gentillesse" in love become the example and analogue of virtuous behaviour generally, so that sin is exposed as base, unreasonable, and stupid rather than condemned as deadly.

Gower was certainly aware of the effectiveness of the dramatic scheme he had

6 Prologue 782, 799, 830, 851, 889, 893, 896, 966, 971, etc.

devised, and he exploits it with dry humour. The very assumption by the poet of the role of lover is like the slipping on of a mask, and his confession throughout is timid, hopeless, rueful, in the manner of one who had "hopped always behind" in love. His response to his Confessor's admonitions is often pathetically wistful, suggesting that he only wishes he had the chance to be sinful. He admits the justice of the Confessor's remarks about Sloth and unpunctuality, but tells him that his own problem is not keeping appointments but getting them:

> Mi fader, that I mai wel lieve.
> Bot me was nevere assigned place,
> Wher yit to geten eny grace,
> Ne me was non such time apointed;
> For thanne I wolde I were unjoynted
> Of every lime that I have,
> If I ne scholde kepe and save
> Min houre bothe and ek my stede,
> If my ladi it hadde bede.
> (IV.270–278)

Elsewhere there are moments of tentative self-assertion: he complains, for instance, when questioned about the sin of ingratitude, that if anything it is his lady who is ungrateful (V.5190), and he suggests too that it is she who is guilty of usury in love:

> Be large weyhte and gret mesure
> Sche hath mi love, and I have noght
> Of that which I have diere boght,
> And with myn herte I have it paid;
> Bot al that is asyde laid,
> And I go loveles aboute.
> (V.4508–13)

The lover has a mind of his own and, after the Confessor has been exhorting him to seek his lady's favour by winning glory in battle against the heathen, he stoutly maintains that killing heathens is not the best way of saving their souls, and anyway,

> What scholde I winne over the Se,
> If I mi ladi loste at hom?
> (IV.1664–65)

There is a flicker of wit sometimes in the lover's literal-minded responses. He thanks his Confessor for his story of Phebus and Daphne, told as an example against over-hastiness,

> Bot while I se mi ladi is
> No tre, but halt hire oghne forme,
> Ther mai me noman so enforme,
> To whether part fortune wende,

> That I unto mi lyves ende
> No wol hire serven everemo.
> (III.1730–35)

When asked to confess any sin of incest, his reply is blandly unoutraged (VIII.169). On this he feels he can at last speak with a completely clear mind.

In a series of longer passages, Gower develops with great sympathy and sensitivity the familiar theme of faithful hopeless love, embodying in lively detailed description the refined and attenuated ideal of the lover's service. The lover describes how he conducts his lady to church:

> Thanne is noght al mi weie in vein,
> Somdiel I mai the betre fare,
> Whan I, that mai noght fiele hir bare,
> Mai lede hire clothed in myn arm:
> Bot afterward it doth me harm
> Of pure ymaginacioun;
> For thanne this collacioun
> I make unto miselven ofte,
> And seie, 'Ha lord, hou sche is softe,
> How sche is round, hou sche is smal!'
> (IV.1138–47)

In her bower, he waits her pleasure, watches her fingers at embroidery, plays with her little dogs or with her birds if she is away; if he has the chance to dance with her, his feet seem hardly to touch the ground, and at night when he has to leave,

> Er I come fulli to the Dore,
> I torne ayein and feigne a thing,
> As thogh I hadde lost a Ring
> Or somwhat elles, for I wolde
> Kisse hire eftsones, if I scholde,
> Bot selden is that I so spede.
> (IV.2826–31)

There is a touching pathos in all this, combined with a wry self-mockery which leaves the poem only at the end, where Gower describes the healing of love's wound. This long passage has a deceptive lightness of touch, for it reaches out beyond the familiar images of darts and wounds to a deeply moving evocation of age and the passing of love. In itself it represents that final controlling of passion by reason which has been Gower's constant theme, but it is a control which is won at bitter cost: "Remembre wel hou thou art old" (VIII.2439). It is, in the end, a "beau retret," and Gower has no songs of joyful love to remember as he returns to his books,[7] only a necklace of black beads inscribed *Por reposer*:

---

[7] As has Chaucer in the *Parlement*. The conclusion of the *Confessio* is well analysed by C. S. Lewis (*Allegory of Love*, pp. 219–222); cf. Fisher, *John Gower*, p. 191.

I stod amasid for a while,
And in my self y gan to smyle
Thenkende uppon the bedis blake,
And how they weren me betake,
For that y schulde bidde and preie.
And whanne y sigh non othre weie
Bot only that y was refusid,
Unto the lif which y hadde usid
I thoughte nevere torne ayein:
And in this wise, soth to seyn,
Homward a softe pas y wente.
                          (VIII.2957–67)

The poem as a whole gains enormously from the dramatic scheme, just as Gower himself gained from the freedom it gave him. It would not be right to claim that it has any of that quality of seemingly organic growth which activates the *Canterbury Tales*, but it makes the *Confessio* something more than a mechanic structure. It is, for instance, an infinitely better frame than that devised by Chaucer for the *Legend of Good Women*, and it retains its hold to the end. However, it is flawed, particularly by long passages where Gower regresses into the informational and overtly didactic, passages which have no internal validity within the structure, such as the long discourse on false and true Religion and the even longer discourse on universal knowledge and the duties of Princes.[8]

It is in the stories that Gower's imagination receives its final and fullest release. It is an imagination in which moral discrimination continues to operate, but operates in an artistically integrated manner. The truth about human nature and human behaviour which Gower tells in the tales is not one that he could have isolated and spoken of in expository fashion, for it is one which depends on the initial response of imaginative sympathy to the human situation, but it is one nevertheless in which his ripest wisdom is embodied, in which virtuous action is not the eschewing of the seven deadly sins but the fine flower of the noble mind, of order, discernment, and "gentillesse."

A simple but telling example of Gower's narrative power is provided by the story of Constantine and Silvester (II.3187–3496). The legend, of Constantine's leprosy, his rejection of the barbarous cure recommended by his physicians, his subsequent conversion and baptismal healing, is a familiar one, and is told, appropriately enough, as an exemplum of charity and pity. Gower's special achievement is to embody, in Constantine's soliloquy and in the description of the workings of his mind and heart, the very substance of human charity and pity, and not only that, but also to convey, through Constantine's meditation on the essential equality of all men in the sight of the "divine pourveance" (3243–73), the justness

---

[8] V.747–1959; Book VII. Admittedly, both are prompted by (somewhat foolhardy) questions from the lover and both questions spring naturally from the dramatic context. But, however skilfully done, it is a patent device. This, though, is not to deny that the passages have external validity, that is, in relation to the moral frame of Prologue and Epilogue and in relation to the world of action.

of moral discrimination which precedes virtuous action. Chaucer has a favourite line, "Pitee renneth soone in gentil herte," which he is fond of playing with in ironic contexts. Gower goes quite simply to the heart of the matter, and gives local, imaginative truth to general, abstract truth. The rest of the legend, of course, passes into a different world of truth, for the moralist's simpler purposes are not served by anything so insubstantial as "Virtue is its own reward"; rather, his theme must be "Hou Merci multiplieth the timliche guodes." So too the Franklin's Tale moves into a different world of truth once Arviragus has gritted his teeth on his principles.

Ovid is Gower's major source of narrative material in the *Confessio*.[9] It is interesting that Ovid's concern in the *Metamorphoses*, Gower's favourite quarry, is to make a mosaic of classical legends and myths, in which every tale is to have its place in a continuing overall narrative; but Gower, in every story he tells, suppresses all the cross-connections and allusions, and re-embeds the pieces of the mosaic in the only overall pattern he knows, that of humane Christian values.[10] The tale of Tereus is an example.[11] Gower's handling of this story is throughout consistent: his aim is to mute the horrors, to eliminate the flamboyant rhetoric of simile and periphrasis, to cut out extraneous allusions,[12] all in the interests of preserving a plausible pattern of human behaviour which will be susceptible of humane moral interpretation. With this in mind, he abbreviates a good deal of the early material and, when he comes to describe the rape of Philomena, omits the whole of Ovid's gruesome description of the mutilation and the second rape:

> Radix micat ultima linguae,
> ipsa iacet terraeque tremens inmurmurat atrae,
> utque salire solet mutilatae cauda colubrae,
> palpitat et moriens dominae vestigia quaerit.
> hoc quoque post facinus (vix ausim credere) fertur

---

[9] He provides 38 of the 133 stories in the poem, or 4,419 lines out of 17,213 (the total length of the *Confessio* is 33,444 lines). There is study of Gower's narrative technique in relation to Ovid (stories of Actaeon and Pygmalion), and also in the tale of Florent, in Ch. vi of Maria Wickert, *Studien*. Quotation of Ovid is from the texts in the Loeb Classical Library.

[10] Christian reinterpretation of classical fable is of course customary in the Middle Ages, though it is usually figural and allegoric, as in the *Ovide Moralisé*. The importance of understanding this kind of medieval reading of the classics is made clear in an interesting essay by R. H. Green, "Classical Fable and English Poetry," *Critical Approaches to Medieval Literature* (Selected Papers from the English Institute, 1958–59), ed. Dorothy Bethurum (Columbia Univ. Press, 1960), pp. 110–133. Gower's rehandling of classical material, however, seems quite distinct from traditional allegoric techniques, except in the treatment of the metamorphoses, and more akin to the vivid, human use of exempla in homiletic writing: see G. R. Owst, *Literature and Pulpit in Medieval England*, 2nd ed. revised (Oxford, 1961), p. 121.

[11] *Confessio* V.5551–6047; *Metamorphoses* VI.424–674.

[12] He omits, for instance, all mention of how Procne uses the Bacchic rites as cover when delivering Philomela from captivity (*Met.* VI. 587).

saepe sua lacerum repetisse libidine corpus.
(VI.557–562)

Out of this, Gower can produce only something like tenderness:

> Bot yit whan he hire tunge refte,
> A litel part therof belefte,
> Bot sche with al no word mai soune,
> Bot chitre and as a brid jargoune.
> (V.5697–5700)

Instead of concentrating on the physical reality, which is essentially discrete in Ovid, a theme for development, Gower concentrates on the mental reality, on what goes through Philomena's mind as she languishes in prison, and by her prayer to Jupiter (V.5741–52), of which Ovid has nothing, gives to the crime a moral context in a finite world.

In Ovid, as soon as Procne hears of her sister's plight, she becomes at once a vengeful fury, possessed as of some elemental passion, and vows her readiness for any crime:

> In omne nefas ego me, germana, paravi:
> aut ego, cum facibus regalia tecta cremabo,
> artificem mediis inmittam Terea flammis
> aut linguam atque oculos et quae tibi membra pudorem
> abstulerunt ferro rapiam aut per vulnera mille
> sontem animam expellam.
> (VI.613–618)

In Gower, Procne prepares for vengeance by first praying to Venus, asserting her own truth and fidelity in marriage and the enormity of Tereus' outrage (V.5821–42), and then to Apollo, begging him to take the vengeance upon himself and to forgive her for having been the indirect cause of it all, in asking Tereus to fetch her sister to see her (V.5846–60). At every point, it will be seen, Gower invests his actors with a sense of being involved in an action larger than themselves, as if they operate as morally responsible creatures in a known and received environment, not as the victims of inhuman lusts and passions.

The murder of Itys, Procne's son, is introduced by Gower with combined explanation – she is "mad Of wo, which hath hir overlad" – and execration: "Withoute insihte of moderhede / Foryat pite and loste drede" (V.5893–94). The blend of sympathy for the perpetrator of a crime and abomination of the crime itself is characteristic of Gower. The actual killing, dismemberment, and cooking of the child is related with the utmost brevity (and without any Chaucerian "horror"), and the serving of Tereus with his son's remains is followed by a discourse from Procne in which the nature of Tereus' outrage and the justness of his punishment is finally driven home. Ovid, on the other hand, makes wanton play of her suppressed mother's and wife's love – "A! quam es similis patri!" – which makes her subsequent behaviour all the more inhuman, and then develops the butchery with relish.

> Satis illi ad fata vel unum
> vulnus erat: iugulum ferro Philomela resolvit,
> vivaque adhus animaeque aliquid retinentia membra
> dilaniant. Pars inde cavis exsultat aenis,
> pars veribus stridunt; manant penetralia tabo.
> (VI.642–646)

Philomela's role, it will be seen, is made gratuitously vindictive, whereas in Gower she plays virtually no part in the revenge. The feast-scene is the occasion of Procne's witty rejoinder to Tereus' call for his son – "Intus habes, quem poscis" – and then, as Tereus looks around puzzled and calls again for his son,

> Sicut erat sparsis furiali caede capillis,
> prosiluit Ityosque caput Philomela cruentum
> misit in ora patris nec tempore maluit ullo
> posse loqui et meritis testari gaudia dictis.
> (VI.657–660)

The transformations, which follow, are nothing in Ovid, but are developed by Gower with great charm and tenderness, as if to mitigate the horror of the story he has just been telling by re-enacting it in a "distanced" world where human emotions and values are poeticized. Tereus becomes a lapwing, notorious for its falseness; Procne becomes a swallow,

> And chitreth out in hir langage
> What falshod is in mariage,
> And telleth in a maner speche
> Of Tereus the Spousebreche.
> (V.6011–14)

Philomena is the nightingale which hides in winter for shame at her lost maidenhood but emerges in spring when she can sing in the concealment of the foliage:

> And seith, 'Ha, nou I am a brid,
> Ha, nou mi face mai ben hid:
> Thogh I have lost mi Maidenhede,
> Schal noman se my chekes rede.'
> (V.5985–88)

Ovid tells a story which, despite the richness of the paraphernalia he surrounds it with, is essentially simple, indeed essentially meaningless. He treats the given material as a series of themes for ornamentation: he uses *sermocinatio* as opportunity for the display of rhetoric and clever wit, and dwells on the horrors for the sake of unrelated, wanton shock. Gower turns it into a humanly complex story, in which what is developed is the meaningfulness of human behaviour and the reality of human motive. He is an artistic simpleton beside Ovid, but his narrative throws out roots and makes connections which make Ovid's tale of Tereus look like a high-powered shocker.

It is worth remarking that Chaucer, in the *Legend of Good Women*, makes little of the story of Tereus. He expresses straightaway his disgust with the story (2238), hurries through it with obvious distaste (2257–58), and has hardly started before he is talking of the need to make an end (2341). He follows Ovid much more closely for as far as he goes, but omits all the last part of the story (2383) and the metamorphoses – certainly, it did not suit his theme of wronged womanhood. He tells the tale in idle somnambulistic fashion, and his narrative intrusiveness, which elsewhere can add an extra dimension to his writing, seems here a merely mechanical trick.[13]

Gower's other Ovidian narratives display the same humane moral and sentimental redirection of purpose as the story of Tereus. The tale of Ceix and Alceone, for instance, makes a similar use of the transformations to suggest human values in poeticized form. Gower's overt concern here[14] is with the truth of dreams, and to this end he makes some skilful changes in the dream-mechanism and its relation to the finding of the body of Ceix on the sea-shore;[15] but his inner and deeper concerns are displayed in the metamorphoses, which provide the opportunity for an affirmation of the pathetic endurance of wifely fidelity:

> Sche fondeth in hire briddes forme,
> If that sche mihte hirself conforme
> To do the plesance of a wif,
> As sche dede in that other lif:
> For thogh sche hadde hir pouer lore,
> Hir will stod as it was tofore,
> And serveth him so as sche mai.
>
> (IV.3109–15)

(Chaucer of course ignores all this in the *Book of the Duchess*, since his purposes in using the narrative are specialised.) In the story of Pyramus and Thisbe, on the other hand,[16] Gower rejects the metamorphosis completely, probably because he

---

13 Comparison of Chaucer, Gower, and Ovid, here and elsewhere below, is not affected by Chaucer's presumed use of the *Ovide Moralisé* in certain legends, for which see J. L. Lowes, "Chaucer and the *Ovide Moralisé*," *PMLA*, XXXIII (1918), 303–319; Sanford B. Meech, "Chaucer and the *Ovid Moralisé* – A Further Study," *PMLA*, XLVI (1931), 182–204. Edgar F. Shannon, *Chaucer and the Roman Poets* (Harvard Studies in Comp. Lit., VII, 1929) makes laborious comparison of Chaucer and Ovid. For comparison of the frames of the *Legend* and the *Confessio*, with discussion of biographical links, see L. Bech, "Quellen und Plan der *Legende of Goode Women* und ihr Verhältniss zur *Confessio Amantis*," *Anglia*, V (1882), 313–382; Fisher, *John Gower*, pp. 235–250. Attempts have been made to interpret the *Legend* as comic is conception, e.g., R. M. Garrett, " 'Cleopatra the Martyr' and her Sisters," *JEGP*, XXII (1923), 64–74. The interpretation is not borne out by the quality of the legends: the imaginative temperature is low, and no amount of dramatic-ironic "interpretation" will make it higher.

14 IV.2927–3123; cf. *Met* XI.410–748.

15 See Macaulay, *Works*, II, 512.

16 III.1331–1494; cf. *Met.* IV.55–166.

could not stomach, any more than Chaucer could, the image of Pyramus' blood spouting high to stain the mulberry,

> Non aliter quam cum vitiato fistula plumbo
> Scinditur et tenui stridente foramine longas
> eiaculatur aquas atque ictibus aera rumpit.
> (*Met*, IV.122–124)

Gower's major change here, apart from some felicitous added details (e.g., III.1387), is to develop Thisbe's speech over the dead body of Pyramus (III.1462–81) as a questioning of justice and divine providence:

> This Piramus, which hiere I se
> Bledende, what hath he deserved?
> For he your heste hath kept and served,
> And was yong and I bothe also:
> Helas, why do ye with ous so?
> (III.1468–72)

The word "deserved" is one which Ovid has little use for, but it provides in itself an index of Gower's preoccupation with human actions as responsible, as part of a meaningful pattern. In accordance with his usual practice, Gower also mitigates the horrors of the tale: he does not, for instance, allow Pyramus to lie writhing in his death agony until Thisbe arrives (*Met*. IV.133–134). Chaucer does, and is led into some ludicrous detail:

> And at the laste hire love thanne hath she founde,
> Betynge with his heles on the grounde.
> (*Legend*, 862–863)

Ovid's tale of Iphis and Anaxarete is extensively developed by Gower.[17] For Ovid it is again essentially a tale of elemental conflict, between the irresistible fire of Iphis' love and the immovable stone of Anaxarete's heart. When he commits suicide by hanging himself at her door, Iphis calls on her to celebrate her triumph, to come and gloat over the physical evidence of her victory:

> Certe aliquid laudare mei cogeris amoris,
> quo tibi sim gratus, meritumque fatebere nostrum.
> (XIV.722–723)

His feet, as he hangs senseless, beat out a sinister tattoo on the door. Gower will have none of this: his people act out to the last a civilised and sentimental morality, and here Iphis explains his decision as a response to what seems the unalterable decree of the gods (IV.3558–68), and reflects in a moment of poignant realisation on their nearness as he stands between life and death:

---

17 IV.3515–3684; cf. *Met*. XIV.698–764.

> Ha, thou mi wofull ladi diere,
> Which duellest with thi fader hiere
> And slepest in thi bedd at ese,
> Thou wost nothing of my desese,
> Hou thou and I be now unmete.
> Ha lord, what swevene schalt thou mete,
> What dremes hast thou nou on honde?
> Thou slepest there, and I hier stonde
> (IV.3569–76)

Ovid's convulsively jerking corpse is forgotten.

> And with that word he tok a Corde,
> With which upon the gate tre
> He hyng himself, that was pite.
> (IV.3592–94)

In Ovid, Anaxarete is completely unmoved by her lover's fate – "Videamus miserabile funus," she says, curious – and her petrification as she watches the bier pass is quite involuntary. Gower's heroine, however, is stricken with remorse, laments her lack of pity, and begs for punishment:

> And as I dede, do to me:
> For I ne dede no pite
> To him, which for mi love is lore,
> Do no pite to me therfore.
> (IV.3627–30)

She behaves, in fact, like a lady.

The comprehensiveness of Gower's humanity is nowhere better displayed than in the story of the incestuous Canacee.[18] There are here none of the stock responses of the narrow moralist, but a sober and compassionate meditation on the blind instinctual nature of sexual passion, on the difference between nature's ordinances and "positive law." Out of this he draws the pathos of her prayer for mercy to her father, and the moving letter to her brother, embodying in them the human dilemma and the human truth. Skilfully, he postpones the exposure of the child, which in Ovid takes place immediately the birth is discovered, so that she can have the child with her as she writes:

> In my riht hond my Penne I holde,
> And in my left the swerd I kepe,
> And in my barm ther lith to wepe
> Thi child and myn, which sobbeth faste.
> (III.300–303)

---

[18] III.143–336; cf. Ovid, *Heriodes* XI.

73

Ovid, who is concerned more with the witty elaboration of conceits, such as the idea of the sword sent to her by her father being her dowry (*Her.* XI.99), and with wantonly indecorous realistic detail, such as her nurse's attempts at abortion (39), misses this completely:

> Dextra tenet calamum, strictum tenet altera ferrum,
> et iacet in gremio charta soluta meo.
>
> (3–4)

It is, as we see, women who draw forth Gower's largest humanity, and his most deeply effective expressions of that humanity. Phillis in her tower watches the sea all night for Demephon's return,

> Bot al for noght, sche was deceived,
> For Venus hath hire hope weyved,
> And schewede hire upon the Sky
> How that the day was faste by.
>
> (IV.823–826)

The reference to Venus is conceived with beautiful irony. In his story of Lucrece, Gower achieves perhaps his most perfect realisation of womanliness.[19] There is no need here for the elucidation of moral patterns, since they are already clearly implied in the narrative, and he concentrates therefore on the human predicament. He dwells at length on her openness and hospitality to the unexpected visitor, her timid questions about her husband's welfare,[20] but cuts out completely the bargaining which precedes the rape. In Ovid, various plans of escape occur to her, only to be dismissed when Tarquin tells her of his intention and of how he will kill a slave and accuse him if she cries out. "Succubuit famae victa puella metu" (II.810). In Gower, every suggestion of acquiescence is eliminated. Tarquin is in bed and has her in his arms before she awakes; in pure fear, she loses her voice, and his threats (no slave is mentioned) cause her to swoon,

> And he, which al him hadde adresced
> To lust, tok thanne what him liste,
> And goth his wey, that non it wiste.
>
> (VII.4988–90)

Her actions on the morrow have the momentous, pre-ordained quality of one who has, like Clarissa, already passed beyond suffering into a different world:

> And sche, which in hire bed abod,
> Whan that sche wiste he was agon,
> Sche clepede after liht anon
> And up aros long er the day,

---

[19] VII.4754–5123; cf. Ovid, *Fasti* II.721–852.
[20] VII.4926–27. This is added, and the whole passage is much expanded from Ovid, *Fasti* II.787–791.

And caste awey hire freissh aray,
As sche which hath the world forsake,
And tok upon the clothes blake.
(VII.4996–5002)

Ovid provides for this only the merest hint:

Iamque erat orta dies: passis sedet illa capillis,
ut solet ad nati mater itura rogum.
(II.813–814)

Chaucer's rendering of the story has Tarquin arriving at her house at dead of night,
unannounced, thus missing all the irony and suspense of Lucrece's welcome. As
Lucrece feels the weight of his body in the bed she remarks, ludicrously, " 'What
beste is that,' quod she, 'that weyeth thus?' " (Legend, 1788). Chaucer keeps all the
debate in her mind, and the conversation with Tarquin makes much of her fear of
slander, but in the end he too has her swoon – though the motive is, incongruous-
ly, as much fear of slander as fear of death. Chaucer has none of Gower's subsequent detail, and omits even Ovid's pathetic account of her successive confused
attempts to begin her story.[21] It is difficult to understand why Chaucer bothered
himself with these stories at all.

The story of Jason and Medea is one of Gower's longest, and illustrates well his
handling of his second major source of exemplary narrative, the Roman de Troie of
Benoit de Sainte-Maure.[22] His technical problem here is to disentangle the
meaningful tale from a much more closely knit total narrative than Ovid's Metamorphoses – it is, in a way, the same problem that Malory faced with the Arthurian
Vulgate. Gower isolates the tale by omitting all mention of Peleus' treacherous
purpose in sending Jason to Colchos and by suppressing the Lamedoun episode,
and at the end he rounds out the narrative by describing, from a different source
(Ovid again), and with great brilliance, Medea's magical rejuvenation of Jason's
father Aeson – which is happily to his purpose, since his moral theme is Jason's
betrayal, and this kindness of Medea's adds to his debt of gratitude. Within the
confines thus laid out Gower concentrates on the love story of Jason and Medea by
eschewing all rhetorical elaboration – description of seasons, the sea-journey, the
city of Jaconites – and by moving away all the time from stereotypes of epic and
romance[23] towards the human situation. His most effective single stroke is to
portray Medea's love as fully returned by Jason, for by this one change he relieves
the main part of the narrative from all external moral pressure and gives himself
the same kind of imaginative freedom – to compare great things with smaller – as
Chaucer gained by refusing to accept the medieval stereotype of Criseyde. In
Gower, Jason's desire to be with Medea is devoid of calculation, and he waits

---

21 Fasti II.823; Confessio VII.5043.
22 Ed. L. Constans, Société des Anciens Textes Français, 6 vols. (1904–12). Gower (Confessio
V.3247–4222) sometimes uses Guido for the Troy story, but not in a way significant for the
following comparisons.
23 Such as the arming-scene, Benoit, ll. 1815–42 (cf. Confessio V.3686–87).

eagerly for her maid to arrive to conduct him to Medea's room. In Benoit, Medea soliloquises as she waits for him and, when half the night has passed, has to send her *vieille* (a much more sinister figure!) to fetch the laggard – who had to be woken up – while she prepares a rich bed for the reluctant lover.[24] In the morning, it is Jason, according to Benoit, who recalls Medea's attention to the essential business in hand, that of winning the fleece, and when he has got the information he wants, he departs abruptly. In Gower, it is Medea who, with womanly practicality, arouses Jason to thoughts of the danger he is in, and, after the briefing, there follows a long and touching farewell scene.[25]

Jason's return from his successful quest is briefly dismissed by Benoit (ll. 1971–82), but in Gower it is described with a joy and delight and sense of victorious release in which even the elements participate:

> The Flees he tok and goth to Bote,
> The Sonne schyneth bryhte and hote,
> The Flees of gold schon forth withal,
> The water glistreth overal.
> (V.3731–34)

Medea stands weeping and sighing, on a tower looking out over the sea:

> Sche preide, and seide, 'O, god him spede,
> The kniht which hath mi maidenheide!'
> And ay sche loketh toward thyle.
> Bot whan sche sih withinne a while
> The Flees glistrende ayein the Sonne,
> Sche saide, 'Ha lord, now al is wonne,
> Mi kniht the field hath overcome:
> Nou wolde god he were come;
> Ha lord, that he ne were alonde!'
> Bot I dar take this on honde,
> If that sche hadde wynges tuo,
> Sche wolde have flowe unto him tho
> Strawht ther he was into the Bot.
> (V.3739–51)

In Benoit, she meets him immediately and arranges a nocturnal rendezvous, and the story is then hastily closed, with dark mutterings as to Jason's treachery, which has never been far from our minds. Gower, however, describes Medea meeting Jason first at the official reception, where she behaves with maidenly modesty (V.3786–92), and then retiring, sending her maid to get all the news:

---

[24] Benoit, ll. 1551–71. The lovemaking, which follows, is treated very briefly by both Benoit and Gower, but with doctrinaire relish by Guido, *Historia*, ed. N. E. Griffin (Cambridge, Mass., 1936), p. 25.
[25] *Confessio* V.3633–69; cf. Benoit, ll. 1764–66.

> Sche tolde hire ladi what sche wiste,
> And sche for joie hire Maide kiste.
>   (V.3799–3800)

They meet again at the banquet, where their private words are precious together and where the idea of another night-meeting seems to arise spontaneously without urging on her part:

> What nede is forto speke of ese?
> Hem list ech other forto plese.
>   (V.3869–70)

The reckoning must of course come, and Gower spares us no detail of Medea's final revenge. To say that Gower has been taking a holiday from morality would be in a way true, but it would miss the deeper truth that in giving rein to his warm imaginative sympathy Gower has achieved expression of a kind of "goodness" which in his cooler moments he could have stared straight in the face without recognising.

Gower's success with these classical stories is due in part to his ruthlessness. He has no respect for antiquity nor for the rich resonance of its allusiveness, and no hesitation at all in re-embodying its narratives in the social and moral contexts he understands. So Narcissus becomes a "lordes sone" and the weariness which causes him to rest by the well is not due to his having been chased all day by young men and nymphs but because he has been out hunting.[26] The consistency of social setting gives added force to the single pattern of moral and sentimental values which Gower draws from the stories. Something is lost of course, and sometimes the sources provide material which Gower is simply not equipped to cope with. It is difficult to know, for instance, exactly what lies behind his telling of the story of Orestes (III.1885–2195). Purportedly an exemplum against murder, it fails completely to make its point or even to extract any single story line, and the pressure to provide motives and to relate cause to effect in a moral sphere results in a sad mangling of high tragedy. Similarly with the story of Dejanira and Nessus, where Gower's attempt to explain Hercules' death as the punishment for "love untrewe" (II.2261) and, it seems, for transvestitism (II.2268–74) is merely trivial. Myth, like tragedy, was not tractable to Gower's method, and he can make nothing of the grandeur and fury of Hercules' dying agonies:

> Saepe illum gemitus edentem, saepe trementem,
> saepe retemptantem totas infringere vestes
> sternentemque trabes irascentemque videres
> montibus aut patrio tendentem bracchia caelo.[27]

---

[26] *Confessio* I.2288–2313; cf. Ovid, *Metamorphoses* III.413.

[27] *Metamorphoses* IX.207–210. Perhaps Gower's reference to "Clerk Ovide" here (II.2297) is a sign that he recognised the inadequacy of his own treatment.

Sometimes, too, Gower's overt moral betrays his own best understanding. He tells the story of Pyramus and Thisbe, for instance, ostensibly against the irrational haste of lovers (Pyramus should have had more sense), and the story of Paris and Helen, in itself a most consummate demonstration of his power of economical narrative (V.7195–7590), is brought in as an example of the inevitable punishment of sacrilegious rape. Perhaps this is understandable, for the medieval moralization of the Trojan story exerted a powerful pressure, but it is more difficult to excuse his similar interpretation of the Troilus story:

> And Troilus upon Criseide
> Also his ferste love leide
> In holi place, and hou it ferde,
> As who seith, al the world it herde.
> (V.7597–7600)

To look on the story of Troilus and Criseyde as a warning against flirting in church is a strange conclusion for a man who must have read Chaucer's *Troilus* (it was dedicated to him, after all), but it does not effect our view of Gower's narrative art, for the point is – and perhaps it need be laboured no further – that Gower, if he had actually *told* the story, would have penetrated a good deal deeper.

Some comparisons of Gower with Chaucer have already been made in passing, especially in respect of the *Legend of Good Women*, and it has been suggested that Gower at his best is better than Chaucer at his worst. It is safe to say this, but perhaps it would be fair to put the matter in its larger perspective by comparing their achievement when Chaucer is working within a frame, that of the *Canterbury Tales*, which suits his dramatic needs. Four of the *Canterbury Tales* have more or less close analogues in Gower, those of the Physician, the Manciple, the Man of Law, and the Wife of Bath.[28] Neither poet makes much of the legend of Appius and Virginia, though Chaucer exploits the situation with far deeper pathos. The Manciple's Tale, on the other hand, is infinitely rich beside Gower's tale of Phebus and Cornide: indeed, it has been suggested that the complex ironic and parodic structure of the Mancuple's Tale includes some satire of Gower's simplicity.[29] Comparison, however, is invidious, since Gower's tale is excessively short. Gower's tale of Constance is long, approximately the same length as the Man of Law's Tale, but seems pale and thin beside it. It is not one of Gower's finest achievements, though it may be that his handling of the episode of the lustful steward, who falls overboard by divine intervention and not in struggling with the heroine, as in Chaucer, has greater propriety.[30] In general, however, Gower's tale lacks the power of rich imaginative and philosophical extension which make Chaucer's legend,

[28] *Confessio* VII.5131–5306, III.782–817, II.587–1598, I.1407–1861.

[29] See R. Hazelton, "*The Manciple's Tale*: Parody and Critique," *JEGP*, LXII (1963), 1–31.

[30] For general comparison of the two versions, and with Trivet, see Margaret Schlauch, *Chaucer's Constance and Accused Queens* (New York, 1927), pp. 132–134; Edward A. Block, *PMLA*, LXVIII (1953), 572–616; Fisher, *John Gower*, pp. 286–292.

whether it achieves full internal or external (i.e., dramatic) validity or not, memorable, and which made it a model for late medieval legendaries.

Gower's tale of Florent represents what we may consider the more "primitive" version of the story.[31] The father of Branchus, whom Florent has killed in battle before being taken prisoner, wishes to revenge his son in quasi-legal manner and so, on the advice of the grandmother, asks Florent to set his life on a question. The old woman whom Florent meets on his quest states her terms straightaway, and when he has agreed to them, tells him the answer to the question, thus placing all the moral stress of the story on his honour and fidelity to his promise. On the wedding night, she shows him her beauty *before* asking him her question, which is a simple one (fair by day and foul by night or *vice versa*), and, having got the right answer, is released from a stepmother's spell, whereby the answer had to be provided by a knight of surpassing honour. By any conventional standards, Gower's realization of the story is much superior to Chaucer's. One ingredient, for instance, that any novice would have recognised the need for, is a loathsome description of the loathsome hag, so that Florent's dilemma can be appreciated. This Gower provides, though not Chaucer (or rather, not the Wife of Bath):

> Hire Nase bass, hire browes hyhe,
> Hire yhen smale and depe set,
> Hire chekes ben with teres wet,
> And rivelen as an emty skyn
> Hangende doun unto the chin,
> Hire Lippes schrunken ben for age,
> Ther was no grace in the visage,
> Hir front was nargh, hir lockes hore,
> Sche loketh forth as doth a More,
> Hire Necke is schort, hir schuldres courbe,
> That myhte a mannes lust destourbe,
> Hire body gret and nothing smal,
> And schortly to descrive hire al,
> Sche hath no lith withoute a lak;
> Bot lich unto the wollesak
> Sche proferth hire unto this knyht.
>   (I.1678–93)

He also portrays Florent acting in a compellingly human manner: after hearing her terms he keeps going away and coming back in an agony of indecision:

> Now goth he forth, now comth ayein,
> He wot noght what is best to sein.
>   (I.1569–70)

---

[31] The situation is not as simple as this, but it does not affect the argument. For comparison, see B. J. Whiting in *Sources and Analogues of Chaucer's Canterbury Tales*, ed. W. F. Bryan and Germaine Dempster (Chicago, 1941); Sigmund Eisner, *A Tale of Wonder* (Wexford, 1957); Fisher, *John Gower*, pp. 295–301.

He solaces himself with the thought that she can not last long:

> And thanne he caste his avantage,
> That sche was of so gret an age,
> That sche mai live bot a while,
> And thoghte put hire in an Ile,
> Wher that noman hire scholde knowe,
> Til sche with deth were overthrowe.
>
> (I.1575–80)

At the court, he tries various other answers he has thought of (I.1641), just in case there may be a way out, but to no avail. He takes her home, riding by night and hiding by day, and smuggles her into his castle:

> And prively withoute noise
> He bringth this foule grete Coise
> To his Castell in such a wise
> That noman myhte hire schappe avise.
>
> (I.1733–36)

Throughout he behaves with scrupulous honour and honesty[32] combined with the most convincing humanity.

In the Wife of Bath's Tale, the offence becomes a rape, so that the knight is put in the wrong from the first, and the verdict of the court (of ladies) is a graceful concession. The withholding by the hag of the terms she is demanding and of the answer to the question until they are actually at the court means that the knight is placed in an impossible situation – he does not get the chance to choose whether to behave honourably or not. The whole thing is being engineered by the hag for his discomfiture, and finally her honeymoon homily leaves him so completely bemused that he is only too ready to concede her sovereignty in the answer to a much more subtly angled question. It is not simply that the Wife of Bath's Tale proves that it is a good idea to concede sovereignty to women: the whole tale itself is a demonstration of woman's inalienable right to that sovereignty, that there is really no alternative. When all this is set in the fully developed context of the Wife of Bath's own character, it is clear that Chaucer is working on a different level altogether from Gower.

Still, perhaps enough has been said to demonstrate that Gower, by any but these, the very highest standards, is an uncommonly fine narrative poet. His power resides partly in his sophisticated handling of narrative structures and partly in his development of a fluent, "natural" poetic style, but, essentially, in the nature of his response to the human fiction, both in the frame and in the exemplary stories. In this response, his own persistent moral preoccupations find, for once, a genuinely poetic expression, and out of this, made whole by art, Gower can speak so as to compel our attention.

---

[32] As Gower emphasizes, I. 1511, 1518, 1667, 1715, 1719–21, 1798.

JOHN GOWER'S NARRATIVE ART

Arno Esch

Translated by Linda Barney Burke

During the late Middle Ages and Renaissance, Gower was ranked equally with Chaucer. In the opinion of Sir Philip Sidney, the two poets had a significance for English literature analogous to that of Dante, Boccaccio, and Petrarch for the Italian.[1] They were the originators of a new English poetry which could compare with classical and continental prototypes. Gradually, however, Gower came to be increasingly overshadowed by his contemporary. In comparison with Chaucer, his poetry now seemed simplistic, dry, and tedious. It lacked Chaucer's skill at characterization, his humor and his deep humanity, his "realism" and the ironic distance of his narrator.

From a modern aesthetic point of view there is undeniably a certain degree of truth to these objections. But apparently the characteristics which the modern reader admires in Chaucer were not at all striking to his contemporaries and successors. Just as an early seventeenth-century reader could group John Donne and Ben Jonson together under the label "strong lined" and contrast them with the mellifluous style of Spenser, so a fifteenth or sixteenth-century reader would not have been conscious of a distinction between Gower and Chaucer. Chaucer was not a master of "realism" or of irony to his contemporaries, but the "flour of rethorique;" readers saw no distinction between the style of the two poets but grouped them together under the rubric "the fresh rethoryens."[2]

Because of such considerations, a new interest in Gower has sprung up in recent years, the object of which was a better understanding of Gower in the context of his time. One might say that there is a new appraisal of Gower, in which, however, he is still underestimated as a narrative artist. Derek Pearsall judges rightly: "The current reappraisal of Gower is doing loyal service to Gower the man, but may be doing less service to Gower the English poet."[3] Likewise, W. F. Schirmer expresses regret, in his discussion of J.H. Fisher's book on Gower, that in this comprehensive study "Gower's great narrative art [remains] so much in the background."[4] Perhaps the most impressive evaluation of Gower's artistry is still C. S. Lewis's brilliant chapter on Gower in his *Allegory of Love*.[5] If we look further for discussions of Gower's narrative and descriptive technique, the results are meager. G. C. Macaulay's great edition of Gower remains of inestimable value for the abundance of its

---

[1] *Elizabethan Critical Essays*, ed. G.G. Smith, 2 vols. (Oxford, 1904), I, 152.
[2] See the overview of contemporary critical judgments by J.H. Fisher, *John Gower: Moral Philosopher and Friend of Chaucer* (London, 1965), pp. 3 ff.
[3] D. Pearsall, "Gower's Narrative Art," *PMLA*, 81 (1966), 475.
[4] *Anglia*, 83 (1965), 356.
[5] *The Allegory of Love* (London, 1936), pp. 198–222.

notes on individual details.[6] Penetrating analyses of the stories of Acteon, Pygmalion, and Florent are found in the closing chapter of Maria Wickert's distinguished book on Gower;[7] P. Fison defended the artistic value of the *Confessio Amantis* in his essay on "The Poet in John Gower;"[8] and Derek Pearsall, in his aforementioned article, recently gave an informative and balanced overview of Gower's narrative art.

The *Confessio Amantis* displays an encyclopedic structure. Gower uses as his principle of classification the schema of the Seven Deadly Sins in all of their subdivisions, he provides an overview of the various religions, and he surveys the entire field of human knowledge with special reference to the duties of princes. His systematic procedure and his comprehensive structure must have agreed exactly with medieval taste. Gower's work corroborates the observation of C. S. Lewis:

> At his most characteristic, medieval man was not a dreamer nor a wanderer. He was an organiser, a codifier, a builder of systems. He wanted "a place for everything and everything in the right place." Distinction, definition, tabulation were his delight.[9]

But even if political, social, and moral ideas were always closest to Gower's heart, he did not conceive of the *Confessio Amantis* as a tract, but as a multifaceted narrative work, which, as indicated in the "Prologue," endeavors to unite the *utile* with the *dulce*:

> But for men sein, and soth it is,
> That who that al of wisdom writ
> It dulleth ofte a mannes wit
> To him that schal it aldai rede,
> For thilke cause, if that ye rede,
> I wolde go the middel weie
> And wryte a bok betwen the tweie,
> Somwhat of lust, somwhat of lore,
> That of the lasse or of the more
> Som man mai lyke of that I wryte: . . .
> (Prol. 12–21)

Hence, *prodesse* and *delectare* are not divided between the frame and the stories, but are tightly bound together throughout the work. Gower's narrative skill is most strongly displayed in the tales, to be sure, but along with entertainment they also provide instruction; and conversely the frame has not only a didactic but also in part an entertaining character, especially in the confessions of Amans.

Although Genius wants all of the tales to be understood as exempla, the

---

6   *The English Works of John Gower*, ed. G.C. Macaulay, 2 vols., EETS e.s. 81–82 (London, 1900–1901; rpt. 1957).

7   *Studien zu John Gower* (Köln, 1953); tr. Robert J. Meindl, *Studies in John Gower* (Washington, D.C., 1981).

8   *Essays in Criticism*, 8 (1958), 16–26.

9   *The Discarded Image* (Cambridge, 1964), p. 10.

connection between the individual stories and the frame is closer in some cases than in others. Besides varying the degree of linkage between the stories and the vices treated in the frame, Gower also adapted inherited literary material to entirely new themes. This required an alteration of emphasis from the original stories and a change of their motivation. For instance, in Ovid's *Metamorphoses*, Vertumnus tells the story of Iphis and Anaxarete by way of example to the nymph Pomona in order to seduce her. He must therefore arouse compassion for the young man, and the death of the beautiful Anaxarete is only the justified punishment of the gods for her coldness. Gower, on the other hand, uses the story as an example of the complicity of Anaxarete in the death of Iphis; the suicide of Iphis leads Anaxarete into an inner conflict, and she longs for death in order to expiate her guilt.

In the following essay only three stories from the *Confessio Amantis* will be examined. They have been selected as follows: The source of the first, the "Tale of Rosiphelee," is unknown to us,[10] and the discussion must be based on the work itself, with only a glance at similar medieval tales. In the second example, the "Tale of Albinus and Rosemund," we are reasonably certain that Gower followed a historian of the early fourteenth century. The artistic inferiority of the source when juxtaposed with Gower's version allows a comparison especially suited to show forth Gower's creative intentions. The legend of Constance, based on an Anglo-Norman chronicle, serves as the third example. Since this story was also told by Chaucer in the "Man of Law's Tale," it offers us the possibility of a double comparison.

I

As the marginal gloss indicates, the "Tale of Rosiphelee" (IV, 1245 ff.) is an "exemplum contra istos qui amoris occupacionem omittentes, grauioris infortunii casus expectant" ["an exemplum against those who, neglecting the occupation of love, can look for an unfortunate outcome." – Tr.]. Although Amans can by no means be accused of *oisiveté* in love, Genius tells him the story of a king's daughter who was punished by Cupid for such "ydelnesse."

In the introduction to the tale, the daughter of an Armenian king is described with conventional attributes. She bears the romance name Rosiphelee, she is "a lusti Maide" (1247), "of gret renomee" (1250), "bothe wys and fair" (1251), and she will one day become the heiress of the kingdom (1252). She has only one fault, that of "Slowthe / Towardes love" (1253–54). Right at the beginning, the erotic is closely bound with political significance: in a king's daughter, a failure in the *schola amoris* has consequences which go beyond the private domain and can result in a far-ranging blow to stability and order. Faced with the "unnatural" behavior of the princess, the love goddess intervenes and brings Rosiphelee "into betre reule"

---

[10] A similar story is found in Andreas Capellanus (cf. Macaulay, I, 505). For further analogues, see *Selections from John Gower*, ed. J.A.W. Bennett (Oxford, 1968), pp. 147–48.

(1264) – a line which foreshadows the ending of the story. For to Venus and Cupid it is inconceivable

> how such a wiht,
> Which tho was in hir lusti age,
> Desireth nother Mariage
> Ne yit the love of paramours,
> Which evere hath be the comun cours
> Amonges hem that lusti were.
>
> (1266–71)

It is typical of Gower that he does not give precedence to so-called "courtly" love (the "love of paramours") but to "Mariage," the love which fulfills itself in wedlock. That Gower rejects on principle the "love of paramours" can be surmised from the confessional material attached to the story, in which the poet through the mouth of Genius explicitly distances himself from "amour courtois":

> My ladi Venus, whom I serve,
> What womman wole hire thonk deserve,
> Sche mai noght thilke love eschuie
> Of paramours, bot sche mot suie
> Cupides lawe; and natheles
> Men sen such love sielde in pes,
> That it nys evere upon aspie
> Of janglinge and of fals Envie,
> Fulofte medlid with disese:
> Bot thilke love is wel at ese,
> Which set is upon mariage;
> For that dar schewen the visage
> In alle places openly.
>
> (1467–79)

These words seem remarkable in the mouth of a priest of Venus, but they confirm that Gower stands for a love which is not subject to secrecy or to any of the other precepts of "courtly" love, but which aspires to marriage and thus can show its face openly. This alone is "honeste love" (1484).[11]

With the conventional formula "as thou schalt hiere" (1282), Genius leads on to the story proper and describes how Cupid succeeds in overcoming Rosiphelee's pride and her "wantounesse" (1277). As in numerous other medieval tales, the heroine resolves to go out one beautiful May morning before sunrise, accompanied by only a few of her women:

---

[11] See J.A.W. Bennett, "Gower's 'Honeste Love,'" in *Patterns of Love and Courtesy: Essays in Memory of C.S. Lewis*, ed. J. Lawlor (Evanston, 1966), pp. 107–21. On the problem of courtly love, see J.M. Steadman, "'Courtly Love' as a Problem of Style," in *Chaucer und seine Zeit: Symposion für Walter F. Schirmer*, ed. Arno Esch (Tübingen, 1968), pp. 1–33.

> And forth sche wente prively
> Unto the Park was faste by,
> Al softe walkende on the gras,
> Til sche cam ther the Launde was,
> Thurgh which ther ran a gret rivere.
> It thoghte hir fair, and seide, "Here
> I wole abide under the schawe:" . . .
> (1287–93)

Wishing to linger by herself in this *locus amoenus*, she sends her only companions away:

> And ther sche stod al one stille,
> To thenke what was in hir wille.
> (1295–96)

Solitude, silence, and reflection characterize Rosiphelee's inner state. The passage appears to set the stage for something extraordinary to happen. As in other stories, the solitude topos prepares the way for the thematic center of the tale.[12] As the narrator imperceptibly abandons the form of a neutral report, we view the natural surroundings through the eyes of the princess:

> Sche sih the swote floures springe,
> Sche herde glade foules singe,
> Sche sih the bestes in her kinde,
> The buck, the do, the hert, the hinde,
> The madle go with the femele; . . .
> (1297–1301)

To be sure, the narrator is not excluded, but he retreats somewhat by using the formula "she saw" (sometimes "heard") to let us see nature from the viewpoint of the princess as observer. Dieter Mehl has shown that this technique is conventional in medieval romance,[13] but it is ordinarily found only in short passages, so that one can scarcely speak of a consciously chosen device. In Gower, however, the point of view of the protagonist is sustained effectively over longer sections of the narrative.[14] Since the immediate source of the "Tale of Rosiphelee" is not known to us, it cannot be determined whether the technique of this passage goes back to the source either in whole or in part, or is to be attributed to Gower's artistic insight.[15] In either case, it remains to Gower's credit that he fully under-

---

[12] See, for instance, I, 351 ff. ("Tale of Acteon") or I, 1522 ff. ("Tale of Florent").

[13] " 'Point of View' in mittelenglischen Romanzen," *Germanisch-Romanische Monatsschrift*, 45 (1964), 35–46.

[14] See also I, 1526 ff. ("Tale of Florent"); I, 2038 ff. ("The Trump of Death"); I, 2304 ff. ("Tale of Narcissus"); III, 1235 ff. ("Diogenes and Alexander").

[15] Gower introduces the formula "he saw" into the "Tale of Acteon," in which the bathing Diana, in contrast to Ovid's version, is described from the point of view of the approaching Acteon. It is worth noting that here too the formula has functional significance, for the

stood the artistic value of "point of view," which allows a much more vivid and effective rendering than a simple description. Perhaps it would be going too far to describe this adoption of an observer's viewpoint as an early example of perspective. Let it suffice to say that Gower achieves a greater directness of description and an increase in suspense. Because of his use of this technique, moreover, the depiction of nature does not interrupt the action, but itself becomes a part of the action.[16]

The image of nature which presents itself to Rosiphelee's senses – budding greenery, birdsong, and the mating of animals – is in opposition to her own unnatural restraint, and this picture of a life of love and fertility kindles in her heart a conflict of feelings "Fro which sche couthe noght asterte" (1304). There follows, however, no depiction of her inner struggle; in a sudden transition the natural imagery is replaced by a new, imaginative picture:

> And as sche caste hire yhe aboute,
> Sche syh clad in o suite a route
> Of ladis, wher thei comen ryde
> Along under the wodes syde: . . .
> (1305–8)

The uniformly dressed ladies, who ride on sleek white horses with saddles decorated in pearls and gold, wear white and blue, the colors of true love; they are tall and slender in form, and their faces are of fairy-like beauty:

> The beaute faye upon her face
> Non erthly thing it may desface; . . .
> (1321–22)

This much praised, repeatedly revised couplet discloses in its final version "the working of a fine, and finely self-critical, poetic impulse."[17] Macaulay's list of textual variants for this passage reveals Gower's work on the lines, which in the earlier version give no indication of their later magic:

> The beaute of hire face schon
> Wel bryhtere þan þe Cristall ston.

The enchanting power of the couplet derives from the epithet "faye." Whereas it is said of Medea "Sche *semeth* faie and no womman" (V, 4105), the ladies on horseback are genuinely of fairy-like beauty. They are almost spiritual beings, and belong to the category of "High Fairies," as C.S. Lewis calls them.[18] As is shown

story of Acteon, like the "Tale of Rosiphelee," presents a "vision"; it is, as the marginal gloss points out, an "exemplum de *visu* ab illicitis praeservando."

[16] Maria Wickert has already referred to this point in her interpretation of the tale (*Studien*, p. 177; tr. Meindl, p. 213).

[17] *The Allegory of Love*, p. 204.

[18] *The Discarded Image*, pp. 130, 136; further examples are in J.A.W. Bennett's *Selections*, p. 150.

later, they come from the realm of the dead. Their heads are adorned with royal crowns, and even the smallest crown is more costly than all the gold of Croesus. After this description of the splendid procession, in which the total impression is static despite the slow forward movement, the frame of the picture closes with a partial echo of line 1307: "Thus come thei ridende forth" (1328).

The passage that follows delineates the effect of this "vision" on the king's daughter. The sight of the more than earthly beauty of the ladies bewilders Rosiphelee profoundly: she keeps herself concealed in her hiding place and lets the company pass by in silence:

> For as hire thoghte in hire avis,
> To hem that were of such a pris
> Sche was noght worthi axen there,
> Fro when they come or what thei were: . . .
> (1333–36)

The encounter with the fairies affects Rosiphelee as a *fascinosum* and *tremendum*. She feels herself unworthy to inquire about their origin and nature, yet she would like more than anything in the world to know the secret of these women. Finally she can restrain her curiosity no longer, and she "putte hire hed alitel oute" (1339).

With this intimate little gesture, Gower skillfully creates the transition to the second picture:

> And as sche lokede hire aboute,
> Sche syh comende under the linde
> A womman up an hors behinde.
> (1340–42)

The narrator refrains from explaining the first scene, and instead follows with an equally mysterious picture of a lone woman on a black horse, still from the viewpoint of the watchful Rosiphelee, with the result of a heightening of suspense. In contrast to the sturdy horses of the earlier company, hers is "al lene and galled on the back, / And haltede, as he were encluyed" (1344–45). In spite of his lamentable condition, this limping horse has in the middle of his forehead "a sterre whit" (1348), and although the saddle appears "wonder badde" (1350), his bridle is richly decorated with gold and precious stones. Following the pattern of the preceding scene, the woman's clothing is described next. Her dress is torn, and around her waist she wears "twenty score / Of horse haltres and wel mo" (1356–57). The mysterious symbol of the halters raises the suspense anew. As the stranger herself comes closer into Rosiphelee's field of vision, Rosiphelee perceives that the unknown woman is young and beautiful. Now the king's daughter overcomes her shyness. She steps out of her hiding place and asks the stranger to explain the mysterious procession:

> "Ha, Suster, let me hiere,
> What ben thei, that now riden hiere,

87

And ben so richeliche arraied?"
(1369–71)

The appellation "Suster" immediately suggests the similarity of situation between the two ladies, and the replies of the forlorn woman mirror almost exactly the inner condition of Rosiphelee.

The dialogue is made up of three parts. In the first reply (1374–82), Rosiphelee learns that the beautiful ladies whom she saw first were all servants of love while they were alive. With this answer, the unhappy woman quickly takes her leave in order to return at once to her assigned duties. But her reference to her duties arouses two additional questions, concerning what her duties are and why she carries the halters. The repeated salutation "goode Soster" (1383) expresses even more pointedly the connection between Rosiphelee and the fate of the lone woman. Her second reply, with twenty lines (1386–1405), is twice as long as the first. The unhappy woman was also – and here the parallel with Rosiphelee becomes obvious – a king's daughter, and disobedient to the commandments of love. She now regrets this bitterly. For this reason her horse is "fieble and badde" (1392) and her clothing torn, and on this account she must follow the procession of the "lusti ladis" during May of each year and carry the halters like a stableboy. This is her punishment because in life she was "slow in loves lore" (1402).

Rosiphelee's last question concerns the "riche bridel" (1406–7). The answer of her interlocutor, who bursts into tears, extends over twenty-five lines (1410–34), and proves even on the basis of length to be the most important part of her statement. The inner agitation of the afflicted woman is immediately evident in the anacoluthon of the first lines:

> "This bridel, which ye nou beholde
> So riche upon myn horse hed, –
> Ma Dame, afore, er I was ded,
> Whan I was in mi lusti lif,
> Ther fel into myn herte a strif
> Of love, which me overcom,
> So that therafter hiede I nom
> And thoghte I wolde love a kniht:
> That laste wel a fourtenyht,
> For it no lengere mihte laste,
> So nyh my lif was ate laste."
> (1410–20)

Here for the first time occurs the word already implied by "whilom" (1375) and long since suspected by the reader: "ded" (1412). While the lady was still alive, there was once in her heart a "strif of love" (1414–15) – here appears the parallel to the aforementioned "quarrel" in Rosiphelee's heart (1302–4). Although she decided in favor of love, the decision stands under the heading "Too late": death snatched her away before the fulfillment of her love. But since her intention was good, she is allowed to have the beautiful bridle (1426–29).

Thus are Rosiphelee's questions answered, the disturbing images explained.

One last time the unhappy woman turns to the king's daughter and takes her leave with an *adhortatio*:

> "To godd, ma Dame, I you betake,
> And warneth alle for mi sake,
> Of love that thei ben noght ydel,
> And bidd hem thenke upon mi brydel."
> (1431–34)

With this admonition she disappears as suddenly as a cloud "out of this ladi sihte" (1437), a phrase which emphasizes yet again the sustained significance of point of view in the artistic arrangement of the story. The lady's request, that a warning be given to all, emphatically intensifies the personal affliction of Rosiphelee:

> And tho for fere hire herte afflihte,
> And seide to hirself, "Helas!
> I am riht in the same cas.
> Bot if I live after this day,
> I schal amende it, if I may."
> And thus homward this lady wente,
> And changede al hire ferste entente,
> Withinne hire herte and gan to swere
> That sche none haltres wolde bere.
> (1438–46)

With great discretion, carefully proceeding step by step, the narrator has led his story to the climax. What follows the climax is movingly expressed in the narrowest space. Rosiphelee's affliction shows itself not in a strong agitation of feeling, in sighs, in pathetic gestures, or in tears of repentance, but in a thoughtful utterance in which she simply and restrainedly expresses the heaviness of her heart. The moral of the story lies in Rosiphelee's reaction to her visionary experience. What remains at the end is not punishment, as in the case of the unfortunate lady of the vision, but a reversal of the will and inner change. And the resolution to act differently from the unfortunate woman is communicated not in the form of an abstract didactic treatise, but in the simple and affecting picture of the halters which the princess wishes not to carry – a beautiful, quiet finale.

To sum up: the "Tale of Rosiphelee" is skillfully constructed, suspensefully narrated, and evidently painstakingly revised. It is remarkable for the economy, the straightforwardness, and the purposefulness of its development; the balance of commentary and dialogue is handled convincingly; and the centering of the events in the consciousness of the heroine is particularly impressive. To be sure, the description from the viewpoint of the protagonist is not unknown elsewhere in medieval narrative, but seldom is it employed with such consequence as an artistic device. The parallel situations of the two princesses are stressed through delicately nuanced turns of expression, and the entire story is overlaid with a fine net of correspondences. One might almost speak of irony, when it is said of Rosiphelee at the beginning that she could be brought to love "thurgh non ymaginacion"

(1258), and yet at the end her insight and reversal are brought about precisely through "ymaginacion." This story, so simple and charming on the surface, is yet profound, and reveals "moral Gower" to be a subtle psychologist, who succeeds equally in creating the punishment of "slowness in love" in the fate of the unfortunate woman, and the change to a positive solution to the problem in the heroine Rosiphelee.

II

The source for the second tale, "Albinus and Rosemund" (I, 2459 ff.), is a work by Godfrey of Viterbo, *Pantheon sive Memoria Saeculorum*,[19] which Gower also used in another passage.[20] Godfrey follows for his part the "History of the Lombards" of Paulus Diaconus.[21] He narrates the episode of Albinus and Rosemund in prose as well as verse.

Godfrey's short poem first establishes the historical situation, the seizure of upper Italy by the Lombards, then introduces Albinus, the first king of the Lombards, and reports on his victory over the Gepts. After the battle, Albinus has the skull of Gurmond, the fallen king of the Gepts, made into a drinking cup, out of which he irreverently drinks "pocula chara sibi" (15). When his wife dies, he takes Gurmond's daughter Rosemund in a second marriage. She soon experiences the wickedness of the king. One day he spitefully offers her the artfully decorated goblet, and then explains to the unsuspecting woman that she has drunk out of her father's skull. Rosemund bursts into tears at the monstrosity of the crime, and resolves to avenge the outrage inflicted on her and to kill her detestable husband (1–30).

The remainder of the poem (31–69) is devoted to the planning, execution, and consequences of her revenge. Rosemund orders her chambermaid to secure the king's cupbearer by granting him her favors. On the following night the queen takes the place of the girl without being recognized, and in this way makes the unsuspecting cupbearer her accomplice. Faced with the choice of either killing the king or being killed himself, the cupbearer murders Albinus and then flees with Rosemund to Ravenna, where they murder each other with poison.

Gower followed the order of events in his source, but he completely changed the motivation for the plot. He used the story as an example of *avantance*, i.e. boastfulness about success in love. This form of Pride was of no import in Godfrey. Godfrey's Albinus was much more of an *impius* who treated his wife cruelly and was therefore punished. This theme was of no use to Gower. His Albinus could be no inhuman criminal; his deed must be caused by his unbounded love. In Gower, Albinus plunges into the abyss because he violates a commandment of love by

[19] Migne, *PL*, 198, 936–8.
[20] Cf. Macaulay, I, 476.
[21] *Pauli Historia Langobardorum*, Lib. II, cap. 28–30, Scriptores Rerum Germanicarum in usum Scholarum editi ex Monumenta Germaniae Historica (Hannover, 1878), p. 104 ff.

boasting about his success in love and thus lapsing into *superbia*. The loss of Rosemund's love signifies a fall from the highest happiness to the deepest unhappiness. Without love, the world of Albinus collapses and turns to chaos, much as in the case of Othello. In comparison with this "tragedy,"[22] the murder is almost unimportant.

From this difference in basic conception results a distinct shift in the main focus of Gower's narrative. Godfrey's principal theme was the curse that springs from the evil deed. For this reason he devotes an entire third of his lines to Rosemund's decision to commit murder and to her plot with the chambermaid and the cupbearer. The assassination itself – unlike the version of Paulus Diaconus – is treated briefly, in only one and a half lines; the flight and punishment of the accomplices, however, are portrayed at greater length (15 lines). Gower's main subject is the transgression of Albinus against a commandment of love. Thus almost three-quarters of his story is devoted to this central theme, while Rosemund's revenge, the murder of Albinus, and the flight and death of the conspirators are summarized in just a few lines.

Consequently Gower's Albinus already appears in the opening lines as a man "of gret chivalerie" (2462), and he has the goblet prepared out of Gurmond's skull "for Gurmoundes sake, / To kepe and drawe into memoire / Of his bataille the victoire" (2474–76). Where the source had alluded to Albinus's love of drinking, Gower refers instead to his love of glory. And the beautiful Rosemund no longer serves simply as a replacement for the deceased first wife, for Albinus marries her out of a deeply felt love:

> His herte fell to hire anon,
> And such a love on hire he caste,
> That he hire weddeth ate laste;
> And after that long time in reste
> With hire he duelte, and to the beste
> Thei love ech other wonder wel.
> (2484–89)

Albinus's innermost being is fulfilled in his love for Rosemund. To please her, he decides to put on a great celebration so that she may share in his happiness and become known to his followers.

Thus we touch on Gower's most important alteration relative to his source. In Godfrey there was only a brief reference to a celebration, and that only in his prose version. Gower has expanded the mere mention in his source into a great scene of splendor and has made it into the very center of his narrative.[23] As Albinus

---

22 Cf. J.H. Fisher, p. 195: "The tale of Albinus and Rosemund . . . is a genuine love tragedy in spite of its clerical descent."

23 It is well known that Chaucer avoids the description of festive occasions; indeed the Man of Law treats such subjects with obvious irony (*Canterbury Tales* B1 701–7). However, we should not necessarily conclude from the portrayal of the feast scene in "Albinus and Rosemund" that Gower has a predilection for such themes. In the story of Constance he too

summons his guests to the feast, he is at the pinnacle of happiness; in his private as in his public life he has accomplished everything that he aspired to:

> This king, which stod in al his welthe
> Of pes, of worschipe and of helthe,
> And felte him on no side grieved,
> As he that hath his world achieved,
> Tho thoghte he wolde a feste make; ...
> (2495–99)

The feast will be a splendid expression of consummate joy, perfect harmony, and outer and inner peace. It serves likewise as background for Albinus's ruin and therefore provides a point of comparison for the later events. In the lines which directly precede the feast scene, the narrator leaves no doubt that the downfall of Albinus threatens to occur at any moment, for the goddess Fortuna is accustomed to set her wheel in motion just as her minions find themselves at the absolute high point of their lives:

> Bot sche which kepth the blinde whel,
> Venus, whan thei be most above,
> In al the hoteste of here love,
> Hire whiel sche torneth, and thei felle
> In the manere as I schal telle.
> (2490–94)

The shadows of the impending disaster are hidden for the time being, however, and the poet describes with obvious enjoyment the preparation for the feast and the splendor of the tournament:

> The grete Stiedes were assaied
> For joustinge and for tornement,
> And many a perled garnement
> Embroudred was ayein the dai.
> The lordes in here beste arrai
> Be comen ate time set,
> On jousteth wel, an other bet,
> And otherwhile thei torneie,
> And thus thei casten care aweie
> And token lustes upon honde.
> (2508–17)

All the guests are in high spirits, and when they later gather in the banquet hall and the heralds praise the victors in the tournament, there rings out the basic theme of all romances: "Al was of armes and of love" (2528).

At the high point of the noisy feast, when the talk on all sides is about deeds of

---

passes over the description of the feast. The decisive factor is rather that the courtly feast in "Albinus and Rosemund" has a definite function.

valor and love, the king too is carried away by the mood of his surroundings, and his heart is moved by pride:

> That of the merthe which thei made
> The king himself began to glade
> Withinne his herte and tok a pride, . . .
> (2531–33)

With this, *superbia* rears her head, and the fall into sin is imminent. As if by accident, Albinus's glance falls on the drinking cup, which provides the stimulus for his action. The artistic perfection and glistening beauty of the vessel are described once again, this time from the viewpoint of Albinus (2534). While in Godfrey these qualities are noted with terse objectivity ("Arte scyphum fieri statuens, auroque ligari" [20] ["Commanding an exquisite goblet to be made and to be wreathed with gold" – Tr.]), Gower revels in the seductive charm of this work of art, of its decoration with gold and precious stones, of its engraving and its radiance, which conceal the skull so well that it appears to be a griffin's egg:

> And was with gold and riche Stones
> Beset and bounde for the nones,
> And stod upon a fot on heihte
> Of burned gold, and with gret sleihte
> Of werkmanschipe it was begrave
> Of such werk as it scholde have,
> And was policed ek so clene
> That no signe of the Skulle is sene,
> Bot as it were a Gripes Ey.
> (2537–45)

The temptation is so strong that the king cannot withstand it. He immediately orders the cup standing before him to be replaced with the marvelous vessel, and he offers the latter to the queen:

> The king bad bere his Cuppe awey,
> Which stod tofore him on the bord,
> And fette thilke. Upon his word
> This Skulle is fet and wyn therinne,
> Wherof he bad his wif beginne:
> "Drink with thi fader, Dame," he seide.
> (2546–51)

The precision, severity, and directness of these words, which make no reference at all to the imminent disaster, are extremely impressive. The concise objectivity of the command dramatises the incident with the utmost suspense; and after Rosemund has imbibed at Albinus's ambiguous invitation, trouble breaks loose. In a boastful speech the king announces to his guests:

> it was hire fader Skulle,
> So that the lordes knowe schulle

93

> Of his bataille a soth witnesse,
> And made avant thurgh what prouesse
> He hath his wyves love wonne,
> Which of the Skulle hath so begonne.
> (2557–62)

Albinus brags of his successes in battle and in love. There is a causal relation between the two, for Rosemund's love is the result of Albinus's victory over her father. Just as the victors in the tournaments were praised earlier by the heralds, so Albinus extols himself. Here rightful praise is sharply contrasted with false. Albinus is as it were his "own herald" and confirms through his behavior what Genius in the frame narrative had named as the distinguishing features of *avantance*:

> The vice cleped Avantance
> With Pride hath take his aqueintance,
> So that his oghne pris he lasseth,
> When he such mesure overpasseth
> That he his oghne Herald is.
> (2399–2403)

The close connection of the story with the frame is also reflected in the key words "pride" and "avant" in lines 2563–69, which describe the effect of Albinus's boastful speech on the festive gathering. Likewise, Rosemund bases her decision to take revenge not on the ghastliness of the crime, but rather on the vice of *avantance*. She will give herself no more peace "Til that sche se him so bestad / That he nomore make avant" (2584–85).

Significantly, Fortune again uses love as the agent of the characters' destruction. The intrigue is set into motion by way of the liaison beween the chambermaid and the cupbearer. After the unsuspecting cupbearer has slept with the queen, Rosemund gives him (in Godfrey's version) two choices, either to die or to cooperate with her plans: "Elige, quod cupias, duo sunt quae conspicis in te, / Aut regem perimes, inquit, vel rex perimet te" (46–47) ["Choose what you want, you have only two choices before you: either you will kill the king, she said, or the king will kill you." – Tr.]. Although Gower too adopts the theme of coercion, he adds as a much more important factor the cupbearer's burning passion for Rosemund:

> Anon the wylde loves rage,
> In which noman him can governe,
> Hath mad him that he can noght werne,
> Bot fell al hol to hire assent: . . .
> (2620–23)

Just as the narrator foreshadows the coming disaster before the beginning of the feast, so at this turning point, which seals Albinus's fate, he takes up the symbol of Fortune's wheel once again:

> And thus the whiel is al miswent,
> The which fortune hath upon honde . . .
> (2624–25)

94

The repetition of the image of Fortune in this passage reinforces the earlier observation that the primary catastrophe for Albinus is not his death, but the irreplaceable loss of his love. At the same time, however, the formula "al miswent" also anticipates the downfall of the conspirators. In the final analysis, the breakdown of love is only a symptom of the deeper *discordia* of a world threatened with dissension and anarchy, and is thus a variation on a basic theme of Gower's writing.

If Gower only briefly summarizes the subsequent events and passes over the details of the flight and the death of the conspirators, this is not a weakness in Gower's narrative art. As Macaulay rightly perceived, an embellishment of the closing events would only have been a digression from the central theme of the story.[24] Similarly, at the end of "Pyramus and Thisbe" Gower omits the metamorphosis, surely not because he was offended at the blood of Pyramus spurting up and spattering the mulberry tree,[25] but because the metamorphosis could contribute nothing more to his theme of "rashness in love." By contrast, where the conclusion of the story was suited to emphasize the theme, Gower not only adopted it but developed it at length. The Ovidian story of "Ceyx and Alcyone" offers an example. Here too the metamorphosis of the two spouses, which Ovid savors in great detail, is irrelevant for Gower, but their reunion is not. In Gower, Ceyx and Alcyone are metamorphosed at the same time without the actual event being described more closely. Instead, Gower paints a lovingly detailed picture of their life together as birds so that the ending of the story turns out to be an exaltation of marital fidelity beyond death, and the final picture with its "joie" represents the counterpoint to Alcyone's previous sorrow:

> And whan sche sih hire lord livende
> In liknesse of a bridd swimmende,
> And sche was of the same sort,
> So as sche mihte do desport,
> Upon the joie which sche hadde
> Hire wynges bothe abrod sche spradde,
> And him, so as sche mai suffise,
> Beclipte and keste in such a wise,
> As sche was whilom wont to do:
> Hire wynges for hire armes tuo
> Sche tok, and for hire lippes softe
> Hire harde bile, and so fulofte
> Sche fondeth in hire briddes forme,
> If that sche mihte hirself conforme
> To do the plesance of a wif,
> As sche dede in that other lif:
> For thogh sche hadde hir pouer lore,
> Hir will stod as it was tofore,

---

24 Macaulay, I, 477.
25 As D. Pearsall believes (p. 480).

And serveth him so as sche mai.
(IV, 3097–3115)

Returning to "Albinus and Rosemund": in Gower's hands, Godfrey's rather thread-bare episode is transformed into a suspenseful narrative. Gower has given the story, moreover, a theme which was not at all present in his source. To be sure, he was able to adopt the plot of his source in broad outline, but the transformation into a "tragedy of love" required a complete change of motivation and a shift in the placement of emphasis in the plot. The transformation appears at its most impressive in the grandiose arrangement of the feast scene.

Gower narrates concretely and directly, without digressions or moralizing commentary, and he adds an air of fatality (in the classical sense) to the fall of his hero. Although his characters are depicted conventionally on the surface, they are lifelike because their behavior is convincingly motivated. Here again the restrained description of emotions is striking. Rosemund remains in control even during the frightful revelation. Godfrey reports,: "Pectora pessundat, lacrymae vehementer inundant" (26) ["She beats her breasts, her tears vehemently flow" – Tr.]. In the same passage Gower has only the the subdued hint, "and sche was softe, / Thenkende on thilke unkynde Pryde" (2564–65); and a few lines later, "Sche soffreth al til thei were uppe" (2570). He is a master of understated effects.

III

As the third example, let us turn to Gower's "Tale of Constance" (II, 587–1598), which allows comparison both with its source, the Anglo-Norman chronicle of the Dominican monk Nicolas Trivet,[26] and with Chaucer's treatment of the story in the "Man of Law's Tale" (Canterbury Tales B¹ 134–1162).[27] Gower's version probably antedates Chaucer's,[28] but this question is of lesser importance for our consideration, for we are not concerned with priority, but with the characteristic features of Gower's narrative art.

The substance of the legend is the life of Constance, the sorely tested daughter of an emperor, who with exemplary faith and God's help overcomes all afflictions and perils, and who closes her earthly existence as the paragon of constancy and loyalty. Fate leads Constance from Rome to Syria, where she is to marry the Sultan, but the Sultan's diabolical mother destroys the marriage plans. The welcoming feast ends in a horrible bloodbath, and Constance is put out to sea in a rudderless boat. After long wandering she reaches Northumbria, where the constable Elda takes her in. She converts Elda's wife Hermyngheld and later Elda himself, and she marries the Northumbrian king Allee. After the birth of a son,

---

26 Text in Sources and Analogues of Chaucer's Canterbury Tales, ed. W.F. Bryan and G. Dempster (London, 1958), pp. 165–81.
27 The Works of Geoffrey Chaucer, ed. F.N. Robinson, 2nd ed. (London, 1957), pp. 63–75.
28 See the discussion of the research in this area by J.H. Fisher, pp. 290 ff.

she again suffers the fate of exile through the intrigue of her evil mother-in-law Domilde. She drifts again for years on the sea until, once more saved through divine Providence, she is sheltered in Rome by Senator Arcennus. Here she is reunited with her husband and her father – the influence of the late antique romance is evident on all sides. Constance travels with Allee to England, and after his death she returns to Rome, her place of origin. The legend ends with the death of her father, her own demise, and the coronation of her son Moris.

In this sequence of events (which might be expounded at much greater length) as in the interpretation of Constance as a Christian saint, Gower follows his source very closely. But he has not only left out superfluous passages, he has above all emphasised the parallelism in the story much more than is the case in Trivet's version. The events of the first part, from the beginnings in Rome and the journey to Syria to the expulsion and the landing in Northumbria, appear in fuller instrumentation in the second part, which includes both the events in England and Constance's second expulsion and rescue. The preliminary character of the first part is evident not only from the fact that it is only a third as long as the second; significantly, all of the major figures besides Constance and her parents remain nameless, while in the second part all the important characters and even many minor ones are called by name. As the proposed wedding with the Sultan stands at the center of the first section, the marriage with King Allee stands at the center of the second. The conversion of the Syrian merchants corresponds to the conversion of Hermyngheld and Elda; the message of the merchants to the Sultan to that of Elda to Allee; the conversion of the Sultan to that of the Northumbrian king. The mothers of the Sultan and Allee are the evil intriguers. Twice Constance is exiled, twice she wanders for years upon the sea, and twice she is kindly sheltered. Through the emphasis on the parallel structure, Gower binds the different episodes together and makes the basic pattern of divine guidance transparently clear.

The effort at parallelism can be traced in detail. In Gower, Constance is expelled and wanders in the same ship[29] for exactly three years, while in Trivet her voyages last three years and eight months in the first instance and five years in the second. Even the circumstances of the discovery of the ship are similar in each case. The assaults of the "false knihts" upon Constance (the first of whom incidentally remains nameless again) are both miraculously thwarted in Gower's version, while in Trivet and Chaucer the first villain is executed and only the second dies through divine intervention. And just as Constance's father at the beginning of the story is characterized as a "worthi kniht in Cristes lawe" (587), so is her son Moris on assuming his inheritance "the cristeneste of alle" (1598).

Also noteworthy is the allusive character of many images and episodes. For instance, the healing of the blind man is also to be understood as a figurative expression of the conversion of the heathen Northumbrians to Christianity. Just as the blind man receives back his natural sight through the miracle, so the heathens are freed from spiritual blindness through Constance's power to convert. When Constance later returns to England with Allee, the theme of blindness is explicitly

---

[29] In Chaucer too Constance is placed in the same ship, but not in Trivet.

resumed. The narrator emphasizes that through Constance's missionary effort the Christian faith was imparted to those "that whilom were blinde" (1571).

A less successful example of foreshadowing is offered by the episode in which Elda and Lucius read Domilde's letter, and are overcome by such grief,

> As thei here oghne Moder sihen
> Brent in a fyr before here yhen.
> (1047–48)

The image has an abrupt and awkward effect;[30] precisely for this reason one can be certain that Gower inserted it into this passage in order to refer to the subsequent death by fire of Allee's mother:

> And tho sche was to dethe broght
> And brent tofore hire Sones yhe: . . .
> (1292–93)

Elsewhere in Gower's work, there is much more effective foreshadowing of later events by means of imagery. An example might be drawn from the "Tale of Tereus." In the *Metamorphoses*, Ovid has the following image of the disgraced Philomela's extracted tongue:

> radix micat ultima linguae,
> ipsa iacet terraeque tremens inmurmurat atrae,
> utque salire solet mutilatae cauda colubrae,
> palpitat et moriens dominae vestigia quaerit.
> (VI, 557–60)

["The mangled root quivers, while the severed tongue lies palpitating on the dark earth, faintly murmuring; and, as the severed tail of a mangled snake is wont to writhe, it twitches convulsively, and with its last dying movement it seeks its mistress's feet." Frank Justus Miller, trans., *Metamorphoses*, Loeb Classical Library (Cambridge: Harvard University Press, 1977).]

Gower does not adopt Ovid's expressive picture of the still twitching tail of a mutilated snake, but he seizes on imagery which anticipates the later metamorphosis into a bird:

> Bot yit whan he hire tunge refte,
> A litel part therof belefte,
> Bot sche with al no word mai soune,
> Bot chitre and as a brid jargoune.
> (V, 5697–5700)

---

[30] Much more appropriate is the anticipatory comparison in lines 1274–76, which describe the rage of Allee when he seizes his mother: "And lich the fyr which tunder hente, / In such a rage, as seith the bok, / His Moder sodeinliche he tok . . . " Cf. a similar anticipatory comparison with fire in the tale of "Deianira and Nessus" (II, 2256–57 and 2291 ff.).

But let us return to the story of Constance and examine several episodes somewhat more closely. The opening lines in Gower's narrative serve as the conventional description of the heroine (587–610). We hear of Constance's parentage and of her faith, which is so great that she converted some Saracen merchants to Christianity. With that, the introduction is concluded. The lines that follow (611–19) prepare for the beginning of the action: the Sultan has the merchants summoned in order to ask the reason for their change of religion.

Chaucer's opening (134–68) begins entirely differently. Here the narrator describes in a leisurely manner the rich Syrian merchants and their magnificent wares, and then their journey to Rome, where they take lodging and where one day the news of the emperor's beautiful daughter comes to their ears. The effect of this carefully detailed account is strongly emphasized by the use of the rhyme royal stanza. While Gower's introduction was tersely factual and his merchants, whose wares were not even mentioned, served only to bring the main characters into action, Chaucer first of all provides an impression of the background and of the setting. Indeed the opening lines of the "Man of Law's Tale" are exceptional for Chaucer; as a rule, he too begins his stories with an introduction of the main characters.

It is remarkable that Chaucer never mentions Constance's conversion of the merchants. Chaucer's Constance is praised in the opening lines not for her strength of faith and her missionary zeal, but for her goodness and beauty, and the narrator wishes that "she were of al Europe the queene" (161):

> In hire is heigh beautee, withoute pride,
> Yowthe, withoute grenehede or folye;
> To alle hire werkes vertu is hir gyde;
> Humblesse hath slayn in hire al tirannye.
> She is mirour of alle curteisye;
> Hir herte is verray chambre of hoolynesse,
> Hir hand, ministre of fredam for almesse.
> (162–68)

Constance is characterized as the essence of courtliness, and her specifically Christian virtues, which are mentioned in the last two lines, emerge only gradually into the foreground.[31] In Gower, by contrast, her devotional and saintly qualities are prominent from the beginning and are almost the exclusive center of interest in the tale.

When Chaucer reports the praise of Constance's beauty and virtue as *communis opinio* (155), and at the end of the eulogy has the narrator assert "And al this voys was sooth, as God is trewe" (169), he accomplishes several purposes at once: he brings the city to life, he suggests to us that the unanimous judgment of its citizens is true, and he makes us eager for the first appearance of the woman who is preceded by such a reputation. Gower on the other hand does not seek initially to

---

[31] But on this subject see M. Wickert, "Chaucers Konstanze und die Legende der guten Frauen," *Anglia*, 69 (1950), 91–92.

achieve vividness or a feeling for the background; instead, he introduces his characters only briefly in their pseudohistorical frame in order to make a prompt transition to the action. His introduction is thus rather solidly packed with information and remains fairly abstract.

In order to lead the reader from the Sultan's marriage plans to Constance's exile at the hands of the Sultan's mother, Gower needs only 47 of his brief couplets (620–713). Scarcely has the Sultan heard of Constance when he has already decided on marriage and dispatches his emissaries to the emperor:

> And whan the Souldan of Constance
> Upon the point that thei ansuerde
> The beaute and the grace herde,
> As he which thanne was to wedde,
> In alle haste his cause spedde
> To sende for the mariage.
> (620–25)[32]

While Gower's narrative manner resembles an impersonal report, Chaucer picks out certain incidents from the story and shapes them into vivid, self-contained scenes in which the narrator's commentary can develop fully alongside the dialogue and description.[33] Chaucer's main interest lies not in the sequence of events, but in the behavior of his characters in a given situation. Thus Chaucer discusses the problem of the Sultan's marriage in a separate brief council scene. The councillors bring forward the most diverse arguments and skillfully debate the delicate question of conversion. On the one hand they do not wish to provoke the Sultan's displeasure, but on the other hand they remain true to their ancestral Mohammedan faith:

> Thanne sawe they therinne swich difficultee
> By wey of reson, for to speke al playn,
> By cause that ther was swich diversitee
> Bitwene hir bothe lawes, that they sayn
> They trowe, "that no Cristen prince wolde fayn
> Wedden his child under oure lawe sweete
> That us was taught by Mahoun, oure prophete."
> (218–24)

---

[32] In the same way Aruns's consideration of Lucretia's "image" in the "Rape of Lucrece" quickly merges with a decision to act: "And up he sterte, and forth he wente / On horsebak . . . " (VII, 4907–8).

[33] Gertraud Walter, in her dissertation "Grundtypen der Erzähl- und Darstellungstechnik bei Chaucer" (Munich, 1964), has demonstrated that the creation of dramatic scenes is a characteristic of Chaucer's narrative art. She describes Chaucer's concept of a scene in the following way: "In Chaucer, a scene consists of a single concrete situation lifted from the flow of the story and an enclosed frame which introduces and concludes the scene. The basic supporting element in each scene is personal speech, whether it be in the form of a brief utterance, an extensive dialogue, or a monologue" (p. 81).

The smooth transition from indirect to direct quotation is masterly. Through this device, not only is the description made more vivid, but the defense of Islam is skillfully placed in the mouths of the Mohammedans. Finally, the Sultan naturally rejects the arguments in order to seek the proposed marriage, and commands that the negotiations with emperor and pope be initiated immediately.

In a similar fashion, Chaucer transforms the departure of Constance from Rome into a great crowd scene with lengthy speeches. The narrator introduces it with ominous sounding lines which create an anxious undertone. At the same time, this pathetic scene is touched with subtle irony when the narrator comments that it is the lot of young girls to leave their parents' homes and to be subjected to a husband unknown to them, but

> Housbondes been alle goode, and han ben yoore;
> That knowen wyves; I dar sey yow na moore.
> (272–73)

Gower devotes little interest to Constance's departure. His attention is directed almost exclusively at the conversion of the Sultan, with the result that the actual reason for this conversion, namely the marriage, recedes entirely into the background. When Constance is accompanied by cardinals and noblemen, it is less to give the emperor's daughter a suitable escort than "To se the Souldan be converted" (638). Their journey into "Barbarie" is a political-religious affair.

Parellel to the scene of the Sultan's council, Chaucer introduces a scene in which the Sultan's mother summons her councillors and reveals to them her diabolical plan to murder the wedding party. Again, Gower is satisfied with a terse report which, without a hint of a definite setting, renders the thoughts of the Sultan's mother in direct quotation:

> The Moder which this Souldan bar
> Was thanne alyve, and thoghte this
> Unto hirself: "If it so is
> Mi Sone him wedde in this manere,
> Than have I lost my joies hiere,
> For myn astat schal so be lassed."
> (644–49)

Gower's motivation diverges from the source. In Trivet the Sultan's mother fears no loss of power: she is more concerned about the Mohammedan faith. That Gower ignores the religious theme here, after he had earlier stressed the idea of conversion so emphatically, should be ascribed to the confessional frame, which required an example of "Detraccioun." The evil mother-in-law's envy lent itself aptly to that purpose.

Likewise the accompanying conversation between the Sultan and his mother, in which the latter shares her plan to give a welcoming feast for her "daughter," receives in Chaucer's version – in contrast to Gower's – a dramatically effective conclusion, with the kneeling of the grateful son and the farewell gesture of the mother, reminiscent of Judas's kiss: "She kiste hir sone, and hoom she gooth hir weye" (385).

Chaucer mentions the feast and the bloodbath only briefly. Gower differs again in a significant fashion. He too describes the feast in no great detail, for unlike the one in "Albinus and Rosemund," it has no important function; but he gives a graphic and forceful report of the carnage from the viewpoint of the surviving Constance:

> This worthi Maiden which was there
> Stod thanne, as who seith, ded for feere,
> To se the feste how that it stod,
> Which was al torned into blod:
> The Dissh forthwith the Coppe and al
> Bebled thei weren overal;
> Sche sih hem deie on every side;
> No wonder thogh sche wepte and cride
> Makende many a wofull mone.
>
> (695–703)

In deathly fear, Constance sees how the banquet hall has turned into a sea of blood. Her eyes take in the blood-spattered objects on the table, which serve as symbols of the overthrow of order, and on all sides she perceives those slain by the Sultan's raging mother:

> Sche slowh hem in a sodein rage
> Endlong the bord as thei be set,
> So that it myhte noght be let;
> Hire oghne Sone was noght quit,
> Bot deide upon the same plit.
>
> (688–92)

The Sultan's mother appears here as an incarnation of evil. Trivet's description is more "realistic." According to his account, the Sultan's mother engages seven hundred Saracen mercenaries as servants for the feast who, with the help of additional Saracens, are to kill the Christians. After the slaughter, she seeks first to convert Constance to Islam, and when Constance refuses to deny her Christian faith, the Sultaness devises the exile by sea as a new torture. Gower's she-devil on the other hand has thought of everything in advance; she has Constance brought straight to the rudderless ship along with her possessions. In Chaucer too Constance is immediately set adrift, and what is more, with the ironic advice "to sail back to Italy;" the following stanzas, up to the landing in England (442–504), however, typically include an extensive commentary by the narrator in addition to a lengthy prayer (451–62). The miraculous preservation of Constance is considered in agitated rhetorical questions and prolonged biblical parallels, almost in the manner of a devotional image;[34] at the same time, the stylistic devices that Chaucer employs serve the self-characterization of the narrator.

---

[34] See Th. Wolpers, *Die Englische Heiligenlegende des Mittelalters* (Tübingen, 1964), p. 413.

Gower on the other hand scarcely mentions a detail which is not directly connected with the action. In Trivet and Chaucer, for instance, the episode of Hermyngheld's conversion possesses its own intrinsic value, while in Gower, as even the syntactic connection indicates, it clearly has the function only of leading on to the healing of the blind man:

> and fell so,
> Spekende alday betwen hem two,
> Thurgh grace of goddes pourveance
> This maiden tawhte the creance
> Unto this wif so parfitly,
> Upon a dai that faste by
> In presence of hire housebonde,
> Wher thei go walkende on the Stronde,
> A blind man, which cam there lad,
> Unto this wif criende he bad,
> With bothe hise hondes up and preide
> To hire, and in this wise he seide:
> "O Hermyngeld, . . .
>
> (751–63)

In this way event follows event; the thread of the plot is never broken. Let us compare this with Chaucer's introduction to the healing of the blind man, where he first portrays the setting, again with a series of vivid details:

> Bright was the sonne as in that someres day,
> For which the constable and his wyf also
> And Custance han ytake the righte way
> Toward the see a furlong wey or two,
> To pleyen and to romen to and fro;
> And in hir walk this blynde man they mette,
> Croked and oold, with eyen faste yshette.
>
> (554–60)

The contrasts in this passage are jarring. Before the background of a clear, bright summer day, the sudden appearance of the pathetic blind man works so much more movingly, and in the following lines the human situation, namely Hermyngheld's initial fear of her still pagan husband and of his reaction to the miracle, is exploited emotionally by Chaucer just as in Trivet's version. Gower's account, in contrast, is to the point; human feelings have no place here. The miracle remains something inexplicable. It operates simply through its result; it has, as the conversion of Elda shows, power to inspire belief:

> Bot Elda wondreth most of alle:
> This open thing which is befalle
> Concludeth him be such a weie,
> That he the feith mot nede obeie.
>
> (775–78)

103

Finally, let us consider an episode which both Chaucer and Gower choose to embellish: Constance's banishment from England. Chaucer describes her departure in a highly pathetic scene in which the helpless Constance, surrounded by her lamenting subjects, kneels on the shore and offers a rhetorically stylised prayer to God and the Virgin Mary. She entreats compassion most of all for her son, and bids Elda to kiss him in the name of his father. Unlike Trivet's longsuffering heroine, she cannot submit dutifully to the king's will; instead, she speaks to her son of "thyn harde fader" (857) and calls to her absent, supposedly cruel spouse a bitter "Farewell, housbonde routhelees!" (863). Again in this passage Gower's tale differs fundamentally. Not only does his version of Constance's prayer, which in Chaucer takes up more than two stanzas, comprise just four lines, but it is also spoken on the high sea and not before a weeping throng on the beach. Gower detaches his heroine from her milieu in such a way that she seems more solitary, grander, less sentimental. He wishes less to arouse the compassion of his audience than to establish the certainty of the belief that God is nearest to the person in distress.

The portrayal of Constance's behavior to her child also differs in a characteristic way. Chaucer embellishes the portrait of the mother in an almost affected manner:

> Hir litel child lay wepyng in hir arm,
> And knelynge, pitously to hym she seyde,
> "Pees, litel sone, I wol do thee noon harm."
> With that hir coverchief of hir heed she breyde,
> And over his litel eyen she it leyde,
> And in hir arm she lulleth it ful faste,
> And into hevene hire eyen up she caste.
> (834–40)

It is a touching scene in which Chaucer borders on sentimentality, but his Constance makes an unforgettable, individual little gesture. Gower aims at a typical and conventional picture. After Constance has been strengthened by her prayer, she takes her child in her arms "And yaf it sowke" (1079).

The comparison between Chaucer's and Gower's legends of Constance reveals a difference in artistic purpose. One can admire the variety, the narrative richness, and the vitality of Chaucer's fictional art and still appreciate the simple form of Gower's legend as the fulfillment of a different intention. Chaucer wishes to portray a religious but at the same time a deeply human theme. For this reason one enjoys the intrusions and the patronizing comments of the narrator, when he remarks, for instance, with delicate irony on Constance's and Allee's wedding night:

> They goon to bedde, as it was skile and right;
> For thogh that wyves be ful hooly thynges,
> They moste take in pacience at nyght
> Swich manere necessaries as been plesynges
> To folk that han ywedded hem with rynges,
> And leye a lite hir hoolynesse aside,

As for the tyme, – it may no bet bitide.
(708–14)

Gower, on the other hand, would not and could not bind together earnestness and irony, or courtliness and the piety of a saint's life. His objective was to write a simple, straightforward saint's legend, and to this end he correctly believed a chronological report to be the most suitable form. Consequently, he strove for an austere, symmetrical structure; for this reason his main character has a certain stiffness, for this reason psychological analysis is dispensed with.

That Gower was entirely capable of writing with psychological insight is shown not only by numerous other stories, but also by a figure like King Allee. To be sure, he embodies the ideal of the good and sensible ruler, but he has enough individual traits to make him real to us. He does not fall head over heels in love with Constance like the Sultan; he thinks before he acts. The narrator remarks on the behavior of the king, with regard to God's judgment of the Saxon knight:

> He tok it into remembrance
> And thoghte more than he seide.
> (894–95)

When the messenger brings him the forged letter, Allee cannot hide his displeasure, but he answers "in wys manere" (992). After he finally realizes that Constance has become a victim of Domilde's intrigue, he furiously swears revenge against his mother:

> "O beste of helle, in what juise
> Hast thou deserved forto deie,
> That hast so falsly put aweie
> With tresoun of thi bacbitinge
> The treweste at my knowlechinge
> Of wyves and the most honeste?
> Bot I wol make this beheste,
> I schal be venged er I go."
> (1278–85)

In the same scene in Trivet, Domilde can only briefly confess her shameful deed to Allee before he beheads and dismembers her:

> Et ele [Domilde] . . . en priaunte mercy, recunisoit toute sa felonie. Et le rey a grant fierte ly dist que nul merci ne en auereyt mes come sa tresoun demaunda. "Qar de moy, ne de ma femme, ne de moun enfaunt vous ne nauiez pite, ne ioe de vous ia pite naueray." E a ceo ly coupa la teste e le corps tut a pecees, come ele iut nue en soun lit.[35]

> [And praying for mercy, she confessed all her evil deeds. And the king in great anger told her that he would have no mercy on her except as her

---

35 *Sources and Analogues*, pp. 176 f.

treason required. "For you had no pity on me, nor on my wife, nor on my child, and now I will have no pity on you." And with that he cut her head and body all to pieces as she lay naked in her bed. – Tr.]

Allee also slaughters his mother in Chaucer's version, but as might be expected, the narrator spends little time on the bloody event:

> Th'effect is this, that Alla, out of drede,
> His mooder slow – that may men pleynly rede –
> For that she traitour was to hire ligeance.
> Thus endeth olde Donegild, with meschance!
> (893–96)

Gower's Allee, by contrast, has a funeral pyre built, and he has Domilde thrown onto it only when she has given a detailed confession of her misdeed. The king does not act spontaneously as in Trivet: he imposes a severe but just punishment which is expressly approved by the eyewitnesses to her death by fire (1294–1301). Thus the evil is eradicated, but the sorrowful king cannot be happy as long as he knows nothing of his wife's fate.

Another episode which demonstrates Gower's gift for psychological characterization is the one in which Allee rediscovers his son in Rome. When the king learns that Moris's mother is called Constance, he is pulled this way and that by conflicting emotions, and longs for the truth as a soul in purgatory longs for entrance into paradise:

> For he was nouther ther ne hiere,
> Bot clene out of himself aweie,
> That he not what to thenke or seie,
> So fain he wolde it were sche.
> Wherof his hertes privete
> Began the werre of yee and nay,
> The which in such balance lay,
> That contenance for a throwe
> He loste, til he mihte knowe
> The sothe: bot in his memoire
> The man which lith in purgatoire
> Desireth noght the hevene more,
> That he ne longeth al so sore
> To wite what him schal betide.
> (1412–25)

Gower knows how to depict dramatically the exciting moment in which the king almost loses his composure. If there is little room in Constance for human emotions, and if some of her reactions – her grief, her fear, her sorrow – are repeated stereotypically, one must conclude that Gower did not wish to psychoanalyze his protagonist but to portray her as a saint. For that reason Constance always retains something cool, strange, impersonal. Her essence is defined by her *constantia*, and a detailed study of her motives is unnecessary to Gower (just as her evil enemies are

106

simply "false" or "thurghout untrewe"). Instead we find all the essential elements of a Christian saint's life: the heroine's missionary zeal, the miracles, and after her death, Constance's assumption into heaven. There is even a brief hint of her venerable status, when it is said of Constance's father,

> Bot what that eny man him bad
> Of grace for his dowhter sake,
> That grace wolde he noght forsake;
> And thus ful gret almesse he dede,
> Wherof sche hadde many a bede.
> (1468–72)

The last line should be understood as referring to prayers of thanks from recipients of alms, which provides the hint of the theme of pious veneration which is indispensable to the saint's legend.

In all three versions, Constance keeps noticeably silent on her origin. It is obvious that Trivet, who wrote for a nun of royal birth, could not keep the theme of the original story, in which the heroine must flee from her father who intends to rape her. In place of the incest theme, he explains that the shameful deed of the Sultan's mother had already become widely known.[36] Gower does not take up the hint; in his legend, Constance's silence on her origin has instead the effect of a motif from a fairy tale. Perhaps the mystery of her origin should also explain why her husband found believable the claim in Domilde's letter that Constance was "of faierie" (964),[37] an evil spirit who had brought a monstrous child into the world. The term arises again at Constance's death, this time however in a striking reversal:

> [God] fro this worldes faierie
> Hath take hire into compaignie.
> (1593–94)

Constance is not "faie" (1019), but the world is. At the end Constance leaves the realm of false appearances to enter the world of true reality.

The connection of the story with the vice of *detraccioun* is loose, for only in two cases is there a discussion of slander, and even here it is not in the special sense of slander by a lover against a rival as defined in the confessional frame. On the other hand, much like the two stories previously discussed, this story is closely connected with the overall theme of the *Confessio Amantis*, for Constance suffers not only for

---

[36] "E entre sez dys riens ne voleit reconustre de Tyberie lemperor, soun piere, ne del soudan; quar laauenture del mourdre del soudan et de les Cristient estoit ia conue par totes terres" ["And from her words she wanted nothing to be known of her father Tiberius the emperor nor of the sultan, for the episode of the murder of the sultan and the Christians was now known through all nations." – Tr.] (*Sources and Analogues*, p. 168). In Trivet three Christians were able to escape from the slaughter and bring the news back to Rome (*ibid.*, p. 167).
[37] Trivet's wording of this passage runs as follows: "Maueise espirit en fourme de femme" (*Sources and Analogues*, p. 173).

her faith, but also for her love. The sorely tested king remains true to his love just as the unjustly suffering Constance does, and their love in spite of all the wickedness of the world proves itself not an empty illusion, but a secure rock in the sea of falsehood, as Genius repeats impressively at the end of the tale:

> And thus the wel meninge of love
> Was ate laste set above;
> And so as thou hast herd tofore,
> The false tunges weren lore,
> Whiche upon love wolden lie.
> (1599–1603)

In retelling the legend of Constance, Gower and Chaucer each had different objectives, and each of the two poets has fulfilled his artistic intention in his own way. Gower was less concerned with the human side of spiritual events than in the depiction of the absolute in the life of his heroine. He wanted to narrate a straightforward, edifying saint's life, and the simple structure always favored by him was very much to his purpose. In order to make the transcendent visible, objective reporting and a strictly chronological sequence of events were the only suitable and convincing means.

It was naturally not our intention to prove Gower the equal of Chaucer. That would be an impossible undertaking, for Chaucer is a unique phenomenon not only in English but in the European literature of his time. Our goal was more modest: to understand Gower's artistic purpose, and to point out some of the most characteristic features in the structure and development of his tales.[38]

---

[38] The author wishes to thank the participants in his 1967–68 graduate seminar, especially Achim Böker, Detlef Boldt, Rudolf van den Boom, and Ingrid Reufels.

THE CHARACTER GENIUS IN ALAN DE LILLE, JEAN DE MEUN, AND JOHN GOWER

GEORGE D. ECONOMOU

One of the most obvious aspects of the career of the character Genius in medieval allegory is his association with that great and meaningful figure the Goddess Natura. It is, in fact, quite probable that Genius, as we know him in medieval allegory, would not have developed into a traditional figure were it not for the prominence of his mistress, the *vicaria Dei, Natura pronuba et procreatrix*. A number of scholars, particularly C.S. Lewis and G. Raynaud De Lage, have already carefully traced and listed the uses and definitions of *genius* in late Roman and early Christian literature.[1] My concern is with the figure that appears in the allegorical poems of Alan of Lille, Jean de Meun, and John Gower, with the figure appropriated from the Roman god of generation by Christian poets interested in the purpose, meaning, and morality of sexual love in the world. Genius appears in close connection with Natura in the *De planctu naturae* of Alan and in the continuation of the *Roman de la Rose* of Jean, but not in Gower's *Confessio Amantis*, where he is introduced by Venus as "Genius myn oghne Clerk" (I, vs. 196).[2] My intention in examining the Genius figures in these poems is to demonstrate that we cannot fully understand or appreciate them unless we consider them in light of their tradition, which is, basically, the tradition of the Goddess Natura. It is possible to read these three poems, and Chaucer's *Parlement of Foules* as well, as a continuing debate on the question of love from the twelfth to fourteenth centuries. We can be better critics in this case if we are good historians, we can understand Jean better if we look at Alan, we can understand Gower better (and perhaps clear up a long-standing misgiving about his work) by looking at Jean and Alan. In doing so, particularly with the *Confessio Amantis*, I shall be trying to find a more unusual relation-

---

1. C.S. Lewis, *The Allegory of Love* (London, 1936), pp. 361-63; G. Raynaud De Lage, *Alain De Lille* (Montreal and Paris, 1951), pp. 89-93. For other discussions of Genius, see also, Edgar C. Knowlton, "The Allegorical Figure Genius," *Classical Philology*, XV (1920), 380-84, and "Genius as an Allegorical Figure." *MLN*, XXXIX (1924), 89-95. Genius is discussed in John H. Fisher's *John Gower* (New York, 1964), pp. 161-63 *et passim*.
2. All quotations from the *Confessio Amantis* are from the edition by G.C. Macaulay, *The Complete Works of John Gower* (Oxford, 1901), Vols. II and III.

ship between that poem and the *Roman de la Rose* than one of our greatest critics and scholars was willing to allow; for this one time I shall ignore the excellent and usually sound admonition that fools rush in where Lewis declined to tread.[3]

Although a figure identified in part as *genius* appears in the *De mundi universitate* of Bernard Silvestris,[4] an early contemporary of Alan, it was Alan in his *De planctu naturae* who established the medieval characterization of Genius from which later poets were to draw their own. Genius enters the narrative near the end of the work in order to excommunicate those who disobey Natura's laws.[5] At this point in the action of the poem, Natura has completed her complaint and has gathered about herself her company of virtues, including Hymen, the god of marriage. We should note here that Alan insisted that the only lawful expression of sexual love was within the institution of marriage and under the guidance of reason, Natura's supreme gift to man; he makes this quite clear in other sections of the work and emphasizes the point here by showing Hymen, the husband wronged by the second Venus, who represents unbridled passion (*cupiditas*), in close association with the Goddess Natura, who appears in the poem as *pronuba* as well as *procreatrix*. It is Hymen that she sends to Genius with her letter asking her priest to come to anathematize all offenders against her laws.

We may best understand the Natura-Genius relationship by considering what she herself says of it in her letter. Genius is her other self (*sibi alteri*); she sees herself in him as if she had looked into her own mirror—so marked is the resemblance; they are bound to each other by the knot of love (their daughter is Truth); so much is she with him that they fail or succeed together. This definition of their relationship is echoed by Genius in his address to Natura when he arrives. It is no wonder to him if in the union of their wills he discovers the melody of concord, for one idea and thought conforms his will to that of the goddess and brings them into the same mind. Their resemblance comes into even sharper focus in the physical description of Genius. On his robes the images of things live for a moment and then vanish, a sight, the poet reports, barely perceptible to the viewer. In his left hand he carries an animal hide which he has scraped

---

3. See *The Allegory of Love*, pp. 198-222.
4. Bernard Silvestris, *De mundi universitate*, ed. Barach and Wrobel (Frankfurt, 1964), II, iii, 38.
5. Thomas Wright, ed., *The Anglo-Latin Satirical Poets and Epigrammatists* (*Rerum Britannicarum Medii Aevi Scriptores [Rolls Series]* 59), II, 511 ff.

clean of its hair. In his right hand he carries a fragile reed with which he continuously draws images on the hide. These images, like those Natura drew earlier, would fade away; as soon as they had faded and died, Genius drew others to replace them.

It is evident, then, that Genius was intended as a kind of double to Natura; however, we should note that he shares with her only those features which pertain to her as *procreatrix* of the sublunary world. None of her celestial features have parallels in his description. Thus, when Genius lays aside his common garment and dons his sacerdotal vestments in order to pronounce his excommunication, he is acting as the priest, as the representative on earth, of *Natura procreatrix.* It has been suggested that Alan introduced the character Genius because he could not possibly assign to Natura the priestly office of excommunication.[6] This is certainly logical enough, for she is goddess and *vicaria Dei* as *signum* but a woman as *res*, but it does not fully explain why Genius is characterized as being so similar to Natura. When he condemns the abominators he is in fact acting as her priest, but he is asked to do this not only for reasons of propriety but also because, as everything in his description clearly implies, he is an aspect of Natura herself, possibly that part of her that has been abused and perverted by the lust of men. If this is so, then it is quite fitting that he pronounce the anathema in behalf of them both.

When we turn to Jean de Meun's Genius, we notice immediately that the French poet has expanded the role of Genius to include the function of confessor as well as that of priest and official spokesman of Natura. And Gower in turn borrowed these activities but applied them to his Genius in relation to Venus and the Amans in his poem. But to consider these developments without considering as well the attitudes towards love that in fact have in good part caused them would be, as I have already suggested, to consider them in a vacuum. In the *De planctu naturae*, Genius acts as a kind of enforcer of natural law as well as priest to Natura, and by virtue of his close identification with the sublunary realm of her domain he is himself a wronged party because of mankind's failure to keep the dictates of Natura's law. This law, to summarize it briefly, requires that sexual activity come under the rule of reason and that it be expressed only in the marriage bed. In this way man helps Natura fulfill her duty by ensuring the continuity and plenitude of God's creation. Man's failure to keep this law, represented allegorically by the story of the second

---

6. De Lage, p. 92.

Venus' adultery with Antigamus, loosed upon the world not only the vices of heterosexual promiscuity and homosexuality but other sins of excess such as gluttony and avarice as well. It is unfortunate and therefore especially pertinent at this moment that some scholars have studied more literature *about* the Chartrian poets than they have studied the works of those poets, for it is commonly assumed that the Christian institution of marriage does not occupy an important place in their moral philosophies. This is clearly not the case in Alan, nor is it in Bernard Silvestris' *De mundi universitate,* a work described by an eminent scholar as being "bathed in the atmosphere of a fertility cult,"[7] for in his tribute to the male genitals' effective battle against man's mortality, Bernard suggests that these weapons, which restore nature and perpetuate the race, are at one and the same time the weapons of generation and marriage.[8] Deriving their power from Genius, they are used with pleasure at the proper time and place.

This philosophy of love which Natura and her priest serve in Alan's poem, is also given voice in Jean de Meun but not through the characters of Natura and Genius. For Jean de Meun significantly altered the philosophical position of the two characters in addition to adding the role of confessor to Genius. This latter development of the character by Jean enabled the goddess to reveal the scope and glory of her realm and to make her complaint against mankind and enabled the poet to exploit humorously and ironically the relationship between Natura and Genius as lady penitent and confessor.[9] The changes the French poet made are central to our understanding of Genius and his lady.[10] First, the Christian cosmological and moral conception of sexual love as it is expresssed in Alan is assigned to the character Raison rather than to Natura and Genius;[11] Genius, in his famous sermon to Amor and his barons, completes the presentation of his mistress' position.[12] Second, Natura and Genius in the *Roman* represent the procreative instinct without reference to the institution of marriage or a thorough awareness of Christian morality. This important alteration

7. Ernst Robert Curtius, *European Literature and the Latin Middle Ages,* trans. Willard Trask (New York, 1953), p. 112.
8. II, xiv, ll. 161-62, p. 70: "Cum morte invicti pugnant genialibus armis,/Naturam reparant perpetuantque genus."
9. See Lionel J. Friedman, "Jean De Meung, 'Antifeminism', and 'Bourgeois Realism'," *MP,* LVII (1959), 19-20.
10. I have pursued more thoroughly the implications for the *Roman* of Jean de Meun's changes in The Goddess Natura in Medieval Literature, a book-length study based on my Columbia dissertation, 1967, now in preparation.
11. Ernest Langlois. ed., *Le Roman de la Rose* (Paris, 1920-24), ll. 4221-7231.
12. Ibid., ll. 19687-704, where Genius summarizes his own argument.

is underscored by a significant change of detail which has far-reaching implications for the poem: the Goddess Natura denies having any authority over man's reason—it was not one of her gifts to him—but reason, as we have already seen, was the primary gift of the goddess to man in Alan.[13] What we have here, then, is a Goddess Natura and a priest speaking in her behalf with forceful eloquence who stand for sexual but not for rational power. Furthermore, Natura in Jean de Meun, though still *vicaria Dei* and *procreatrix,* is no longer *pronuba.*

Once Jean de Meun's personal artistic use of the Natura tradition is understood, it provides a meaningful context in which the activities of his goddess' representative and spokesman can be appreciated. Like the Goddess Natura whom he represents, Genius is concerned with procreation, with the battle against Death on a level that does not take into account the moral demands expressed by Alan's Natura and Genius or by Jean's own Raison. Because he is literally a priest, he delivers a sermon before Love's host in which he promises the true paradise to all men who will follow their natural inclinations to the end, but since his concern is exclusively with procreation he fears and, indeed, attacks the Christian virtues of abstinence and chastity. Although Genius' position may at first seem shocking, it is perfectly consistent with Jean's characterization of the goddess whom he represents. No apologies for Jean are necessary. Nor is it necessary to find the poet guilty of espousing heretical views, for such an attitude is based on the assumption that Natura and Genius speak for the poet. It makes just as good sense for a Genius who is almost obsessed with unrestrained sexuality to fear chastity as it does for the same Genius who is the advocate of a Natura stripped of her traditional association with reason to fail to see that the real enemy is not man's chastity but his cupidity, his desire to enjoy sex as an end in itself rather than as a means to the divinely ordained end that Genius and his mistress serve.

This cupidity is represented in the poem by Venus and her son Amor. And it is they, in what is one of the most ingenious and significant episodes in the *Roman,* who turn the exhortation of Genius to their own use. Before Genius leaves Natura to go before the barons of Love, he exchanges his priestly garments for secular clothing, exactly the opposite of what his counterpart in the *De planctu naturae* does prior to reading his excommunication before Natura and her company.[14] If this is an instance of Jean's ironic use of details from Alan,

---

13. Ibid., ll. 19055-062.
14. Ibid., ll. 19428-438; Wright, p. 520.

it is also a deliberately artistic tactic in the poet's preparation for Genius' ironic treatment by the God of Love and his mother.[15] Having put aside his priestly robes, which signify his office in the religion of Natura, he comes, appropriately dressed in secular clothes, before Love's host only to be newly arrayed by the God of Love in a chasuble and supplied with ring, cross, and miter. The god of Love has thus made Genius into his own priest, and Venus, who is unable to restrain her laughter, gaily places in his hand a candle which, we are told, was not made of virgin wax. The priest of procreation has unwittingly become the priest of Love, and his message and promise of paradise becomes the means through which Venus and Cupid inspire the barons to begin their victorious assault on the castle. The natural—I am inclined to add, innocent—inclination for sexual reproduction has been made to serve a cause which has only the act of love and not its proper end as its objective.

That Venus and Natura can work at cross purposes, I believe, is one of Jean's most clearly made points, especially when we understand that Jean's Venus figure is presented in a way that quite simply separates her intentions from those of Natura and from those of Raison. In Jean, Venus is the descendant of Alan's fallen Venus, she is more a figure of *luxuria* than she is the goddess of love that helps Natura in her forge. It is, therefore, of the utmost importance that we recognize that Gower wished to restore the old accord between Venus and Natura, which is to say, Gower basically sees the Natura-Venus relationship in a way that is similar to Alan's original Natura-Venus relationship. Near the end of the eighth and final book of the *Confessio Amantis*, the goddess explains to Amans that those men who disobey Natura's laws are not welcome in her court.

> Bot of these othre ynowe be,
> Whiche of here oghne nycete
> Ayein Nature and hire office
> Deliten hem in sondri vice,
> Wherof that sche fulofte hath pleigned,
> And ek my Court it hath desdeigned
> And ever schal; for it receiveth
> Non such that kinde so deceiveth.
>
> (VIII, 2337-44)

Besides disavowing all offenders against Nature, Gower's Venus speaks

---

15. *Roman*, ll. 19477 ff.

of reason as a necessary guide to lovers (VIII, 2367 ff. and 2912 ff.), and, indeed, it is through her appeal to reason that the elderly Amans recognizes that it is futile and senseless for one his age to persist in "the olde daunce." Gower's Venus, thus, represents an attitude towards love much more like Alan's than Jean's, and very like that expressed by his friend Chaucer in the *Parlement of Foules*, where Nature also speaks the language of reason and where the critical distinction is made between Venus the heavenly, planetary goddess of love and Venus *luxuria*.[16] Gower's goddess of love, "Enclosid in a sterred sky,/ Venus, which is the qweene of love,/Was take in to hire place above" (VIII, 2942-44), is also conceived of as a heavenly planet, an identification not even hinted at in Jean.

This vision of Venus as an important and legitimate part of the cosmology and this realignment of Venus with Natura and reason in the *Confessio Amantis* suggests that Gower was consciously using and altering as he saw fit and right the Natura tradition which he had inherited from Jean de Meun and Alan of Lille. With this in mind, we can approach the question of why he introduces Genius as Venus' clerk and not Natura's. The answer is that that is where he found him in Jean's *Roman*, in the Natura tradition as it had come to him. Genius, tricked and used by a different court of love in the French poem, has been accepted as Venus' priest by an English poet not generally admired for his slyness with the significant difference that the Venus he serves in Gower's poem is quite a different one from the Venus who laughingly placed her votive candle in his unsuspecting hand. The traditional priest of procreation can serve such a Venus who is in basic agreement with a Nature strongly resembling his original Chartrian mistress. In fact, his doctrine of "honeste love," for marriage and childbearing, recently discussed thoroughly by Professor J.A.W. Bennett,[17] not only emphasizes his significance in a Christian moral context, it also emphasizes the poet's belief in the need for such moral awareness in matters of love between man and woman, the domain of Venus. In this sense, his dual role as Christian priest and priest of Venus, as she is defined by Gower, does not create a problem, for Genius is the moral agent that bridges the worlds of true religion and the religion of love, that greatest of medieval literary artifices, which, though man-

---

16. See *The Works of Geoffrey Chaucer,* ed. F.N. Robinson, 2nd ed. (Boston, 1957), 113-19, and 260 ff.
17. J.A.W. Bennett, "Gower's 'Honeste Love,'" in *Patterns of Love and Courtesy, Essays in Memory of C.S. Lewis,* ed. John Lawlor (Evanston, 1966), pp. 107-21.

made, is never divorced in its poetic conception from man's awareness of his universe and its Creator.

I would not pretend for a moment that this investigation eliminates all of the difficulties the character Genius raises in our minds, particularly those that turn up in the *Confessio Amantis*. I would insist, however, that Genius in Gower's poem is just as important a character as he is in the other allegorical poems in which he appears. I do not believe that we can any longer entertain the views that, despite his importance to other aspects of the work, he is to be taken for granted or regarded as insignificant as an allegorical figure.

RHETORIC AND FICTION:
GOWER'S COMMENTS ON ELOQUENCE
AND COURTLY POETRY

GÖTZ SCHMITZ

> Full of high sentence, but a bit obtuse;
> At times, indeed, almost ridiculous –
> Almost, at times, the Fool.

I

The first book of John Gower's *Confessio Amantis* begins on a note of resignation;

> I may noght strecche up to the hevene
> Min hand, ne setten al in evene
> This world, which evere is in balance:
> It stant noght in my sufficance
> So grete thinges to compasse,
> Bot I mot lete it overpasse
> And treten upon othre thinges.
> Forthi the Stile of my writinges
> Fro this day forth I thenke change
> And speke of thing is noght so strange,
> Which every kinde hath upon honde,
> And wherupon the world mot stonde,
> And hath don sithen it began,
> And schal whil ther is any man;
> And that is love, of which I mene
> To trete, as after schal be sene.
>   (I, 1–16)[1]

With these words, John Gower the mentor of royalty hands in his resignation in favour of Amans, the lover to be shriven by a priest of Venus. The shrift that follows is apparently to be conducted in a less lofty style than that of Gower's former works, and it will treat a more familiar subject ("thing . . . noght so strange"). Its subject will be love, not love in general, nor love in its higher sense of caritas, but *amor naturatus*, the kind of love "which every kinde hath upon honde". The Latin note in the margin makes Gower's distinction between *amor* and *caritas* explicit:

> Postquam in Prologo tractatum hactenus exstitit, qualiter hodierne condicionis diuisio caritatis dileccionem superauit, intendit auctor ad presens suum libellum, cuius nomen Confessio Amantis nuncupatur, componere

---

[1] Quotations are taken from G.C. Macaulay's edition of the *Confessio Amantis* in *The English Works of John Gower*, 2 vols., EETS e.s. 81–82 (London, 1900–1901; rpt. 1957).

de illo amore, a quo non solum humanum genus, sed eciam cuncta animancia naturaliter subiciuntur. (I, i, 13–19, margin)

[After the Prologue, which contained a treatise on how the present
division in the world has extinguished the love of charity, the author
intends to deal in his new book, which is called The Lover's Shrift, with
that kind of love which rules not only men but every living creature by
force of nature].[2]

In his earlier works Gower had touched on greater things in an appropriately grand
style: the implied reference is to the Prologue which dealt with the general
division in the world, in particular the Schism of 1378, and to the *Vox Clamantis*, a
visionary poem which dealt with matters of state such as the Peasants' Rising of
1381. The *Vox Clamantis* was written in Latin and in a highly elaborate style. The
new subject, love of the animal kind, is an inferior subject and calls for an
appropriately modest style.

The change of style is obvious if one compares the highly-wrought Latin of the
Vox Clamantis with the plain vernacular of most of the *Confessio Amantis*. There
are, however, some traces of the former style left in that later work, most notably in
the intricate, and sometimes obscure, Latin elegiacs prefixed to the numerous
subdivisions of the *Confessio Amantis*, but also in its more learned parts, in particular the encyclopaedic Book VII. Compare, for instance, the Latin head-piece to
the Prologue of the *Confessio Amantis* with the English lines just quoted from the
beginning of Book I:

> Torpor, ebes sensus, scola parua labor minimusque
>   Causant quo minimus ipse minora canam:
> Qua tamen Engisti lingua canit Insula Bruti
>   Anglica Carmente metra iuuante loquar.
>   (Prologue, Latin verses i, 1–4)

[Inertia, insensibility, little schooling and less perseverance cause me, the
least of poets, to sing of minor things, and since the island of Brutus sings
in the tongue of Hengist, I will, with the help of Carmentis, speak in
English metres.]

Although these distichs contain a *captatio benevolentiae* similar to that of the
English couplets, the series of self-deprecating synonyms in the first line, the
word-play on 'minimus' and 'minor' in the next, the reference to Hengist, the Jute
who founded the Kingdom of Kent, and the invocation of Carmentis, the prophe-
tess who brought the Latin language from Arcadia to Italy, show off the author's
ingenuity as well as his erudition and make his modesty look rather affected.

There are similar verse-headings at the beginning of each major section of text
in the *Confessio Amantis*. They sum up in a condensed form what is unfolded in the
English dialogue. The epigrammatical terseness and the rhetorical pattern of these
verses is intensified by the elegiac metre and finds a sharp contrast in the steady

---

2 Translations throughout this chapter are my own, unless otherwise indicated.

flow of the vernacular text. Distichs create, of course, a certain artificiality of their own, in particular in the Middle Ages, and writing in Latin automatically places an author in a more learned and sophisticated tradition than the vernacular, which had only recently been allowed to enter the aristocratic and the judiciary courts. Nevertheless, the way Gower reminds his reader of the contrast between the Latin and English parts of his poem reinforces his contention that he deliberately changed his style with the new subject matter when entering on the *Confessio Amantis*.[3] That the difference in style is not the result of forces inherent in the languages and their traditions only becomes evident if one compares Gower's Latin verses with the marginal summaries in the *Confessio Amantis*, which are written in the dry, repetitious Latin of a medieval handbook. There we have the sort of plain style which is also found in contemporary texts written for satirical or homiletic ends. In Langland's *Piers Plowman*, for instance, and – to a lesser extent – in Chaucer's 'Parson's Tale', we find a fusion of the 'lered' with the 'lewed' on a lower level, where Latin phrases blend in with the vernacular in an almost macaronic mixed style which is characteristic of homiletic literature. As Maria Wickert has shown in her study of the *Vox Clamantis*, Gower was familiar with the homiletic tradition,[4] but he prefers to keep his styles apart. When in the earlier poem Gower raises his voice as mentor of his king and country, he tries to lift it to the level of classical poetry. His distichs in the *Vox Clamantis* are only a foot short of epic grandeur, and long passages of this satire read like patchwork stitched together with Ovidian lines.

Apart from the Latin headpieces, there is little to remind one of this style in the *Confessio Amantis*, although the Prologue and the Regiment of Princes in Book VII are spoken in the more weighty voice of a *sapiens* and *poeta doctus*. The dignity of these hortatory parts is of a simpler, rather Old Testament kind, and even this has created problems of integration with the rest of the poem. As in the transition from the Prologue to Book I, Gower has marked the change of subject in the Latin head-piece preceding Book VII. He particularly stresses the doctrinal content of what is to come:

> Omnibus in causis sapiens doctrina salutem
> Consequitur, nec habet quis nisi doctus opem.
> Naturam superat doctrina, viro quod et ortus

---

3   With a poet well versed in Virgil's poetry the invocation of a rustic Muse and the phrase "minora canam" would even suggest an inversion of the first line of Eclogue IV: "Sicelides Musae, paulo maiora canamus" ["Sicilian Muses, let us sing of greater things for a while!"]. But though this eclogue was by far the best known part of the *Bucolics* in the Middle Ages and developed a life of its own on the strength of its association with the Incarnation, this seems rather unlikely. Gower shows little, if any, acquaintance with Virgil's works, and Virgil is for him the lover and the sorcerer of the *Vitae Vergilianae* (see *Confessio Amantis*, V, 2031–2224; VIII, 2714–17) rather than the eminent poet. He may have come across quotations from the *Bucolics*, however, together with extracts from the *Vitae*, in medieval florilegia.

4   *Studien zu John Gower* (Köln, 1953), esp. chap. 3, pp. 32–109; tr. Robert J. Meindl, *Studies in John Gower* (Washington, 1981), pp. 69–130.

Ingenii docilis non dedit, ipsa dabit.
(Latin verses VII, i, 1–4)

[In cases of doubt, the wise man seeks remedy by way of doctrine, and no
one but the learned is truly competent. Doctrine overcomes Nature, and
if a man was not given talent by birth, she will supply it.]

The doctrines which follow in the English text are those that Aristotle is said to
have handed on to his pupil Alexander. They are delivered, however, by Genius,
who has by now established the authority and the voice of a sage but not overly
doctrinal confessor, and they are passed on to Amans, who has made it perfectly
clear by now that philosophy is not foremost in his mind. Genius senses the
awkwardness of the situation; he feels ill at ease with his task of imitating the voice
of Aristotle:

> I am somdel therof destrauht;
> For it is noght to the matiere
> Of love, why we sitten hiere
> To schryve, so as Venus bad.
> (VII, 6–9)

This introductory passage, by pointing to the double role that Genius has to play
(rather reluctantly, as it seems), lays bare some of the stylistic tensions inherent in
the poem and gives proof of Gower's appreciation, or at least awareness, of the
problems this tension creates. In particular, he is concerned about the correlation
of subject matter and speaking voice – in a word, about decorum – to a degree
which invites closer attention. In this chapter, I will try to outline Gower's position on questions of stylistic propriety with regard to classical and medieval notions of rhetoric. I will then try to trace some of the consequences which Gower's
modification of rhetorical precepts has had on his treatment of love, and in
particular courtly love, in his *Confessio Amantis*.

II

In Book VII of his *Confessio Amantis* Gower addresses the problem of decorum or
propriety directly. From ancient times the appropriateness of subject matter,
speaker and style has been discussed in handbooks of rhetoric; in particular, it
comes in under the heading of *dispositio*, the part which deals with the most
advantageous order of a speech. Every speaker has to find arguments and figures
(*res* and *verba*) apt to further his cause, and to arrange them in a convincing order.
Rhetoric is one of the subjects treated in Gower's short encyclopaedia of the arts
and sciences in Book VII, and disposition is placed at the centre of interest.[5] The
historical implications of this short treatise on rhetoric are discussed elsewhere in

---

5 Rhetoric is dealt with in lines VII, 1507–1640; for its importance in the development of
rhetorical theory in England see James J. Murphy, 'John Gower's *Confessio Amantis* and the

my study;[6] here, I will concentrate on the importance of the treatise for Gower's ethical concept of style and I will connect it with related remarks on the propriety of language throughout the *Confessio Amantis*.

The gist of Gower's concept of style is again anticipated in the verse heading to his discussion of rhetoric:

> Compositi pulcra sermonis verba placere
> Principio poterunt, veraque fine placent.
> Herba, lapis, sermo, tria sunt virtute repleta,
> Vis tamen ex verbi pondere plura facit.
> (Latin verses VII, v, 1–4)

[At first, the beauty of the words in a set speech will please, but in the end their truth only. Herbs and stones, like words, are full of virtues, but the power of words outweighs them all.]

The first distich stresses the importance of matter (*res*) over style (*verba*), and it seems to diminish the importance of the aesthetic aspect of rhetoric. In a way, a statement like this questions that part of a well-composed speech which brings it close to poetry (or poetry in its modern sense); pushed to its logical extreme, it raises questions about the validity of rhetorical poetry altogether. However, this question-mark behind the aesthetic quality of a well-set speech does not, in Gower's view, diminish the importance of eloquence; on the contrary: in the great chain of being speech (*sermo*) carries more weight than anything else, dead or alive.

The high esteem of rhetoric that informs these lines goes back to Cicero's *De inventione*, and ultimately to Aristotle's *Rhetoric*. The material for Gower's treatise is taken from the *Livres dou Tresor*, an encyclopaedia which the Florentine notary Brunetto Latini wrote shortly after the middle of the thirteenth century while in exile in France.[7] Gower has introduced the political concept behind the Aristotelian rhetoric, which was little known at his time, to England, but he has also adapted it to the purposes of his *Confessio Amantis*. This concept differs in both theory and practice from the idea of medieval rhetoric conveyed in the better-known thirteenth-century handbooks of poetry by Anglo-French authors such as Geoffrey of Vinsauf's *Poetria nova* or John of Garland's *Poetria*. Whereas handbooks of that kind present little more than a collection of rhetorical figures, the *Rhetorica vetus*, as Cicero's *De inventione* was called in the Middle Ages,[8] gives the art of rhetoric a theoretical basis in the Aristotelian system of philosophy and an emi-

---

First Discussion of Rhetoric in the English Language', *Philological Quarterly*, 41 (1962), 401–11.

[6] See the Appendix in my *The Middel Weie* (Bonn, 1974), pp. 168–97.

[7] For details of its composition see the introduction to Francis J. Carmody's critical edition of *Li Livres dou Tresor*, University of Los Angeles Publications in Modern Philology 22 (1948; rpt. Geneva, 1975).

[8] Cicero's *De inventione* has, in fact, deeper roots than the Pseudo-Ciceronian *Rhetorica*

nent practical importance for the development of civilisation. In this system (or its interpretation by medieval commentators), rhetoric is usually assigned a sector in the field of politics, which in turn forms part of practical philosophy. With Cicero and Latini, rhetoric almost overshadows its parent, the art of government: in Latini's *Tresor*, which makes the government of a city its main concern, eloquence is considered one of the essential requirements of a *podestà*, and its treatment fills the best part of Livre III. In spite of its encyclopaedic character, the *Tresor* can be called a Regiment of Princes, and something similar could be said of Book VII in the *Confessio Amantis*. The instructions ascribed to Aristotle cover the whole field of philosophy, but more than two thirds of Book VII are concerned with practical (i.e. political) philosophy, and most of the tales woven in exemplify points of policy. It should be noted, however, that Gower places the subject of rhetoric on a level with and in a central position between theoretical and practical philosophy, thus elevating it to an even higher rank in the system of philosophy and releasing it from its subservient position as a mere handmaid of practical politics.

As in the whole of Book VII, policy comes into Gower's discussion of rhetoric mainly by way of *exempla*. He mentions two in the course of his short treatise: the eloquence of Ulysses which led to the destruction of Troy (VII, 1558–63), and Caesar's plea in the trial against Catiline which led to the pardoning of the conspirators (VII, 1595–1628); this last *exemplum*, which is taken from Latini's *Tresor* (III, xxxiv–xxxvii), deserves particular attention.

The Catiline trial is particularly well suited to demonstrate the Aristotelian concept of rhetoric because it asked for speeches of a practical and political kind. Traditionally, the whole of the art of rhetoric was divided into three disciplines according to its main fields of application: the *genus demonstrativum*, the *genus deliberativum* and the *genus iudiciale*; Latini calls them "demoustrement, conseil, et jugement" (III, ii, 8). The first aim in all of these disciplines is to win the favour of an audience; "toute sa entention est a dire paroles en tel maniere que l'en face croire ses dis a ceaus ki les oient" (*Tresor*, III, ii, 1) ["All its (i.e. rhetoric's) intention is to set words in such a way that those listening believe in them"]. A good orator should be able to win his audience regardless of the cause for which he pleads and regardless, too, of his own conviction. The purely instrumental character of a speech, and in particular of its initial stages, is most obvious in the court room, the field of the *genus iudiciale*, because more often than not an advocate has to find arguments in support of a case of criminal conduct. This is clearly so in the case of Catiline and his fellow conspirators, at least in the eyes of Sallustus, Latini's witness for the proceedings. Now Latini, who is writing on rhetoric, not on history, shows little interest in the arguments brought forth in the case, not even in its outcome. He is interested only in the means employed by the most effective speaker, in this case by Julius Caesar who came in for the defence. Latini barely mentions that Decimus Iunius Silanus, the prosecutor, called for the death penalty (III, xxxiv, 3), but quotes at length from Caesar's plea for mercy (III, xxxv, 1–12).

nova, which became a main source for the lists of rhetorical figures that dominated the field of rhetoric in the later Middle Ages.

He then goes on to point out in detail how much more skillful Caesar's speech had to be because his case was 'vile', and the judge hostile,[9] whereas Decimus Silanus could count on common support for his just demand (III, xxxvi, 1). Caesar had to plead guilty and could, at best, hope to arouse the sympathy of his audience:

> Sillanus, s'en passa briement a poi de parolles sans prologue et sans coverture nule, pour ce que sa matire estoit de honeste chose, si comme de livrer a mort les traitors dou commun de Rome. Mais Julle Cesar qui repensoit autre chose se torna as covertures et as moz dorés, por ce ke sa matire estoit contraire, car il savoit bien ke li cuer des oïeurs estoient commeu contre sa entention, et por ce li covient il aquerre la lor bienweillance; et d'autrepart restoit sa matiere douteuse et oscure par plusours sentences et couvertures k'il voloit consillier, et sor ce li estevoit il doner as oïeurs talent de savoir et d'oïr ce k'il voloit dire. (III, xxxvi, 1).

> [Since his case was honest, Silanus contented himself with giving a few words, without prologue or any kind of blandishment, to the effect that the traitors of the Roman people should be put to death. But Julius Caesar, who answered him, turned to blandishment and gilded words because his matter was adverse and he knew well that the hearts of his listeners were moved against his purpose, and so he was forced to solicit their good will; and besides, he placed his doubtful and difficult case in so many sentences and insinuations because it wanted support, and because he would arrest the attention of his listeners and make them wish to know and hear what he had to say.]

Gower's report of the proceedings is obviously indebted to Latini's analysis:

> Cillenus ferst his tale tolde,
> To trouthe and as he was beholde,
> The comun profit forto save,
> He seide hou tresoun scholde have
> A cruel deth;
> [. . .]
> Bot Julius with wordes wise
> His tale tolde al otherwise,
> As he which wolde her deth respite,
> And fondeth hou he mihte excite
> The jugges thurgh his eloquence
> Fro deth to torne the sentence
> And sette here hertes to pite.
>   (VII, 1607–11; 1615–21)

---

[9]   The degree of difficulty depends on the attitude of the audience (in this case the judge), and the credibility of the cause. There are, traditionally, five degrees or *modi causarum*: a high degree (*genus honestum*), a medium degree (*genus dubium*), and several low degrees (*genus humile, genus obscurum*, and *genus turpe*). Latini had termed them "honeste", "douteus", "vilh", "oscur" and "contraire" in his *Tresor* (III, xvii, 4–9); he sees elements of all the lower degrees in Caesar's cause, and calls it "contraire" as well as "douteuse et oscure" (III, xxxvi, 1).

At first sight, Gower's account looks like a fairly literal rendering of the passage in Latini's *Tresor*. A closer inspection reveals, however, a number of minor, but nevertheless significant alterations. Before considering these differences it should once more be stressed that Gower (following Latini) takes his example for the art of persuasion from the courtroom or, in rhetorical terms, from the *genus iudiciale*. With him, this was an even less obvious choice than with Latini. As Ernst Robert Curtius has shown, medieval rhetoric had developed away from its practical origins and the more practical *genera* (*iudiciale* and *deliberativum*) towards the more decorative function it has in the *genus demonstrativum*.[10] In consequence, the rhetorical rules determining the structure of a speech were neglected in favour of those concerned with its ornaments. In rhetorical terms, of the five steps to be followed in composing a speech, *elocutio* (the point at which it is garnished, in particular with *colores*, the tropes and figures subsumed under the heading of *ornatus*) was given much more scope than any of the others. In particular, invention and disposition, the parts that Latini found most interesting, receded into the background.[11] The effects of this focussing on the ornamental phase in the compositional process are apparent in the thirteenth-century handbooks mentioned above. Geoffrey of Vinsauf's *Poetria nova*, for instance, which is often taken to represent the medieval idea of rhetorical poetry, has about 2000 lines, of which more than 1200 are devoted to tropes and figures. For the most part Geoffrey's *Poetria* is as much a *Summa de coloribus rhetoricis* as the shorter treatise of that title which is attributed to him in a Glasgow manuscript.[12] In ordinary speech, the ornamental concept of rhetoric lying behind such treatises has been dominant ever since the Middle Ages: we still think of rhetorical figures or *colores* primarily when speaking of rhetorical style.

Not only our concept of rhetoric, but also our understanding of rhetorical colours has become narrower than it was originally. In the old rhetoric, *color* could mean two different things: it was used as a synonym of *ornatus* (this is its meaning in Geoffrey's *Summa*, and in Chaucer's 'Franklin's Tale')[13], and it could mean the glossing necessary to give a fair appearance to a dubious case (this is what Caesar

---

[10] *European Literature and the Latin Middle Ages*, tr. W.R. Trask (New York, 1953), Chap. 4, *passim*.

[11] The preparation of a speech is traditionally divided into five steps, with *elocutio* in the middle; these steps correspond with the five parts (*partes artis*) of the old rhetoric: *inventio* (finding appropriate arguments or *res*), *dispositio* (selecting and ordering the material), *elocutio* (finding the right words or *verba*), *memoria* (learning the speech by heart) and *pronuntiatio* (delivering a speech with appropriate intonation and gestures). Latini's *Tresor* has a chapter on the steps which begins: "En ceste science [i.e. rhetoric] ce dist Tuilles sont .v. parties, ce sont truevement, ordre, parables, memores, et parleure" (III, iii, 1).

[12] Both these treatises are published and analyzed in Edmond Faral's *Les Arts poétiques du XIIe et du XIIIe siècle: Recherches et documents sur la technique littéraire du moyen age* (Paris, 1924; rpt. 1971).

[13] "I sleep nevere on the Mount of Pernaso, / Ne lerned Marcus Tullius Scithero. / Colours ne knowe I none", 'The Franklin's Prologue', *Canterbury Tales*, V, 721–3; Chaucer quotations are taken from *The Riverside Chaucer*, gen. ed. Larry D. Benson, based on *The Works of Geoffrey Chaucer*, ed. F.N. Robinson (Boston, 1987). The current rhetorical sense of 'col-

did in his defence of Catiline).[14] So Gower is right in using the term (in the second sense) when he contrasts Caesar's plea in the case of Catiline with the demands of Silanus and Cato:

> Thei spieken plein after the lawe,
> Bot he the wordes of his sawe
> Coloureth in an other weie
> Spekende,
> (VII, 1623–6)

Applying colours in this second sense has certain moral implications which Latini evades by keeping strictly to their technical sense. Latini analyses the situation in purely rhetorical terms which give scarcely a hint of the moral or political questions involved in calling for the death penalty or in asking for pity in a case of high treason. The task of Silanus was easy because his case was honest (in the technical sense of *genus honestum*), and Caesar had to use subterfuge and embellishments ("covertures" and "moz dorés") because his case was adverse, doubtful and difficult ("contraire", "douteuse et oscure"). Latini, in other words, accepts without scruples the purely instrumental character of rhetoric. It is on points like these that Gower's paraphrase differs in a few significant details from his source. By adding phrases like "Cillenus first his tale tolde / To trouthe" and "Thei spieken plein after the lawe" (VII, 1607–8, 1623) to his source and ascribing them to the prosecutors, Gower alerts his reader to the fact that Caesar's use of rhetorical colouring obscures the truth and runs counter to the law. Caesar's practice also contradicts the conclusion which Gower draws at the end of his chapter on rhetoric about the proper use to be made of eloquence:

> Ther mai a man the Scole liere
> Of Rethoriqes eloquences,
> Which is the secounde of sciences
> Touchende to Philosophie;
> Wherof a man schal justifie
> Hise wordes in disputeisoun,
> And knette upon conclusioun
> His Argument in such a forme,
> Which mai the pleine trouthe enforme
> And the soubtil cautele abate,
> Which every trewman schal debate.
> (VII, 1630–40)[15]

ours' is still that of the Franklin; it is defined in the OED as "rhetorical modes or figures; ornaments of style or diction, embellishments" (*s.v.* colour, III. 13.).

[14] See Heinrich Lausberg, *Handbuch der literarischen Rhetorik* (Munich, 1960), p. 511. With respect to Gower's *Confessio Amantis*, it is worth mentioning that Quintilian applies the second meaning to confessions in hopeless cases, "quodsi nulla contingit excusatio, sola colorem habet paenitentia" (*Institutio oratoria*, 11,1,81) ["when there is no other excuse, penitence can lend colour to a confession"].

[15] The impression that Gower had doubts about the use of rhetorical colouring is also

125

This conclusion emphasizes once more the two points in which Gower's view of rhetoric differs from that of Latini: he lifts it to a higher, philosophical plane (it occupies one of the major divisions of philosophy), and he does not separate it from considerations of morality. In Gower's *Confessio Amantis* the art of persuasion gains an even more fundamental position than in Latini's *Tresor*.

Gower's ethical concept of rhetoric is rooted in his view of the importance of speech or, as he puts it, of the word. The faculty of speech is what distinguishes man from beast; it is, like reason, a gift of God, and like reason it is a faculty that can be abused. There is a hint of the sublime style of the Book of Genesis when Gower comes to extol the importance of the word at the beginning of his chapter on rhetoric:

> Above alle erthli creatures
> The hihe makere of natures
> The word to man hath yove alone,
> So that the speche of his persone
> Or forto lese or forto winne,
> The hertes thoght which is withinne
> Mai schewe, what it wolde mene;
> And that is noghwere elles sene
> Of kinde with non other beste.
> So scholde he be the more honeste,
> To whom god yaf so gret a yifte,
> And loke wel that he ne schifte
> Hise wordes to no wicked us;
> For word the techer of vertus
> Is cleped in Philosophie.
> Wherof touchende this partie,
> Is Rethorique the science
> Appropred to the reverence
> Of wordes that ben resonable:
>   (VII, 1507–25)

The idea that man is raised above the rest of the created world by his faculty of speech goes back to classical sources; it had become commonplace already by the time of Cicero, who uses it repeatedly in his writings on oratory.[16] From there it found its way into Latini's *Tresor*, where it is used twice (I, iv, 9; III, i, 11). Gower, in turn, was prompted to his eulogy on the power of words by Latini; he added,

strengthened by the example he adds to Latini's chapter to document the influence of rhetoric, namely the eloquence with which Ulysses persuaded the Trojan prince Antenor to deliver his home town into the hands of the Greeks. Though Ulysses is praised for "his facounde / Of goodly wordes" (VII, 1560–1), Gower leaves do doubt about the moral quality of this achievement: "Such Rethorique is to despise" (1556). Gower shares, of course, the medieval point of view about the fall of Troy which was defined by Dares Phrygius and Dictys Cretensis rather than by Homer: in his eyes Troy was won "with treson" (VII, 1563).

[16] See the note in H.M. Hubbell's edition of *De inventione. De optimo genere oratorum. Topica* in the Loeb Classical Library (London, 1949, rpt. 1960), p. 12.

however, not only the biblical overtones, but also a warning not to abuse this power. With Cicero, wielding the power of words had been an aristocratic responsibility; in his *De inventione*, he draws a line not only between man and beast, but also between the man who is gifted with eloquence and the majority who are not:

> Ac mihi quidem videntur homines, cum multis rebus humiliores et infirmiores sint, hac re maxime bestiis praestare, quod loqui possunt. Quare praeclarum mihi quiddam videtur adeptus is qui qua re homines bestiis praestent ea in re hominibus ipsis antecellat. (*De inventione*, I, iv)

> [Furthermore, I think that men, although lower and weaker than animals in many respects, excel them most by having the power of speech. Therefore, that man appears to me to have won a splendid possession who excells men themselves in that ability by which men excel beasts. (Hubbell's translation)].

Latini follows Cicero in this respect, too; he distinguishes between language ("parleure"), which is given to every man, and eloquence ("bien parler"), the skill or the talent of a few particularly gifted men, and he adds by way of example the myth of Amphion, the bard who raised the walls of Thebes with his music. The myth is probably taken from Horace, who explains it euhemeristically by turning Amphion into a poet who civilized a barbaric people by force of his eloquence.[17] This civilizing function is the first point that Latini, like Cicero before him, wishes to make: eloquence is part of the art of government; moreover, it is the prime requisite of a *podestà*: "Et Tuilles dist que la plus haute science de cité governer si est rectorique, c'est a dire la science du parler" (*Tresor*, III, i, 2) ["And Tullius (Cicero) says that the highest skill in governing a city is rhetoric, that is the art of speaking well"]. The second point is that rhetoric is an art that can be learned; both Cicero and Latini answer the question of whether eloquence is a natural talent or an art in favour of art: "noureture passe nature" (*Tresor*, III, i, 12).

On all these points Gower differs from his predecessors. He levels both the distinctions between language and eloquence and between the few and the many by speaking of the 'word' as an ability conferred on every man. He thus broadens the issue at hand: rhetoric is no longer a concern of politicians only, but a matter of concern for every responsible person. At the same time he deepens the issue at stake by making 'the word' a gift of God comparable to the gift of reason. The collocation of terms like "hihe makere" and "alle erthli creatures" evokes the scene of the first creation and equates the gift of the word with the gift of the soul: it is a sign of man's being created in the likeness of God.[18] It follows that when exercising his faculty of speech, man's prime responsibility is towards his creator, not towards his fellow men. In Latini's *Tresor* it is the civilising quality of eloquence which makes man capable of becoming a second God ("comme .i. secons

---

17 *Ars poetica*, 391–401; Latini gives Cicero as his source for the myth, but then he also says that Amphio raised the walls of Athens, not of Thebes; see *Tresor*, III, i, 5–8.
18 The connecting link between the word and the soul is man's reason. Both speech and soul should be governed by reason; cf. VII, 517 and VII, 1525.

Dieus, ki estora le monde par l'ordene de l'umaine compaignie", III, i, 7) ["like a second God who created the world according to the laws of human society"] – a claim, incidentally, that is even higher than Cicero's and makes Latini look like a forerunner of Machiavelli, whereas Gower sounds rather like a follower of Augustine.

The main moral distinction to be drawn out of these corresponding passages in *De inventione*, the *Tresor* and the *Confessio Amantis* is that between a political concept of the art of speech in Cicero and Latini, "la plus haute science de cité governer", and a personal one in Gower, who demands that a man's speech disclose his innermost motives, "the speche of his persone" and his "hertes thoght". By concentrating on man's personal responsibility Gower does not diminish the importance of the spoken word. On the contrary: he places a eulogy on the power of words at the centre of his short treatise on rhetoric which includes political consequences:

> The wordes maken frend of fo,
> And fo of frend, and pes of werre,
> And werre of pes,
>   (VII, 1574–6)

His main concern is with the ambiguity of words and with the danger inherent in the fact that words can be used to both good and evil ends. Being interested in personal motives, not in political aims, Gower cannot accept the functional definition of rhetoric which says that a speech is good if it succeeds in persuading an audience. The eloquence of Ulysses is despicable, not only because it led to the fall of Troy, but mainly because it was treacherous. Ulysses deceived Antenor, and therefore his "goodly wordes" were evil:

> For whan the word to the conceipte
> Descordeth in so double a wise,
> Such Rethorique is to despise
> In every place, and forto drede.
>   (VII, 1554–7)

The words of Ulysses only seemed to be good; in a functional concept of rhetoric like that of Latini, this is acceptable as long as it is successful; Gower, however, is not content with asking for verisimilitude, he demands veracity, or "trouthe" (VII, 1552).

In the light of this ethical concept of rhetoric, every word that glosses over the truth of a matter is suspect. *Res* and *verba* have to agree, and this is why Gower does not even mention those parts of the art of rhetoric that deal with *colores* or any other means of giving an argument a more favourable appearance. Of the five phases of preparing a speech he mentions composition and delivery and skips over *elocutio* altogether:

> Bot forto loke upon the lore
> Hou Tullius his Rethorique

> Componeth, ther a man mai pike
> Hou that he schal hise wordes sette,
> Hou he schal lose, hou he schal knette,
> And in what wise he schal pronounce
> His tale plein withoute frounce.
>
> (VII, 1588–94)

Gower's main concern is with sincerity; this is stressed time and again in the course of his short treatise on rhetoric.[19] The only style that accords with this concern is a plain style. Classical rhetoric held precepts for this kind of style: *sinceritas* or, significantly again, *confessum* is a possible attitude in defending a cause, but it needs little art and is therefore barely mentioned in handbooks of rhetoric – unless, that is, an attitude of sincerity is struck for tactical reasons only. Latini's analysis of the pleas in the trial of Catiline in Chapter III, xxxvi of the *Tresor* is a case in point: he devotes one sentence to the honest cause ("honeste chose", III, xxxvi, 1) of Silanus, but almost a page to the masterly blandishment of Caesar ("Julle Cesar parla par coverture maistrielement", III, xxxiv, 3).

Latini, then, admires the artful concealment in Caesar's plea. This is where Gower disagrees with him. Defending a proved traitor goes against his sense of justice. In his summary of Latini's analysis Gower forbears to condemn Caesar's coloured defence, but an attentive reader can have little doubt that his sympathies rest with the prosecution and their outspoken plea in support of justice and the common weal. His sympathies for the possible victims of a death sentence are much more in doubt: in Book III of the *Confessio Amantis* the Confessor, not a draconian character, had asserted the right of man to slay in the interest of law and order:

> Lo thus, my Sone, to socoure
> The lawe and comun right to winne,
> A man mai sle withoute Sinne
>
> (III, 2230–2)

Disrespect of common profit and the law leads to chaos, as Gower indicates several times in his own person in those parts of the *Confessio Amantis* which deal with corruption in official ranks of society.[20] Colouring one's words in order to obtain personal advantages is not, however, restricted to those occupied in public offices, and it is one of the consequences of Gower's more personal definition of the uses of rhetoric that it enables him to transfer his criticism to those parts of his *Confessio Amantis* that employ Gower in the role of Amans, not of mentor. Even the more trivial aims of an elderly lover come under the suspicion, as we shall see, of being pursued with the use of too much colour.

---

[19] See once more VII, 1510–13, 1532–5 (where it is applied to the art of logic, which Gower makes subservient to rhetoric), and 1550–3, the passage that leads up to the example of Ulysses.

[20] See, for instance, Prol. 370–7, 795–801; VII, 1991–2002, 3073–83.

III

In the light of Gower's chapter on rhetoric one will have to take more seriously not only the first, but also the last of his *captationes benevolentiae*. Near the end of the *Confessio Amantis*, Gower dissociates himself once more in no uncertain terms from the sort of rhetoric that recommends the use of colours, and he mentions the name of Cicero as an advocate of such arts:

> And now to speke as in final,
> Touchende that y undirtok
> In englesch forto make a book
> Which stant betwene ernest and game,
> I have it maad as thilke same
> Which axe forto ben excusid,
> And that my bok be nought refusid
> Of lered men, whan thei it se,
> For lak of curiosite:
> For thilke scole of eloquence
> Belongith nought to my science,
> Uppon the forme of rethoriqe
> My wordis forto peinte and pike,
> As Tullius som tyme wrot.
> Bot this y knowe and this y wot,
> That y have do my trewe peyne
> With rude wordis and with pleyne,
> In al that evere y couthe and myghte
> This bok to write as y behighte,
>   (VIII, 3106–24)

Self-effacing statements of this kind are to be found throughout medieval literature; as we have seen, they are particularly numerous at the beginning of a poem; Curtius has therefore numbered them among his "exordial topics".[21] Chaucer's Franklin, for instance, in the Prologue quoted from above, asks his listeners to bear with his lack of eloquence in similar terms, and he also mentions Cicero and the colours of rhetoric in the same breath.[22] In Gower's *Confessio Amantis*, however, the profession of a plain style appears to be more than an instance of affected modesty. Terms such as 'rude' or 'plain' and their antonyms such as 'colour' or 'paint' occur with a frequency throughout the *Confessio Amantis* which suggests that they function as ever-present poles of reference not only

[21] See Chapter 5 of his *European Literature* for *topoi* in general, and Appendix 2 for the *topos* of humility in particular. Maria Wickert deals with topical material in the Prologue to Gower's *Vox Clamantis* in a chapter of her *Studien zu John Gower* (1953, pp. 87–109; tr. Meindl, pp. 91–115).

[22] For an example from the most rhetorical poet of the following age see John Lydgate's Prologue to the first book of his *Fall of Princes*, 452–5 (ed. Henry Bergen, *Lydgate's 'Fall of Princes'*, Part I, EETS e.s., 121 (London, 1924), p. 13).

stylistically but also structurally. The word 'plain' and related terms are particularly common, and they are almost invariably linked with matters of speech and the moral attitudes of speakers. Phrases like 'pleinly forto telle' or 'the pleine trouthe' occur with formulaic regularity in the instructional parts as well as in the confessional framework and the tales of the *Confessio Amantis*.[23] They stand guard at passages of the greatest import such as this one on the division of the earth after the Flood;

> Of what matiere it schal be told,
> A tale lyketh manyfold
> The betre, if it be spoke plein:
> Thus thinke I forto torne ayein
> And telle plenerly therfore
> Of therthe, wherof nou tofore
> I spak . . .
> (VII, 521–7)

and they are made to watch over the Regiment of Princes, for 'trouthe' is said to be one of the essential virtues of a prince:

> He scholde of trouthe thilke grace
> With al his hole herte embrace,
> So that his word be trewe and plein,
> Toward the world and so certein
> That in him be no double speche:
> For if men scholde trouthe seche
> And founde it noght withinne a king,
> It were an unsittende thing.
> (VII, 1729–36)

As before in theory, Gower refuses to allow differences between manners and morals, as a rhetorician like Latini might have done. There is to be no dissembling, not even in the public interest; the word should always be the expression of a person's, and in particular a prince's, innermost conviction: "The word is tokne of that withinne" (VII, 1737). The wording sounds commonplace, almost proverbial, but it expresses one of Gower's central concerns, and in his view the high road to personal and public peace in a troubled world. In the Prologue to the *Confessio Amantis*, he had ascribed the peace now lost to a remote Golden Age which knew no difference between word and thought:

> Of mannes herte the corage
> Was schewed thanne in the visage;
> The word was lich to the conceite

---

[23] Nearly all of the more than 100 entries s.v. 'plein' and its derivatives are of this kind; see *A Concordance to John Gower's 'Confessio Amantis'*, ed. J.D. Pickles and J.L. Dawson (Woodbridge, 1987), pp. 477–8.

Withoute semblant of deceite:
(Prol. 111–14)[24]

Gower's demand for sincerity is thus linked up with the governing ideas which he had set out in the framework of the *Confessio Amantis*; some of these ideas are compressed into the distichs of the second Latin head-piece in the Prologue:

> Tempus preteritum presens fortuna beatum
> Linquit, et antiquas vertit in orbe vias.
> Progenuit veterem concors dileccio pacem,
> Dum facies hominis nuncia mentis erat:
> Legibus vnicolor tunc temporis aura refulsit,
> Iusticie plane tuncque fuere vie.
> Nuncque latens odium vultum depingit amoris,
> Paceque sub ficta tempus ad arma tegit;
> Instar et ex variis mutabile Cameliontis
> Lex gerit, et regnis sunt noua iura nouis:
> Climata que fuerant solidissima sicque per orbem
> Soluuntur, nec eo centra quietis habent.
>
> (Latin verses Prol. ii, 1–12)

[Our present fortune leaves the happy past behind and turns the ancient customs upside down. When the face of a man was the herald of his mind, unanimous love brought forth the peace now lost. The laws of the past shone in unbroken clarity, and the ways of justice were plain. Now hidden hatred shows a face of love, and under the pretext of peace the present hides its weapons. Justice acts as variably as if it wore the guise of a chameleon, and every reign brings new laws.]

Gower sketches two worlds in these verses; an ancient world of peace and stability, "the world that whilom tok" (Prol. 54), and the present which is subject to mutability and unrest, "the world that neweth every dai" (Prol. 59). The realisation that the breach between the old world and the new is irreparable will induce Gower to announce his change of subject matter at the beginning of Book I. This change from the great theme of charity to the smaller one of love is anticipated here in the distinction between *dilectio* and *amor*. With respect to the discussion of rhetoric and Gower's change of style it is interesting to note that Gower employs

---

[24] 'Visage' and 'corage' are one of Gower's favourite pairs of rhyme-words; A *Concordance to John Gower's 'Confessio Amantis'* lists eleven instances. It should be noted that Gower's demand for a correspondence between word and thought is different from the demand for an appropriate facial expression in the delivery of a speech. The latter is one of the rules of rhetoric (dealt with under the head of *pronuntiatio*) and does not regard a speaker's mind; this rule became a stock element of the poetical *decorum* (see, for instance, Chaucer's 'Squire's Tale', 102–4, or his *Troilus and Criseyde*, I, 12–14). Gower's demand is related to Chaucer's proverbial "The wordes moote be cosyn to the dede" ('General Prologue' to the *Canterbury Tales*, 742; cf. 'Manciple's Tale', 207–8), but, again, Chaucer's apology for the plain style of some of his pilgrims, though voiced in similar terms as Gower's repeated demands, is used as a dramatic device and sometimes spoken with tongue in cheek.

the Latin equivalents of 'paint' and 'feign' ("depingit" and "ficta") to characterize the present, and antonymic expressions such as 'unicolor' and 'plana' for the stable past. The present world of love appears to be as superficial as a layer of make-up on an otherwise ill-favoured face. If the connection of love in the 'modern' sense with fiction in the sense of disguise and deceit is more than coincidental, its negative connotations are bound to affect the treatment of love in the main part of a poem, which, after all, introduces the author disguised as a lover ("fingens se auctor esse Amantem", I, 61, margin). To put this assumption to the test, it should be worthwhile following the use of vernacular equivalents of terms connected with make-up and make-believe throughout the poem.

The negative connotations marked above are quite obvious in the case of 'feigne' and its derivatives, both in the parts concerned with the duties of a ruler and in the confessions of Amans. Such terms are rife, of course, in the section dealing with hypocrisy, and are applied to princes and lovers alike: Genius castigates many a great man "which spekth of Peter and of John / And thenketh Judas in his herte", as well as lovers "that feignen hem an humble port, / And al is bot Ypocrisie" (I, 656–7, 673–4). But this is not surprising since 'to feign' takes on a negative colouring in almost any context and is habitually, if not proverbially, equalled with petty deceit (the false shepherds in the Prologue, for instance "feignen chalk for chese", 416). Gower's distrust of anything colourful extends, however, to more neutral terms as well, such as 'queinte' and 'peinte' (One of his favourite rhyme couples). These frequently assume negative significance too in the *Confessio Amantis*, especially when used in connection with matters of speech. The story of Echo provides an example. The hapless nymph who covers up the escapades of Jupiter by diverting Juno with her prattle is severely reproached in the *Confessio Amantis* for her deceit and thoroughly deserves her punishment:

> Thou hast gret peine wel deserved,
> That thou canst maken it so queinte,
> Thi slyhe wordes forto peinte
> Towardes me, that am thi queene,
> (V, 4623–5)[25]

The story is taken from Ovid's *Metamorphoses*, but "the circumstances are somewhat modified to suit Gower's purpose", as Macaulay put it.[26] The purpose is to supply an example of love-brokerage, and Gower lays stress on the slyness of Echo's language which helped Jupiter conceal his affairs. Ovid had only hinted at this with a single word, calling Echo "prudens"; otherwise she is for him a guileless chatterer ("garrula"; see *Metamorphoses*, III, 362–9). Gower turns her into a shameless creature who deceives her mistress "with queinte wordes and with slyhe" (V, 4593). Echo makes up words, and this puts her in the ranks of the misusers of speech.

Now not only concealing, but also making love in its traditional sense is

25 See also I, 284; II, 2852–4.
26 See his note to *Confessio Amantis*, V, 4583 ff., *English Works*, II, 501.

traditionally connected with making up in its various senses, and both Ovid and Gower are very much aware of this connection. Ovid was generally regarded as the greatest authority in matters of love, and Gower acknowledges "the grete clerc Ovide" as his master in that respect. In a way the *Confessio Amantis*, and in particular its confessional framework, is an *Ars amatoria* which also contains the *Remedia amoris*.[27] It is not surprising, then, that the question of making up words for amatory purposes plays a significant part in the conversation between the lover and his confessor. Amans freely confesses that he has tried to impress his lady with songs of love on several occasions, and the same rhyme-pair of 'peinte' and 'queinte' occurs that we met with in the Tale of Echo:

> And also I have ofte assaied
> Rondeal, balade and virelai
> For hire on whom myn herte lai
> To make, and also forto peinte
> Caroles with my wordes qweinte,
> To sette my pourpos alofte;
> (I, 2726–31)

The confession looks innocent enough, at least at first sight. In the light of the connotations registered above, however, one comes to wonder if a passage like this is not, in the eyes of Gower, as revealing about the lover's state of mind as the similarly worded one was of Echo's. Shortly before the lines just quoted the new-fangledness of Vain-Glory is compared to a chameleon's habit of changing its colour,

> Lich unto the Camelion,
> Which upon every sondri hewe
> That he beholt he moste newe
> His colour,
> (I, 2698–2701)

and that in turn is related to the composing of fashionable songs: "And ek he can carolles make, / Rondeal, balade and virelai" (I, 2708–9). The passage is thus linked up with the Latin verses in the Prologue which describe the lawless and loveless present. The similarity in terms and imagery can hardly be coincidental: the more fashionable aspects of making love in the courtly sense are connected with the decay of love in its Christian sense. One may even be tempted to ask whether the list of fashionable love-poetry contains a hint at actual pastimes of the age. Similar references to French love-songs are to be found in Chaucer's poetry, and there are indications that such entertainment had fallen into disrespect or was

---

[27] See III, 736 and VIII, 2266; Genius invokes Ovid more than twenty times in the course of the *Confessio Amantis*; most of his references are to the *Metamorphoses*, but his story of Vulcan and Venus (V, 635–725) may have been taken from the *Ars amatoria*, and in IV, 2668–74 he explicitly recommends the *Remedia amoris*.

thought to be a thing of the past, at least in other than courtly circles.[28] Gower certainly has his reservations about such poetry, if not about the whole "besynesse" (as Chaucer's Alceste puts it) of courtly love.[29] That all this business is tainted with a touch of folly, or of self-deception, is discovered in Gower's *Confessio Amantis* not only in the end, when Senex Amans is finally cured of "loves rage" (VIII, 2863) and, incidentally, Chaucer is reminded of his advanced age (VIII, 2941*–57*), but already in the early parts of his confession. There is again the long section on hypocrisy, one of the daughters of Pride, in Book I, which is, of course, particularly suited to demonstrate the negative effects of putting on too much colour in love-making. In the Latin head-piece to that section, personified Hypocrisy is presented as endowed with almost histrionic skills at facial and verbal expression:

> Laruando faciem ficto pallore subornat
> Fraudibus Ypocrisis mellea verba suis.
> (Latin verses I, v, 5–6)

[Hypocrisy masks his face with made-up paleness and hides his frauds with mellifluous words.]

In the conversation which follows this presentation, Amans is told more about the masquerading of a hypocritical lover:

> The colour of the reyni Mone
> With medicine upon his face
> He set, and thanne he axeth grace,
> As he which hath sieknesse feigned.
> (I, 692–5)

This looks innocent, if not ludicrous, again, but one of the examples given by Genius for the workings of hypocrisy is that of Antenor and Eneas, who brought about the fall of Troy with their false counsel (I, 1123–5). The passage is thus linked with the discussion of rhetoric in Book VII and with one of Gower's central concerns in the *Confessio Amantis*.

An equally obvious chance of demonstrating the evil consequences of coloured speech is given and taken in Book II, when Genius presents False-Semblant, the schemer who employs the "derke untrewe Ypocrisie" (II, 1892) as his chief counsellor. False-Semblant is one of the agents of Envy in the *Confessio Amantis*; in the *Roman de la rose*, Amour accepts him at his court, even before his long confes-

---

[28] The love-sick Squire Aurelius in the 'Franklin's Tale' is said to have composed "manye layes, / Songes, compleintes, roundels, virelayes" (*Canterbury Tales*, V, 947–8), and I think this has to be kept in mind when Chaucer is credited with a similar list in the Prologue to his *Legend of Good Women* (F, 422–3). Short catalogues like these had become commonplace in contemporary French poetry; see Aage Brusendorff, *The Chaucer Tradition* (Copenhagen, 1925), pp. 430–3.

[29] See the Prologue to *The Legend of Good Women*, G, 412, where "besynesse" replaces "holynesse" in the revised version.

sion.[30] Characteristically, Gower introduces False-Semblant as a double-talker ("Nil bilinguis aget, nisi duplo concinat ore, / Dumque diem loquitur, nox sua vota tegit", Latin verses II, iv, 1–2 ["The double-dealer will achieve nothing except with double talk; he keeps speaking during the day, while night covers his intentions"]). Amans confesses that he sometimes takes to "coverture" and "colour" (II, 1939, 1963) in order to further his cause against a rival:

> I wol me noght therof excuse,
> That I with such colour ne steyne,
> Whan I my beste Semblant feigne
> To my felawh,
>
> (II, 1962–5)

Not much is made of this confession, but it is striking that the terms 'coverture' and 'colour' are the technical terms employed by Latini for the sort of blandishment that Gower found obnoxious. There are many more such more or less hidden links between courtly love and the carelessness with which its servants make use of the gift of speech. Taken together these links serve to prepare an attentive reader for the dénouement after the confession. They could also be added up into an indictment of at least the more superficial side of the courtly style of poetry. The courtly code is apparently not much different from the chameleonic law that Gower had mentioned in his Prologue, and at least with hindsight it becomes clear that Amans is gradually being prepared to see that following *amor* is tantamount to courting trouble; this was expressed in a series of oxymora, the most unstable of rhetorical figures, at the very outset of the confession: "Est amor egra salus, vexata quies, pius error" (I, i, 7) [Love is an ill health, a troubled rest, a pious fraud"]. It is only by accepting the rosary inscribed "Por reposer" that Amans can find personally the centre of rest which the troubled climate which he described in the Prologue can no longer provide.

As a final consequence, then, Gower's misgivings about the language of fiction lead him to the renunciation of courtly love poetry. This applies, apparently, to lyrics of the "Rondeal, balade and virelai" variety as well as to romances. Romances are a colourful genre, and by their erratic structure they are closely related to the world of instability. Amans speaks of them as the food of love (or of 'lust', as he terms it in Book VI, 896–8), and he ranges them with other short-lived delicacies that appeal primarily to the senses:

> Fulofte time it falleth so,
> Min Ere with a good pitance
> Is fedd of redinge of romance
> Of Ydoine and of Amadas,
> That whilom weren in my cas,
>
> (VI, 876–80)

[30] See *Le Roman de la rose*, 10928–30 (the approbation) and 11003–11976 (the confession); tr. Charles Dahlberg, *The Romance of the Rose* by Guillaume de Lorris and Jean de Meun (Princeton, 1971), pp. 193, 194–209.

The unstable world of romance is ruled by the goddesses Venus and Fortuna; in one of his romance-like tales, that of Albinus and Rosemund, Genius conflates these two and makes Venus turn the fatal wheel:

> Both sche which kepth the blinde whel,
> Venus, whan thei be most above,
> In al the hoteste of here love,
> Hire whiel sche torneth, and thei felle
> (I, 2490–3)[31]

In that tale, "the basic theme of all romances", as Arno Esch puts it, is trumpeted by heralds at the beginning of a splendid feast: "Al was of armes and of love" (I, 2528).[32] The tale, however, is told as an *exemplum* for the vice of magniloquence, and the feast affords the occasion for Albinus to overreach himself by boasting of his deeds of arms in front of his wife whose father fell victim to his prowess: he makes her drink out of a cup made from her father's skull, "And thus the whiel is al miswent" (I, 2624).[33] When next the theme of "Hou love and armes ben aqueinted" (IV, 2137) is sounded in the *Confessio Amantis*, it is in the course of a discussion of the martial service necessary to prove worthy of a lady's love. As an example of knighthood Genius tells, somewhat surprisingly, the story of Penthesilea who entered the battlefield of Troy for love of Hector. Amans is not impressed; he is wary of military exploits, even if undertaken for worthier causes. Earlier on he had questioned even the benefit of crusades, and said that he would rather pursue his love at home: "What scholde I winne over the Se, / If I mi ladi loste at home?" (IV, 1664–5). Now he admits that he prefers to have the matter of Troy in bottled form, as it were, and to read of knightly deeds at the feet of his lady:

> And whanne it falleth othergate,
> So that hire like noght to daunce,
> Bot on the Dees to caste chaunce
> Or axe of love som demande,
> Or elles that hir list comaunde
> To rede and here of Troilus,
> Riht as she wole or so or thus,
> I am al redi to consente.
> (IV, 2790–7)

---

[31] Amor and Fortuna are similarly coupled at the beginning of the *Confessio Amantis*: "Sunt in agone pares amor et fortuna, que cecas / Plebis ad insidias vertit vterque rotas" (Latin verses, I, i, 5–6) ["Love and fortune are ever in an open battle who is to turn the blind wheel to the destruction of mankind"].

[32] "John Gowers Erzählkunst", *Chaucer und seine Zeit: Symposion für Walter F. Schirmer*, ed. Arno Esch (Tübingen, 1968), p. 221.

[33] Gower generally transforms the material he found in romances by curtailing its haphazard elements and stressing the responsibility of his heroes. This is most notably the case in his handling of the story of Apollonius of Tyre; see Chapter VI of my *"The Middel Weie"* which deals with the tales in the *Confessio Amantis*, in particular pp. 147–54.

The way he sets the reading of romances side by side with the throwing of dice or the discussion of *questions d'amour* reflects once more on the high aspirations of courtly ideals: the knightly service has come down to domestic proportions.

There are bound to be echoes of such domestic scenes when the theme of chivalric romances is struck for the last time near the end of the *Confessio Amantis*, when a procession of courtly lovers passes through the lover's final vision. The lovers, with the Trojan pair of Troilus and Cressida among them, are said to talk of nothing but of arms and love:

> The moste matiere of her speche
> Was al of knyhthod and of Armes,
> And what it is to ligge in armes,
> With love, whanne it is achieved.
> (VIII, 2496–9)

Amans has by that time finished his confession, but is still "fulfilt of loves fantasie" (VIII, 2211). He also hopes to lie in the arms of his own love soon, and this may have coloured his vision. The reader, however, is directed to the true significance of the procession by the vocabulary employed in its description, in particular the references to colour and variety in terms which are connected with the deceit and the instability that Gower has deplored in the instructional parts of his work. The description of Youth and his company – the same party that talks of nothing but love and arms – is particularly revealing:

> I sih wher lusty Youthe tho,
> As he which was a Capitein,
> Tofore alle othere upon the plein
> Stod with his route wel begon,
> Here hevedes kempt, and therupon
> Garlandes noght of o colour,
> Some of the lef, some of the flour,
> And some of grete Perles were;
> The newe guise of Beawme there,
> With sondri thinges wel devised,
> I sih, wherof thei ben queintised.
> It was al lust that thei with ferde,
> Ther was no song that I ne herde,
> Which unto love was touchende;
> (VIII, 2462–75)

One remembers that the aura of the old world of stability was unadorned and plain, 'unicolor' and 'plana', and the eyes of the dreamer, too, will soon be opened to the truth that this world of youth is much too fast, at least for someone of his age. If read with this frame of reference in mind, the topical allusions to Bohemian fashions and the pageantry of the Flower and the Leaf can be read as a gentle critique of pastimes at the court of Richard II and Queen Anne: they change fashions at this court very much like the personified Vain-Glory who was compared to a chameleon in Book I (2681–2717).[34] In any case, the multi-coloured and newfangled society led by Youth belongs to the world of artifice and vanity which is repeatedly connected in the *Confessio Amantis* with the recklessness of a decaying age. The discrepancy between this fast-moving set of lovers and the dazed narrator Amans becomes apparent in a second procession of lovers which is led by Elde. This party is even more remarkable ("queinte" is Gower's term, VIII, 2687) than the company of youths: there is Solomon, for instance, with a hecatomb of wives and mistresses, and even Amans questions his ability to do all of them justice; and there is the Philosopher, Aristotle, whose shrewish wife "made him such a Silogime, / That he foryat al his logique" (VIII, 2708–9). Again, these are variations on a well-worn courtly theme, that of imperial love, but they cannot but look quaint in the light of the roles these wise men have played in their earlier appearances. One of the *exempla* about Solomon, for instance, is summarized like this: "Hic dicit secundum Salomonem, quod regie maiestatis imperium ante omnia sano consilio dirigendum est" (VII, 3914, margin) ["Quoting Solomon, he (i.e. the confessor) says here that the power of royal majesty has to be wielded above all with sound judgement"]. There are tacit contradictions in these final passages which are resolved only in the laughter with which Venus accompanies her gift of the rosary in the end (the lovers led by Elde, incidentally, are not allowed to laugh, VIII, 2685).

Setting Gower's references to courtly love in the context of his opinions on the superficiality of ornament and fiction leads inevitably to the question of how courtly a poet Gower himself is. His poem was, after all, written for a courtly audience. If we trust his own report in the Prologue to the *Confessio Amantis*, the commission for this work came from King Richard himself, and in the beginning of Book I the author clearly stated that love (unruly love or *amor*, not *caritas*) is to be the subject of his poem (Prol., 35*–53*; I, 8–16). This mundane love is inextricably coupled with the variable world of fiction ("Est amor ex proprio motu fantasticus", Latin verse II, i, 9 ["love is by its nature fantastic (i.e. illusory)"]; it is blind and makes blind, as Genius keeps telling us. The leading motive of love in this sense is 'lust', the same force that drives Youth and his company.

Now Gower does not condemn this world of 'lust' outright. Otherwise he would not have given it the scope it has in his *Confessio Amantis*, above all in the Confessor's tales. But he balances it with what he calls 'lore', the learning and the wisdom that provides the stable framework in his poem, and he leaves no doubt which of the two has to prevail at the end of the day. The result is what he had promised at the start, a mixture of almost Horation proportions:

> I wolde go the middel weie
> And wryte a bok betwen the tweie,

---

[34] This is not the place to discuss the relationship of this passage with the Prologue of Chaucer's *Legend of Good Women*, but Chaucer's picking the modest daisy (and not, for instance, the more fashionable marguerite) as an emblem of womanly excellence may contain a comparable element of gentle criticism.

    Somwhat of lust, somewhat of lore,
              (Prol. 17–19)

He repeats the twin formula in similar terms at the end of the *Confessio Amantis* when he says that his English work stands "betwene ernest and game" (VIII, 3109). The antonyms 'lore' and 'lust', or 'ernest' and 'game', repeat on the level of poetical ends what we have distinguished as 'plain' or 'ornate' on the level of stylistic means. It is tempting to associate the various parts of the *Confessio Amantis* with either of these poles: the tales clearly contain an element of game, the Prologue and the Regiment of Princes in Book VII are predominently earnest – but what about the confessional dialogue? Judging from the roles of the interlocutors this should pose no problems: Amans is obsessed with 'lust', the Confessor tries to temper this with 'lore'. In these roles they both have their predecessors, for instance in the *Roman de la rose*. But there are complications, for the interlocutors both move between the poles of 'lust' and 'lore'.

    At first sight Amans is caught in the familiar see-saw of love's "unsely jolif wo" (I, 88; VIII, 2360). His part is obviously that of the languishing, lamenting lover who finds himself subject to the caprices of love in general, and those of his lady in particular. The difference lies in his being a truly, even ridiculously hopeless case. Though his age is kept a secret right to the end (we are led to believe that he himself is blind to the fact until Venus makes him look into her mirror, VIII, 2820–31), his folly and his self-deceit are being signalled to an attentive reader. The style ascribed to the confessions of Amans gives him away by deviating from the plain style advocated and practised by his confessor Genius and by the author himself in the instructional parts of the poem. Thus Amans is prone to the hyperbolic language used in the literature of love-complaints. The tone of such complaints is that of despondency, and Genius characterizes it aptly near the end of Book IV of the *Confessio Amantis* in a caricature of the dejected lover and his outcries of "Helas, that I was bore" (IV, 3406). Amans gives variations of this tone throughout his confession, from his first complaint against the gods of love, "O thou Cupide, o thou Venus" (I, 124), to his formal complaint or Supplication which speaks of "The wofull peine of loves maladie" (VIII, 2217).

    This is all very conventional; now and then, however, Gower allows his Amans a glimpse of his precarious, if not absurd situation, and then he speaks in surprisingly homely terms:

    O fol of alle foles,
    Thou farst as he betwen tuo stoles
    That wolde sitte and goth to grounde.
              (IV, 625–7)

In the end Amans will have to realize, of course, the prophetic meaning of these lines; his stumbling way to that final moment of truth when Venus tells him "thou art ate laste cast" (VIII, 2909) will be followed in a later chapter;[35] a few hints must

---

[35] That moment comes, says Amans, at "the place / Wher Venus stod and I was falle" (VIII,

suffice here to indicate that his wavering between affectation and frankness, and his gradual movement to that celebrated quiet ending, "Homward a softe pas y wente" (VIII, 2967), is accompanied by appropriate changes from the courtly to a homely style.

In the case of Genius a certain vacillation between the poles of 'lust' and 'lore' is implied in his double part as priest of Venus and as advocate of a Christian morality. In this combination he differs from his literary predecessors; he combines, in a way, the parts of Genius and of Reason in the *Roman de la rose*. His ultimate aim in the *Confessio Amantis* is to convert Amans from his foolish ways to the rules of reason, and his immediate function that of a confessor within a framework of the Seven Deadly Sins turned to secular use. As a confessor he asks the penitent Amans to declare his sins in plain terms, and he himself promises to be as plain in his questions. He employs the terms that have by now become familiar:

> For what a man schal axe or sein
> Touchende of schrifte, it mot be plein,
> It nedeth noght to make it queinte,
> For trouthe hise wordes wol noght peinte:
> That I wole axe of the forthi,
> My Sone, it schal be so pleinly,
> That thou schalt knowe and understonde
> The pointz of schrifte how that thei stonde.
> (I, 281–8)

This could, of course, be said in a Shrovetide confession in church as well as on a May morning in the meadow; in fact, the whole procedure of questions and answers is, at first, conducted in an almost sacramental fashion, down to the appropriate forms of address, "Benedicite, / Mi Sone", and "Dominus, / Min holi fader Genius" (I, 205–6; 215–16). In the course of the shrift, however, the confessor is necessarily more concerned with questions belonging to the 'game' of courtly love than is compatible with moral earnestness, and occasionally Gower inserts a note to dissociate himself from the teachings of the priest of love. A double note of caution is given, for instance, to qualify the lesson that Genius draws from the tale of Rosiphelee, probably the most delicate *exemplum* given in the *Confessio Amantis* for the ethics of courtly love. In a marginal note the author dissociates himself from the teaching of Genius, and in particular from the idea which is central to the courtly code, that activity in the service of love is an essential element of gentility: "Non quia sic se habet veritas, set opinio Amantum" (IV, 1454, margin) ["(I tell this), not because it is true, but because lovers believe in it"]. In addition, Genius himself is at pains to dissociate the notion of "love . . . / Of paramours" from the concept of married "love . . . honeste" (IV, 1469–92).[36] The tension between the

2726–7). Chapter V of my *"The Middel Weie"* (pp. 80–109) deals with the confessional dialogue in the *Confessio Amantis*.
[36] See Arno Esch's interpretation of this tale in "John Gowers Erzählkunst", pp. 210–18,

two offices of Genius is all too palpable in passages like this; it finally breaks up in the last book of the *Confessio Amantis*. When at the end of the lengthy Tale of Apollonius Genius urges Amans to embrace 'love honeste' and to renounce all beastly lust (VIII, 2020–6), Amans shows signs of impatience because he fails to see the application of the tale and its lesson to his immediate cause. In the controversy that ensues Genius virtually abjures his religion of love and gives up the game-play connected with his role of a priest of Venus:

> Mi Sone, unto the trouthe wende
> Now wol I for the love of thee,
> And lete alle othre truffles be.
> (VIII, 2060–2)

Amans has to be disenchanted by his look into the mirror of Venus before he can follow suit and see through the cloud that surrounded him when under the influence of love:

> And whan Resoun it herde sein
> That loves rage was aweie,
> He cam to me the rihte weie,
> And hath remued the sotie
> Of thilke unwise fantasie,
> Wherof that I was wont to pleigne,
> (VIII, 2862–8)

After the return of reason Amans no longer even knows what love is, and he goes back to his books with a smile. On a personal level, then, the debate between the forces of 'lust' and of 'lore' has been resolved – ultimately at the expense of love in its carnal and its courtly sense. This does not resolve the public discord denounced in the Prologue. Gower knows this; he has given up the hope of setting the world at large in order, and has turned to the little world of erring man. Like that latter-day Amans, Prufrock, he has not been able to squeeze the universe into a ball, but he has faced the overwhelming question, "Rebus in ambiguis que sit habenda via" (Latin verses I, ii, 3–4) ["which way to take in cases of doubt"], and unlike Prufrock, his Amans bites it off in the end, even with a smile.

esp. p. 211. Gower's concept of marriage is discussed in detail by J.A.W. Bennett, 'Gower's "honeste love" ', *Patterns of Love and Courtesy: Essays in Memory of C.S. Lewis*, ed. John Lawlor (London, 1966), pp. 107–21.

PLEASE LEAVE

These items are to be left out for use tomorrow.

Name:
Date:

Please note the following:

(1) Only books and other study-related items (e.g. notepads, folder may be left. Anything else will be removed to the Lost Property b and may be reclaimed at the front desk. We cannot accept a responsibility for loss of or damage to items.

(2) Books/papers must be left in neat piles and occupy no more th one reader space. If your things occupy more than one reader spa they will be removed.

(3) You should put down **today's date** if you wish your books/pap not to be removed tomorrow. Please do not post-date the form. Y may re-use the form as often as you like by changing the date to current one.

(4) Reference books may not be kept out for you, but will be re-shelv to make them available to other readers.

THE PRIESTHOOD OF GENIUS:
A STUDY OF THE MEDIEVAL TRADITION

DENISE N. BAKER

THE ALLEGORICAL FIGURE GENIUS plays a significant role in three important works of medieval literature: Alain de Lille's *De planctu Naturae,* Jean de Meun's *Roman de la Rose,* and John Gower's *Confessio Amantis.* Although scholars have commented extensively on the meaning and function of Genius in the first two works, the interpretation of this character in the *Confessio Amantis* has proven problematic. The crucial difficulty involves the dual priesthood of Genius in Gower's poem. As a priest of Venus the character is commissioned to instruct Amans about love; but as an orthodox priest he must also teach virtue. This complication of Genius's role is considered the source of the poem's most serious fault, for, as G. C. Macaulay observes, the "conception of a Confessor who as priest has to expound a system of morality, while as a devotee of Venus he is concerned only with the affairs of love, can hardly be called altogether . . . consistent. . . ."[1] More specifically, Gower is accused of inconsistent characterization because Genius's repudiation of Venus's divinity (Book V) and his discussion of the education of Alexander (Book VII) allegedly violate his role as Venus's priest.[2]

Although several critics attempt to vindicate Gower of this charge, their arguments do not adequately explain the dual priesthood of Genius in the *Confessio Amantis.* C. S. Lewis, for example, defends the appropriateness of Genius's denunciation of Venus by defining the allegorical figure in psychomachic terms. "Genius here stands for Love — for that whole complex in the lover's mind which he calls his 'love', and of which he has made his deity and his father confessor. . . ."[3] Lewis identifies Genius as the personification of the lover's own gradual realization that his love is folly. He is "the master passion itself there speaking with a doubtful voice, and presently hinting that it knows (the conscious will shouting it down in vain) — that it knows itself to be all other than the tongue claims of it — that its foundations are crumbling — that its superstructure is but a tissue of illusions and decaying habits. . . . He is simply the lover's deepest 'heart', telling him bitter truths, now no longer avoidable . . ." (p. 220). This psychomachic description of the Genius of the *Confessio Amantis* suggests the character's affinity to the tutelary spirit of the classical period, the Genius B, whose influence on medieval literature Lewis emphatically denies (p. 361). Thus, in his refutation of a common critical objection to Gower's Genius, Lewis raises additional questions about this allegorical figure, for he fails to clarify the relationship between this inner, individual Genius and "the pa-

[1] *The English Works of John Gower,* 1, ed. G. C. Macaulay, EETS (1900; repr. London, 1969), p. xix. All quotations of the *Confessio Amantis* are from this edition.

[2] E. C. Knowlton, "Genius as an Allegorical Figure," *Modern Language Notes* 39 (1924), 90.

[3] *The Allegory of Love* (New York, 1958), p. 220.

tron of generation" of *De planctu Naturae* from whom, he claims, "the Genius of Jean de Meun and of Gower directly descends" (p. 362). Lewis himself seems aware of this problem, for he acknowledges, rather offhandedly, in his discussion of Gower's poem that "if we insist on the original significance of Genius (the god of reproduction) there may be some absurdity," but he offers no suggestion for resolving this contradiction in his argument (p. 219).

Recently, however, the connections between the Genius of the *Confessio Amantis* and the figures depicted in the *De planctu Naturae* and the *Roman de la Rose* have been explored in more detail by George Economou and Donald Schueler. Economou distinguishes between the philosophical position this character represents for Alain de Lille and Gower, on the one hand, and for Jean de Meun, on the other.[4] Gower, he argues, restores "the old accord between Venus and Natura" described in the *De planctu Naturae* which had been inverted for purposes of irony in the *Roman de la Rose* (p. 208). The relationship between Genius and Venus in the *Confessio Amantis* is thus analogous to the relationship between Genius and Natura in the *De planctu Naturae*. The Venus of the English poem is not the Venus *scelestis* of illicit courtly love but Venus *caelestis,* the uncorrupted goddess who originally assisted Alain's Natura in the work of procreation. Although he does not discriminate between Alain's Natura and Jean's, Schueler arrives at a similar conclusion.[5] And both critics agree that as servant of the *vicaria Dei,* Gower's Venus is, by extension, the servant of God. Thus, no tension exists between Genius's roles as Venus's priest and as orthodox priest because, according to Schueler, the "natural love which he serves, and which he is gradually defining, is one wherein the same moral laws obtain which apply in other spheres of human conduct" (p. 248). However, as Economou himself admits, this argument does not resolve "all of the difficulty the character raises in our minds . . ." (p. 210). For if Gower's Venus is the servant of a moral Natura, why then does Genius repudiate her in Book V?[6] Moreover, neither Economou nor Schueler inquires about the characteristic which Gower's Genius shares with his literary precursors since he is no longer associated with procreation (a question which implies, of course, that the description of Genius as "the patron of generation" is too limited to explain the relationship between the three manifestations of this allegorical figure in medieval literature).

The ultimate consideration in a study of the Genius of the *Confessio Amantis* thus must be the way that Gower adapts this figure from the works of his literary predecessors, Alain de Lille and Jean de Meun, to suit his own

[4] "The Character Genius in Alan de Lille, Jean de Meun, and John Gower," *Chaucer Review* 4 (1970), 203–210.

[5] "Gower's Characterization of Genius in the *Confessio Amantis*," *Modern Language Quarterly* 33 (1972), 240–256.

[6] Schueler attempts to explain Genius's repudiation of Venus by differentiating between her allegorical and mythological significance. However, he concludes that the "passage is a muddle, the only one of its kind in this huge poem. . . ." (p. 252).

purposes. Why does he continue to cast Genius as a priest while disassociating him from Natura and ignoring the role he shares with her as *procreatrix*? And what is the significance of Genius's dual ministry in the *Confessio Amantis*? But before these questions can be answered, we must return to the larger tradition and the problem implicit in Lewis's argument. His description of Genius as the personification of the voice of Amans's own "deepest 'heart' " coupled with his antithetical insistence that this figure descends from "the patron of generation" indicates a need to re-examine the medieval concept of Genius to ascertain whether it included any nuance of Genius as tutelary spirit. I will begin, therefore, by studying the references to Genius in the writings of Bernardus Silvestris, Apuleius, and Martianus Capella which provide the basis for Alain's delineation of this character in the *De planctu Naturae*.[7]

I

Alain de Lille emphasizes the significance of Genius in the *De planctu Naturae* by identifying this allegorical figure as Natura's "other self." In the letter she sends to him through Hymen, she writes: "Natura, Dei gratia mundanae civitatis vicaria procuratrix, Genio, sibi alteri, salutem. . . ."[8] As her "other self" Genius participates in Natura's roles as *procreatrix* and moral instructor. These two functions of Genius are represented by his dual commission in the poem as scribe and priest. Like Natura he is *artifex*, an artist who "styli subsequentis subsidio imagines rerum sub umbra picturae ad veritatem suae essentiae transmigrantes, vita sui generis munerabat" (p. 517). Furthermore, Natura considers him the appropriate executor of her moral judgment, for she says to Hymen: "Genium vero qui mihi in sacerdotali ancillatur officio, decens est sciscitari, qui eos a naturalium rerum catalogo, a meae jurisdictionis confinio, meae judiciariae potestatis assistente praesentia, vestrae assentionis conjuvente gratia, pastorali virga excommunicationis eliminet" (p. 510). As priest, then, Genius shares Natura's moral mandate and acts as intermediary between her and man. In his first role as scribe the Genius of *De planctu Naturae* is consonant with the tradition C. S. Lewis cites and is clearly derived from Bernardus Silvestris's *De mundi universitate*. But in ascribing to Genius the duties of priest Alain is

---

[7] For other discussions of Genius see E. R. Curtius, "Zur Literarästhetik des Mittelalters II," *Zeitschrift für romanische Philologie* 58 (1938), 193–194; E. C. Knowlton, "The Allegorical Figure Genius," *Classical Philology* 15 (1920), 380–384; G. Raynaud de Lage, *Alain de Lille* (Paris, 1951), pp. 89–93. The most thorough discussion of the tradition of Genius is a dissertation by Jane Chance Nitzsche, "Classical and Medieval Archetypes of the Figure Genius in the *De Mundi Universitate* of Bernardus Silvestris and the *De Planctu Naturae* of Alanus de Insulis," University of Illinois, 1971. I regret that I could not consult Professor Nitzsche's *The Genius Figure in Antiquity and the Middle Ages* (New York, 1975) which was published after this study was completed.

[8] Alain de Lille, *De planctu Naturae*, in *The Anglo-Latin Satirical Poets and Epigrammatists*, 2, Rolls Series 59, ed. Thomas Wright (1872; repr. New York, 1964), p. 511. All quotations of *De planctu Naturae* are from this edition.

influenced by an aspect of the medieval concept of this figure also evident in Bernardus's work but disregarded by Lewis — the idea of Genius as a tutelary spirit.

Although seldom noted, *genius* in *De mundi universitate* is a generic rather than a proper name referring, in its most general sense, to "that which has spiritual or heavenly quality."[9] More specifically, Bernardus describes four distinct orders of genii who inhabit the various regions of his cosmos. The sphere of the fixed stars and each of the planets are governed by an Oyarses or genius (2.5, lines 45–8, 75–7, 131–7). The garden of Physis, Granusion, in the lower moist air, is also presided over by a genius (2.9, lines 32–4). Both of these classes of genii are involved in the work of creating man. "The genii of the heavens ruled by Urania (the stars and planets) contribute individual form for the soul descending into the first underworld — the sublunary realm. The genius of Physis's Granusion . . . as a principle of plant growth aids the descent of the soul into the second underworld — the body" (Nitzsche, p. 104). The procreative functions of these first two orders of genii in the *De mundi universitate* certainly influence the depiction of Genius as "patron of generation" in the *De planctu Naturae*; but because Alain's dominant interest is the moral meaning of his allegory, he simplifies Bernardus's complex cosmology by expressing the generative work of these genii through Genius's role as scribe.

The prototype for Alain's Genius as scribe in the *De mundi universitate* is, as critics have long recognized, Pantomorphos, a genius whose function in the generative process is symbolized by drawing.

> Hoc igitur in loco pantomorpho persona deus venerabili et decrepitae sub imagine senectutis occurrit. Illic Oyarses quidem erat et genius in artem et officium pictoris et figurantis addictus. In subteriacente enim mundo rerum facies universa caelum sequitur sumptisque de caelo proprietatibus ad imaginem quam conversio contulit figuratur. Namque inpossibile est formam unam quamque alteri simillimam nasci horarum et climatum distantibus punctis. Oyarses igitur circuli quem pantomorphon Graecia, Latinitas nominat omniformem, formas rebus omnes omnibus et associat et ascribit.[10]

Bernardus's Pantomorphos, in turn, is modeled after a figure of the same name in the *Asclepius*. "⟨Decanorum⟩ [[XXXVI quorum vocabulum est Horoscopi]], id est, eodem loco semper defixorum siderum ⟨⟨XXXVI quorum vocabulum est Horoscopi⟩⟩, horum οὐσιάρχης (vel princeps) est quem Παντόμορφον (vel Omniformem) vocant, qui [diversis] speciebus ⟨singulis⟩ diversas formas facit."[11] As ruler of the fixed stars, Pantomorphos is related to the Augustan astrological concept of Genius, the god who, accord-

---

[9] Robert B. Woolsey, "Bernard Silvester and the Hermetic Asclepius," *Traditio* 6 (1948), 343. See also the references to *genius* in Brian Stock, *Myth and Science in the Twelfth Century* (Princeton, 1972).

[10] Bernardus Silvestris, *De mundi universitate*, ed. Carl Sigmund Barach and Johann Wrobel (1876; repr. Frankfurt a. M., 1964), 2.3, lines 89–100.

[11] Walter Scott, ed., *Hermetica*, 1 (Oxford, 1924), p. 324.

ing to Horace, "temperat astrum" and thus determines the temperament and controls the destiny of each individual born (Nitzsche, p. 29). Clearly, then, Alain's characterization of Genius as scribe is derived from the description of Pantomorphos transmitted through the *De mundi universitate* from the Hermetic tradition.

Bernardus's cosmology, however, includes two other orders of genii which provide a means of explaining Genius's priestly role in the *De planctu Naturae*: the intermediary genii who inhabit the upper air (2.7, lines 66–85) and the twin sexual genii residing in the human genitalia (2.14, lines 153–80). In the work of these twin sexual genii charged with regulating human procreation, Winthrop Wetherbee discerns "something like the function of the traditional tutelary guide of the individual soul."[12] And he attributes Alain de Lille's characterization of Genius as priest to a conflation of these microcosmic genii with the cosmic genius Pantomorphos. Although Wetherbee's analysis is a significant contribution to the study of Chartrian thought, his discussion of the priestly role of Alain's Genius requires some modification. For, in citing the sexual genii of the *De mundi universitate* as an influence on the depiction of Genius in *De planctu Naturae*, Wetherbee overlooks the apparent parallelism between Bernardus's description of these figures and Alain's characterization of the uncorrupted Venus, Hymen, and Cupid (p. 470). Like the sexual genii, Venus *caelestis* and Hymen are responsible for insuring the continuity of the human race against the destructive power of Fate by means of the legitimate sexual act; the genital weapons of Bernardus's genii are transformed into the hammer and anvil of Alain's Venus, but the process of reproduction, the transmission of the correct forms from generation to generation, which these figures oversee is the same.

Although Wetherbee is wrong in ascribing Genius's priesthood to these twin sexual genii, he does direct attention to their tutelary function; in this respect they are analogous not to the cosmic genii as he contends, but to the genii of the upper air who mediate between the divine and earthly realms. Bernardus's account of these intermediary genii emphasizes the custodial role associated with them.

> Cum igitur homo condictante quidem providentia novum figmentum, nova fuerit creatura, de clementissimo et secundario spirituum ordine deligendus est genius in eius custodiam deputatus. Cuius tam ingenita, tam refixa benignitas, ut ex odio malitiae displicentis pollutae fugiat conversantem. et cum quid virtutis agendum insumitur, sacris per inspirationem mentibus assolet interesse. . . . genius, qui de nascendi principiis homini copulatus vitanda illi discrimina vel mentis praesagio vel soporis imagine vel prodigioso rerum spectaculo configurat (2.7, lines 67–74, 82–5).

In creating the human body according to the model of the macrocosm,

---

[12] "The Function of Poetry in the 'De Planctu Naturae' of Alain de Lille," *Traditio* 25 (1969), 112–113. See also Wetherbee's discussions of Genius in "The Literal and the Allegorical: Jean de Meun and the 'de Planctu Naturae'," *Mediaeval Studies* 33 (1971), 264–291, and in *Platonism and Poetry in the Twelfth Century* (Princeton, 1972).

Physis duplicates the tutelary function of these intermediary genii in the work of the microcosmic genii who regulate the earthly or sexual region of the body under the auspices of the divine, man's mind (2.13, lines 95–105). And it is this more comprehensive concept of genius as a moral guide rather than the limited role as regulator of sexuality that determines the depiction of this allegorical figure as priest in the *De planctu Naturae*.

A study of Bernardus Silvestris's *De mundi universitate* thus demonstrates that the term *genius* involves a more complex *significatio* in Chartrian thought than the phrase "universal god of generation" implies. Although three of the four orders of genii described are engaged in procreation, the custodial role of the fourth group is clearly expressed. Moreover, Bernardus's depiction of genii as guardian spirits is not, as Lewis contends, alien to the medieval concept of the figure. The tradition of the tutelary Genius is derived from two central texts of the School of Chartres, the *De deo Socrates* of Apuleius and the *De nuptiis Philologiae et Mercurii* of Martianus Capella.

Apuleius establishes for the Middle Ages the precedent of casting Genius as a moral guide by equating this Roman god with the daemons of Platonic cosmology in *De deo Socrates*.

Nam quodam significatu et animus humanus, etiam nunc in corpore situs, δαιμων nuncupatur. . . . Igitur et bona cupido animi, bonus Deus est. Unde nonnulli arbitrantur, ut iam prius dictum est, ευδαιμονας dici beatos, quorum daemon bonus, id est, animus virtute perfectus est. Eum nostra lingua, ut ego interpretor, haud sciam an bono, certe quidem meo periculo, poteris Genium vocare; quod is Deus, qui est animus sui cuique, quamquam sit immortalis, tamen quodammodo cum homine gignitur: ut eae preces, quibus Genium et Genitam precamur, coniunctionem nostram nexumque videantur mihi obtestari, corpus atque animum duobus nominibus comprehendentes, quorum communio et copulatio sumus.[13]

By classifying Genius as daemon Apuleius identifies him as one of the secondary gods who act as mediators between heaven and earth. "Ceterum sunt quaedam divinae mediae potestates, inter summum aethera et infimas terras, in isto intersitae aeris spatio, per quas et desideria nostra et merita ad Deos commeant. hos Graeci nomine δαιμονας nuncupant: inter terricolas coelicolasque vectores, hinc precum, inde donorum; qui ultro citro portant, hinc petitiones, inde suppetias, ceu quidam utriusque interpretes, et salutigeri" (pp. 132–33). Thus, in Apuleius's cosmology, Genius as daemon is an intermediary between man and Deus summus, a precursor of Alain's priestly Genius, the intermediary between man and Natura. Furthermore, Apuleius's discussion emphasizes Genius's tutelary role. While he does not clarify the relationship between Genius and the more exalted order of daemons he describes later as the guardians allotted to each individual, Apuleius does insist that Genius is a good daemon, perfected in virtue, and synonymous with the best desires of the human soul.[14] This depiction of Genius as moral

[13] Apuleius, *Opera omnia*, 2, ed. Franz von Oudendorp (1823), p. 150–152.
[14] Apuleius identifies these guardian daemons with each individual's conscience, pp. 154–156. See also the chapter on demons in Paul Friedländer, *Plato: An Introduction*, 1, Bollingen Series

guide coupled with the reference to him as a spirit who, though immortal, is in some sense created with each man and accompanies him through life attests to the presence of a tutelary Genius in one of the primary sources of medieval Platonism.[15]

Although Apuleius does not clarify the relation between the tutelary spirit and the god of generation (except for a difficult reference to the union of body and soul), it is not unusual for both meanings of Genius to be invoked simultaneously. Augustine, for example, testifies to the prevalence of this usage in the late classical period by citing two seemingly contradictory definitions of Genius in his attempt to discredit paganism. "Quid est Genius? 'Deus,' inquit, 'qui praepositus est ac vim habet omnium rerum gignendarum.' . . . Et cum alio loco Genium dicit esse uniuscujusque animum rationalem, et ideo esse singulos singulorum. . . ."[16] Despite Augustine's objections, the dual meaning of Genius is transmitted to the Middle Ages through the influential Martianus Capella. In the De nuptiis Philologiae et Mercurii, he writes:

> Sed quoniam unicuique superiorum deorum singuli quique deserviunt, ex illorum arbitrio istorumque comitatu et generalis omnium praesul, et specialis singulis mortalibus Genius admovetur, quem etiam Praestitem, quod praesit gerundis omnibus, vocaverunt. . . . Ideoque Genius dicitur, quoniam quum quis hominum genitus fuerit, mox eidem copulatur. Hic tutelator fidissimusque germanus animos omnium mentesque custodit. Et quoniam cogitationum arcana superae annuntiat potestati, etiam Angelus poterit nuncupari. Hos omnes Graeci δαιμονας dicunt. . . .[17]

Martianus's account of Genius is obviously a conflation of the two essential meanings of the term: the Genius of generation is fused with Genius the tutelary spirit. And from this two-fold tradition, also subscribed to by Bernardus Silvestris, Alain de Lille derives the dual commission of Genius as scribe and priest in the De planctu Naturae.

Moreover, in Alain's allegory Genius's functions as artifex and sacerdos are intrinsically related. Because he participates in Natura's procreative duties, he also shares her responsibilities as moral guide. For by virtue of informing the various creatures of the sublunary sphere with "vita sui generis," Genius establishes the innate natural law which governs these creatures. Further-

---

59, trans. Hans Meyerhoff (New York, 1958), pp. 32–58. Calcidius refers to Socrates's protecting daemon in his commentary on the Timaeus. See J. H. Waszink, ed., Plato Latinus, 4 (London, 1962), p. 199.

[15] Apuleius's definition of Genius as "bona cupido animi" apparently influenced the definitions of Servius and Bernardus Silvestris. Commenting on Book VI of the Aeneid, Servius writes, "nam cum nascimur, duos genios sortimur: unus est qui hortatur ad bona, alter qui depravat ad mala." See George Thilo and Herman Hagen, eds., Vergilii Aeneidos commentarius, 2 (1881). Also commenting on the Aeneid, Bernardus casts Euridice as natural concupiscence or "boni appetitus . . . data est enim ad appetendum bonum." See Wilhelm Riedel, ed., Commentum super sex libros Eneidos Virgilii (1924).

[16] De civitate Dei 7.13, PL 41:205.

[17] Martianus Capella, De nuptiis Philologiae et Mercurii, ed. Ulrich Friedrich Kopp (Frankfurt, 1836), pp. 205–207.

more, *genius* is also a philosophical term which Alain equates with this inherent natural law. "Per substantificos genios, id est per substantiales naturas. Genius enim natura vel Deus nature dicitur."[18] In other words, genius denotes not only the god of nature, the traditional scribe who impresses form on matter, but also the nature of the thing created, its essence, and concomitantly, its inherent natural law. For man, this substantifying genius is reason or, according to Apuleius, the soul. Thus, Wetherbee is correct when he writes that "Genius, seeking to preserve man in his ideal relationship with Natura, is the innate principle of rational dignity and vision. . . ." (*Platonism and Poetry*, p. 207). But Genius's tutelary function is due not to his regulation of sexuality, as Wetherbee argues, but to his identification as man's substantial nature, his reason. Alain's definition of genius as "natura vel Deus nature" thus assimilates the two meanings of the term in the medieval tradition: the allegorical Genius in the *De planctu Naturae* is both the tutelary spirit, inherent in each individual as reason, and the god of generation, both priest and scribe.

II

In the *Roman de la Rose* Jean de Meun affirms the same moral position as Alain de Lille does in the *De planctu Naturae*. However, Jean offers this endorsement through the mode of comic irony, for he dramatizes the absurdity of man's sins against reason. And because of this difference of mode, Jean's Natura and Genius are not identical to the figures of the same name in Alain's poem.[19] Jean de Meun divides Natura's dual offices as *procreatrix* and moral guide in *De planctu Naturae* between his Natura and Raison. The authority of the goddess in the *Roman de la Rose* is thus radically diminished. From her man receives

> "Treis forces, que de cors que d'ame,
> Car bien puis dire senz mentir:
> Jou faz estre, vivre e sentir.
> . . .
> Senz faille, de l'entendement,
> Quenois je bien que vraiement
> Celui ne lui donai je mie;
> La ne s'estent pas ma baillie.
> Ne sui pas sage ne poissant
> De faire rien si quenoissant.
> Onques ne fis rien pardurable,
> Quanque je faz est corrompable."[20]

[18] *Textes Inédits*, ed. Marie Thérèse d'Alverny (Paris, 1965), p. 228.

[19] For a similar but more complete discussion of the difference between Alain's Genius and Jean's see George Economou, *The Goddess Natura in Medieval Literature* (Cambridge, Mass., 1972), pp. 105–124. My interpretation of the *Roman de la Rose* agrees with that presented by John V. Fleming in *The Roman de la Rose: A Study in Allegory and Iconography* (Princeton, 1969). However, Fleming does not distinguish between Genius in *De planctu Naturae* and the *Roman de la Rose*.

[20] *Roman de la Rose*, 4, ed. Ernest Langlois (Paris, 1920–24), lines 19036–38, 19055–62. All quotations of the *Roman de la Rose* are from this edition.

Natura's domain, then, is restricted to man's sensitive nature and this limitation is indicated by her identification with the tools of the forge, the hammer and anvil associated in *De planctu Naturae* with the uncorrupted Venus, originally Natura's *subvicaria* in the work of procreation. Consequently, the law Natura enforces in the *Roman de la Rose* is the natural law which governs the animal kingdom rather than the law of reason, unique to man. Thus, her complaint is not, as in Alain's poem, a lament about man's violations of the rule of reason, for morality is clearly beyond her ken.

> "Senz faille, de touz les pechiez
> Don li chaitis est entechiez,
> A Deu les lais, bien s'en chevisse,
> Quant li plaira si l'en punisse."
> (lines 19323–26)

Rather, she tells Genius, she complains of the same men that the God of Love complains, because they refuse to use the tools she has given them (lines 19327–34). Therefore, in an ironic reversal of the *De planctu Naturae,* she commissions her priest Genius to excommunicate those who through chastity sin against nature by refusing to reproduce the species.

The changes which Jean de Meun makes in the figure Natura are paralleled by similar alterations of Genius. In the *Roman de la Rose* the poet emphasizes Genius's role as priest; he adds the confession of Natura and the sermon to Love's barons. But, ironically, Genius's claim to sacerdotal authority has been undermined by Natura's disassociation from her function as moral instructor. Genius, as Natura's "other self," is qualified to share in her work as *procreatrix*; but because she no longer has jurisdiction over man's rational faculties, his activities as spiritual advisor are absurd. And Jean de Meun makes it hilariously clear that Genius is a false priest. The Mass which he offers is a celebration not of the eternal, but "De toutes choses corrompables" (line 16282); and the excommunication he pronounces against celibates is based on a literal interpretation of the Biblical injunction to "increase and multiply." For Genius is, as Fleming indicates, "unregenerately carnal and literal" (p. 210). This priest knows nothing of the supernatural and he believes that God's highest purpose for mankind is physical perpetuation. Furthermore, because of the schism between Genius and Raison, the moral guide in the *Roman de la Rose,* the amoral procreative powers which he represents are easily subverted to Venus's illicit purposes. His investiture as bishop by the God of Love dramatizes this unwitting submission of nature to vice. Thus, in the *Roman de la Rose* the hierarchy established by Alain is inverted; divorced from Raison, Natura and Genius become servants of Venus *scelestis*.[21]

---

[21] Wetherbee views the conception of the child at the end of the poem as a fulfillment of Genius's command to renew the race and as evidence of a providential order which works through man's cupidity and deception. Therefore, he argues that Genius is not merely the hapless tool of Venus. See "The Literal and Allegorical," pp. 282–286. However, as Economou points out, "Whether this means a victory for Natura or for Venus, one thing is certain: Alan's

Genius's inability in the *Roman de la Rose* to make moral distinctions indicates the crucial difference between this false priest and the true one of *De planctu Naturae*. For Jean de Meun's allegorical figure is not the personification of man's innate tutelary spirit, reason, but rather of his inherent concupiscence, identified as Genius by Guillaume de Conches in his commentary on the myth of Orpheus and Eurydice in the *Consolation of Philosophy*.

> Huius est coniunx Euridice, id est naturalis concupiscentia que unicuique coniuncta est: nullus enim sine ea nec etiam puer unius diei in hac vita esse potest. Unde iterum finxerunt poete quemdam deum esse, scilicet genium, qui nascitur cum unoquoque et moritur. Unde Horatius: *deus albus et ater mortalis in unumquodque caput*. Genius est naturalis concupiscentia. Sed hec naturalis concupiscentia merito dicitur Euridice, id est boni iudicatio, quia quod quisque iudicat bonum, sive ita sit sive non, concupiscit.[22]

Guillaume's definition of Genius is different from the traditional concept in the same way that Jean de Meun's Genius is different from Alain's. In both cases, Genius is stripped of his tutelary role. He represents natural concupiscence, that aspect of human nature, distinct from reason, which regards everything it desires to be good, whether or not it indeed is. And because as natural concupiscence Genius's claim to moral authority is spurious, he is easily corrupted by the adulterous Venus.

III

The Genius whom John Gower inherits through Alain de Lille and Jean de Meun is thus an extremely complex allegorical figure. In the works of both Gower's predecessors, Genius plays a dual role as priest and scribe, but his legitimate function as moral guide in Alain's poem is undermined by Jean de Meun for purposes of comic irony. In adapting his Genius from this literary tradition, Gower chooses to disregard the character's conventional association with Natura as *procreatrix* in order to concentrate on his tutelary role which, by the fourteenth century, includes the potential for either a true or a false priesthood.

And it is precisely this potential which accounts for the dual priesthood of Genius in the *Confessio Amantis*.

> "Thi schrifte to oppose and hiere,
> My Sone, I am assigned hiere
> Be Venus the godesse above,
> Whos Prest I am touchende of love.

Natura could never have participated in such a 'cooperative' effort, for in her view, Venus and her son were responsible for the waywardness of man" (*The Goddess Natura*, p. 120).

[22] Cited by Edouard Jeauneau, "L'usage de la notion d'integumentum à travers les gloses de Guillaume de Conches," *Archives d'histoire doctrinale et littéraire du Moyen Age* 32 (1957), 46. Although Bernardus Silvestris also identifies Genius as natural concupiscence, he defines this phrase as a longing for the good rather than an amoral desire. Thus Bernardus's use of the term is very different from Guillaume's. See Nitzsche, pp. 63–64.

> Bot natheles for certein skile
> I mot algate and nedes wile
> Noght only make my spekynges
> Of love, bot of othre thinges,
> That touchen to the cause of vice.
> For that belongeth to thoffice
> Of Prest, whos ordre that I bere."
> (1, lines 233–43)

By attributing this double mission to Genius, Gower skillfully fuses the two different meanings of this allegorical figure which he found in *De planctu Naturae* and the *Roman de la Rose*. As a priest of Venus, Gower's character is similar to Jean's; he is Genius as natural concupiscence, the amoral law of *kinde*. But Gower's Genius, unlike his precursor in the *Roman de la Rose*, also affirms the law of man's complete nature which his prototype in *De planctu Naturae* proclaimed. For, as orthodox priest, Gower's figure is analogous to Alain's; he is Genius as reason, the distinctly human natural law. In his discussion of chastity in Book VII, Genius informs Amans about the relationship between the laws of *kinde* and *reson*.[23]

> "For god the lawes hath assissed
> Als wel to reson as to kinde,
> Bot he the bestes wolde binde
> Only to lawes of nature,
> Bot to the mannes creature
> God yaf him reson forth withal,
> Wherof that he nature schal
> Upon the causes modefie,
> That he schal do no lecherie,
> And yit he schal hise lustes have."
> (7, lines 5372–81)

The dual priesthood of Gower's Genius, then, testifies to the English poet's awareness of the difference between this character's tutelary role in the *De planctu Naturae* and in the *Roman de la Rose*. Genius as priest of Venus teaches Amans the law of *kinde* espoused by his counterpart in Jean de Meun's poem. But the inadequacy of this natural law as a moral standard for man is expressed by Genius the orthodox priest. Through this union of the laws of *kinde* and *reson*, Gower restores the moral authority which Genius originally exercised in the *De planctu Naturae*.[24]

---

[23] I am indebted to Professor Kurt Olsson of the University of Idaho for these observations about the importance of the distinction between *kinde* and *reson* in the *Confessio Amantis*. In his manuscript, *The Major Poems of John Gower: An Interpretation*, Professor Olsson demonstrates the skill with which Gower develops the distinction between these two laws as a structural principle in the *Confessio Amantis*. Because the poet clearly differentiates between *kinde* and *reson*, Schueler's contention that the natural law is identical with morality in the English poem is mistaken.

[24] Although Economou identifies Gower's Genius with Alain's, his discussion ignores the sophisticated understanding of this complex literary tradition which the dual priesthood of Genius in the *Confessio Amantis* reveals.

A brief analysis of the lesson on wrath in Book III reveals the skillful manner in which Gower uses the dual priesthood of Genius to demonstrate the moral fallibility of natural inclinations. Genius begins the instruction about wrath with an exemplum which depicts this vice as a sin against nature as well as reason. After Amans confesses to anger resulting from his melancholy or moodiness, Genius responds with the story of Canace and Machaire. Although King Eolus is harshly condemned for his merciless ire, Genius's attitude toward the incestuous children is curiously sympathetic. He partially exonerates them because the couple succumbs to incest in youth,

> "Whan kinde assaileth the corage
> With love and doth him forto bowe,
> That he no reson can allowe,
> Bot halt the lawes of nature:
> For whom that love hath under cure,
> As he is blind himself, riht so
> He makth his client blind also."
>
> (3, lines 154–60)

In the brief allusion to the Ovidian tale of Tiresias and the snakes which follows, Genius again emphasizes that wrath is a more heinous sin than lust because it violates the law of *kinde*.

> "Lo thus, my Sone, Ovide hath write,
> Wherof thou miht be reson wite,
> More is a man than such a beste:
> So mihte it nevere ben honeste
> A man to wraththen him to sore
> Of that an other doth the lore
> Of kinde, in which is no malice,
> Bot only that it is a vice:
> And thogh a man be resonable,
> Yit after kinde he is menable
> To love, wher he wole or non."
>
> (3, lines 381–91)

Genius's argument, of course, conforms to the medieval hierarchy of the Deadly Sins; lust is the least reprehensible because the most natural. But in emphasizing the irresistibility of love rather than its sinfulness, he endorses a position similar to that of Genius in the *Roman de la Rose*. Through this initial section of Book III, then, Genius's role as priest of Venus dominates and tempers his responsibility as orthodox priest.

As Book III continues, however, Genius assumes his second role as priest of reason and gradually demonstrates the limitations of natural concupiscence as a moral guide. In the confession of contek and homicide, sins against patience and mercy, Genius again refers to the law of *kinde,* but his attitude toward it is altered. Acknowledging his guilt of contek, or foolish haste, Amans describes the inner conflict between reason and will which love makes him suffer.

"Reson seith that I scholde leve
To love, wher ther is no leve
To spede, and will seith therayein
That such an herte is to vilein,
Which dar noght love and til he spede,
Let hope serve at such a nede."
(3, lines 1179–84)

Although Genius remains sympathetic to Amans's plight, he counsels the lover to abide by reason rather than will.

"Thou dost, my Sone, ayein the riht;
Bot love is of so gret a miht,
His lawe mai noman refuse,
So miht thou thee the betre excuse.
And natheles thou schalt be lerned
That will scholde evere be governed
Of reson more than of kinde."
(3, lines 1193–99)

And in the succeeding stories of Diogenes and Alexander, Pyramus and Thisbe, and Orestes, Genius argues for the need to follow the law of *reson* even if it conflicts with the law of *kinde*. In the first of these three tales, the priest makes his point in general terms. Diogenes, a surrogate for Genius, convinces Alexander that willfulness is the cause of sin, but no specific mention is made of lust (3, lines 1270–92). However, in the tale of Pyramus and Thisbe, Genius begins to repudiate love itself.

"For love is of a wonder kinde,
And hath hise wittes ofte blinde,
That thei fro mannes reson falle;
Bot whan that it is so befalle
That will schal the corage lede,
In loves cause it is to drede."
(3, lines 1323–28)

And Genius denounces love outright through the character of Thisbe.

"O thou which cleped art Venus,
Goddesse of love, and thou, Cupide,
Which loves cause hast forto guide,
I wot now wel that ye be blinde,
Of thilke unhapp which I now finde
Only betwen my love and me.
This Piramus, which hiere I se
Bledende, what hath he deserved?
For he youre heste hath kept and served,
And was yong and I bothe also:
Helas, why do ye with ous so?"
(3, lines 1462–72)

The blindness of love which signifies the irresistible force of natural law in the story of Canace and Machaire is given a more sinister meaning in this tale, for it refers to the cruelty of Venus and Cupid. Nevertheless, the lovers are sympathetically portrayed. In the story of Orestes, however, the lover is depicted as the villain. This tale is a reversal of the initial one, for Climestre, like Eolus, is guilty of murder, but her sin of homicide is incited by lust. Thus, Genius teaches Amans that obeying the law of *kinde* can, paradoxically, lead to *unkinde* acts; through this tale the priest reveals the inadequacy of the natural law as a moral guide.

Genius reiterates the need to obey both *kinde* and *reson* in his condemnation of war at the end of Book III.

> "Men schal noght finde upon his liche
> A beste forto take his preie:
> And sithen kinde hath such a weie,
> Thanne is it wonder of a man,
> Which kynde hath and resoun can,
> That he wol owther more or lasse
> His kinde and resoun overpasse,
> And sle that is to him semblable.
> So is the man noght resonable
> Ne kinde, and that is noght honeste,
> Whan he is worse than a beste."
>
> (3, lines 2588–98)

In the case of homicide these two laws correspond, for murder violates the precepts of both nature and reason. But such accord is not always achieved; lust, for example, is prompted by nature, but this sexual urge must be regulated by man's reason. Throughout the *Confessio Amantis*, then, Gower distinguishes between the law of *kinde* and the law of *reson*, between the values of Genius in the *Roman de la Rose* and those of his precursor in *De planctu Naturae*. For, as this examination of Book III demonstrates, the English poet uses the dual priesthood of Genius to correct the unorthodox position enunciated by the false priest in Jean de Meun's poem and to restore to this figure the moral authority exercised by Alain's true priest.

This examination of the dual priesthood of Genius also refutes the charge of inconsistency leveled against Gower, for this character's discussion of the education of Alexander and his repudiation of Venus's divinity are not inappropriate to his role in the poem. Genius's double ministry qualifies him to teach Amans in Book VII about both *kinde* and *reson*, about natural science (the domain of Jean's Natura) and morality (included in the larger jurisdiction of Alain's Natura). Likewise, the combined office of Gower's Genius explains his seemingly contradictory rejection of Venus in Book V. For the Venus of the *Confessio Amantis* is analogous to the amoral Natura in the *Roman de la Rose* (but not, as Economou and Schueler contend, to the moral Natura of the *De planctu Naturae*). She is natural sexuality divorced from reason and, therefore, vulnerable to perversion. Thus the company of lovers which attends Venus in Book VIII includes not only the four virtuous

156

wives, Penelope, Lucrece, Alceste, and Alcione, but also illicit lovers such as Paris and Helen, Tristam and Isolde, and Narcissus. And although Genius condemns Amans's love because it is unreasonable and, therefore, sinful, Venus objects only because Amans is old and impotent (8.2076–98, 2403–20). The law of *kinde* which Gower's Venus represents is morally ambiguous, for the sexual act which she incites can either be subject to reason and therefore moral or subverted by lust and thus immoral. And it is Venus acting in this last manner that Genius, as the spokesman of man's complete, integrated nature, rejects in Book V.

The Genius of the *Confessio Amantis,* then, is not an inconsistent figure but rather a complex and sophisticated assimilation of his two precursors in the literary tradition — an assimilation which proves Gower's thorough understanding of *De planctu Naturae* and the *Roman de la Rose.* Aware of the restrictions which Jean de Meun had imposed on this character in order to achieve comic irony, Gower establishes the combined priesthood of Genius to demonstrate the limitations of natural concupiscence as a moral guide. By making Genius the representative not only of man's carnal nature but also of his rationality, the English poet reinvests this allegorical figure with the true priestly authority originally bestowed by Alain de Lille and restores him to his legitimate role as tutelary spirit. C. S. Lewis's psychomachic description of Gower's character is thus partially correct, for Genius is Amans's inner voice — the voice, however, of his reason, not his love.

JOHN GOWER, *SAPIENS* IN ETHICS AND POLITICS

A. J. MINNIS

The 'moral frame' of the *Confessio Amantis* (consisting of the *prologus*, the structural device of the Seven Deadly Sins, and the epilogue) has troubled many of its recent readers, including those who are convinced of the worth of many of the stories within the frame.[1] The stock view has been that Gower was misguided in imposing a moral frame on alien material, the material of 'courtly love'. In refuting this view, C. S. Lewis argued that the principle behind Gower's frame was his belief that 'the virtues of a good lover were indistinguishable from those of a good man'.[2] It may be suggested that this principle of Gower's was derived from scholastic literary theory, in particular from commentaries on Ovid and the Sapiential Books of the Bible.[3] In writing the *Confessio Amantis*, Gower seems to have adopted a distinctive authorial role,[4] that of the *sapiens* in ethics and politics, and an understanding of this role enables us to appreciate the essential unity of the diverse materials in his work. The *prologus*, Book VII[5] and the epilogue are in fact 'of a piece' with the rest of the work, and the structural device of the Seven Deadly Sins can be seen as a logical extension of a pattern which mediaeval commentators believed to be inherent in the materials used by Gower.

Gower's debt to the 'Mediaeval Ovid' is well known. Various scholars have pointed out that he took from the *Ovide moralisé* details for his stories of Pyramus and Thisbe, Phoebus and Coronis, and Seys and Alcione.[6] In the most comprehensive study to date, C. Mainzer has emphasised the traditional nature of much *Ovidiana*: we should think in terms of a fund of details which is common to mediaeval glosses, commentaries and indeed to translations.[7] For example, the *Ovide moralisé* is often dependent on earlier glosses. Gower was probably indebted to the 'Mediaeval Ovid' for details in fifteen stories from the *Metamorphoses*;[8] he may have used Pierre Bersuire's *Ovidius moralizatus* in his section on the pantheon in the fifth book of the *Confessio*.[9] Moreover, he seems also to have made use of a commentary on Ovid's *Heroides*.[10]

In commentaries on the *Heroides* one can find literary theory concerning Ovid's patterning of *exempla amantium* which is relevant to the issue of Gower's moral frame. Ovid's profound purpose (*intentio*) in the *Heroides* was usually stated to be the commendation of legal marriage and chaste love, and he was supposed to have done this by showing both the moral utility (*utilitas*) which proceeds from legal love and the misfortunes which arise from foolish love and illicit love:

> Materia ipsius est amor licitus et illicitus et stultus. Intentio sua est commendare quasdam a licito amore sicut Penelopes; aliquos reprehendit sicut Phedram de illicito amore que dilexit priuignum suum Ipolitum; aliquos etiam reprehendit a stulto amore sicut Phillida, Didonem. Stultitia enim

est amare hospites sicut Phillis amauit Demophonta [sic.]... Vtilitas est ut per libri lectionem huius modi amoris notitiam habeamus. Etice suponitur quia agit de moribus.[11]

The basic notion here is that certain stories within the collection work positively by describing legal and chaste love 'in such a way that the reader is made aware of its attractiveness, whereas illegal and foolish kinds of love are described in such a way that they appear obnoxious. The whole book pertains to ethics, because the study of ethics teaches the pursuit of good *mores* and the avoidance of evil.

In this way, generations of commentators on pagan *auctores* met the ancient criticism (which goes back to Plato at least) that poetry inflames the passions,[12] by the argument that it can move the will of its reader in the right moral direction. From the twelfth century onwards, it could be claimed that poetry, both profane and sacred, had a commendable 'affective' quality which was the basis of its *utilitas* in a Christian society.[13] Thus, according to the stock xii c. view of the Psalter, evil things are described therein in order that men may be deterred from them.[14] Such *materia* indirectly serves the *principalis materia* of the whole work:

Quod vero de contrariis, id est daemonibus impiis interseritur, non ideo fit, quod sit de principali materia; sed ut principali materiei subserviat, per quasdam commoditates admiscetur: ut in primo psalmo de impiis adducit, ut per eorum poenam homines ab eorum conformitate deterreat, ed ad Christi conformitatem reducat.[15]

This type of defence was popular throughout the later Middle Ages. For example, Caxton adapted it to explain the *intentio* of a prose work, the *Morte Darthur:*

I ... have doon sette it in enprynte to the entente that noble men may see and lerne the noble actes of chyvalrie, ... and how they that were vicious were punysshed and ofte put to shame and rebuke; humbly bysechyng al noble lordes and ladyes wyth al other estates ... that shal see and rede in this sayd book and werke, that they take the good and honest actes in their remembraunce, and to folowe the same... Doo after the good and leve the evyl, and it shal brynge you to good fame and renommee.[16]

Gower's technique of handling *exempla* in the *Confessio Amantis* has often been related to the technique of *exempla* in religious literature,[17] but such comparisons fail to cope adequately with two points: first, that Gower's *exempla* are in the main exemplary lovers (hence Ovidian *exempla* are relevant in a way that sermon *exempla* are not); and secondly that Gower's *exempla amantum* are patterned in a way which is basically similar to what mediaeval commentators regarded as the *Heroides*-paradigm, where *exempla* of legal lovers are juxtaposed with *exempla* of foolish lovers and unchaste lovers. The significance of these two points will emerge clearly if the *Confessio* is approached by way of a very different work, Chaucer's *Legend of Good Women*.

In composing the *Legend*, Chaucer used a glossed copy of the *Heroides*.[18] Indeed, from the *Introduction to the Man of Law's Tale* one may gain the impression that he regarded his work as a 'modern' *Heroides*. The Man of Law claims that Chaucer

... hath toold of lovers up and doun
Mo than Ovide made of mencioun
In his Episteles, that ben ful olde
(II 53-5)

– and then proceeds with a substantial discussion of the *Legend*. From the overall context it is clear that, for the Man of Law, the *Legend* is Chaucer's main attempt to overgo Ovid's 'Episteles' (= the *Heroides*).

The *Heroides* may be considered as a source not only for many of Chaucer's individual legends but also for the literary form or structure (what commentators called the *forma*)[19] of his work. The love-letters in the *Heroides* follow no particular order of sequence. Likewise, Chaucer's stories of good women could be re-arranged without doing violence to any method of deployment. The God of Love tells the narrator to include the story of Alceste, without specifying where it should be included (G 530-9). He is told also to begin with Cleopatra – then the God of Love adds a vague 'and so forth':

At Cleopatre I wol that thou begynne,
And so forth, and my love so shalt thow winne.
(G 542-3; cf. F 566-7)

However, while Chaucer may have been influenced by Ovid's *forma*, it is clear that he did not follow Ovid's precedent for the way in which (according to the mediaeval commentators) diverse *materiae* were juxtaposed within that *forma*. Chaucer's stories are all about good women, as the Man of Law's discussion of the *Legend* makes clear:

Whoso that wole his large volume seke
Cleped the Seintes Legende of Cupide,
Ther may be seen the large woundes wyde
Of Lucresse, and of Babilan Tesbee...
(II 60ff.)

Eight of the heroines named by the Man of Law are not treated in the *Legend* as we have it: the above passage is usually understood to be a description of Chaucer's complete plan for the *Legend*, which, at the time of writing, he planned to finish. *Exempla* of bad women have deliberately been excluded:

But certeinly no word ne writeth he
Of thilke wikke ensample of Canacee,
That loved her owene brother synfully;
(Of swiche cursed stories I sey fy!)
Or ellis of Tyro Appollonious,
How that the cursed kyng of Antiochus
Birafte his doghter of hir maydenhede,
That is so horrible a tale for to rede,
Whan he hir threw upon the pavement.
(II 77-85)

160

Chaucer's disgust (or is it the Man of Law's disgust?) is evident in the very way he paraphrases the stories. The story of Canace is Ovidian: the *Heroides* includes an epistle from Canace to her brother and lover, Macareus,[20] and the commentators regarded Canace as one of Ovid's main *exempla* of illicit love (a point to which I shall return). Hence Chaucer's practice in the *Legend* may be regarded as an important modification, even a simplification, of what the commentators regarded as the *Heroides*-paradigm of juxtaposed *exempla* of virtuous and vicious lovers. Chaucer chose not to provide stories of the loves of women both good and bad, but produced a collection of homogeneous stories, of the loves of good women.

At the end of *Troilus and Criseyde*, Chaucer had begged 'every gentil womman' not to blame him because Criseyde was untrue, and promised to redress the balance with stories which revealed the truth and goodness of other women:

> ... gladlier I wol write, yif you leste,
> Penelopees trouthe and good Alceste.
> (v 1777-8)

This promise was kept in the *Legend*, which Chaucer may have intended as a sequel and complement to *Troilus*. In both versions of the prologue to the *Legend*, the God of Love accuses the narrator of having defamed womankind by writing of the faithless Criseyde and by translating Jean de Meun's scurrilous *Roman de la Rose* (F 329-35; G 255-72). The narrator protests, affirming that he drew on his sources in all good faith: whatever his *auctour* may have meant, he knows what he himself meant. A true lover

> ... oght me not to blame,
> Thogh that I speke a fals lovere som shame.
> They oghte rather with me for to holde,
> For that I of Creseyde wroot or tolde,
> Or of the Rose; what so myn auctour mente,
> Algate, God woot, yt was myn entente
> To forthren trouthe in love and yt cheryce,
> And to been war fro falsnesse and fro vice
> By swich ensample; this was my menynge.
> (F 466-74)

This idiom seems to be dependent on the way in which commentators described the *utilitas* of love-poetry. The professed *utilitas* of Chaucer's works is 'to forthren trouthe in love and yt cheryce'; his declared *intentio* ('entente') is to encourage readers to follow the good ('trouthe in love') and to flee the evil ('falsenesse' and 'vice' in love).

With reference to *Troilus*, the narrator appears to be saying that he held up Criseyde as an *exemplum* of the faithless lover: he taught the doctrine of virtuous love by speaking this 'fals lovere som shame'. This type of defence is found in commentaries on the *Heroides*.

Materia ipsius est amor illicitus et stultus. Intentio sua est quasdam puellas commendare in licito amore sicut Penelopem, alias reprehendere ab illicito sicut Phedram que dilexit Yppolitum privignum suum, alias reprehendere a stulto sicut Phillidam et Oenonem.[21]

'Penelopees trouthe' appears even more attractive than it would do in isolation, because the reader is able to contrast it with the illicit love of Phaedra and the foolish loves of Phyllis and Oenone. The narrator's point is probably that in *Troilus* he wished to recommend virtuous love by pointing out the unpleasantness of faithless love: Criseyde therefore functions as an *exemplum* of faithless love in the same way as (according to the commentators) Ovid's Phaedra functions as an *exemplum* of illicit love and Ovid's Phyllis and Oenone function as *exempla* of foolish love. Readers may 'ben war fro falsnesse and fro vice / By swich ensample'. Having provided this *exemplum* of the faithless lover, Chaucer's narrator must now redress the balance by providing *exempla* of good lovers only, in his *Legend*.

It would appear, then, that Chaucer, perfectly familiar with the stock explanation of the Ovidian paradigm of juxtaposed *exempla*, deliberately chose not to adopt it in his *Legend*. By contrast, Gower adopted and expanded it in his *Confessio Amantis*. The unease which certain critics have felt about Gower's supposed imposition of a moral frame on the apparently alien material of 'courtly love' is quite unfounded. Gower was not original in placing the *materia* of love in a moral perspective – that had already been done in the scholastic study of Ovid's erotic works. His personal achievement consists rather in the fact that he widened the moral perspective which he found in the 'Mediaeval Ovid'. Two aspects of this widening of perspective may now be discussed, beginning with the way in which Gower seems to have encapsulated the commentators' stock moralisations within stories which he re-directed to exemplify other points of morality.

For the Ovid-commentators, Penelope was the prime *exemplum* of lawful and chaste love.[22] Gower tells the story of Penelope as an *exemplum* of the sin of Sloth which is the main subject of Book IV (147-233).[23] The difference is mainly one of emphasis. Gower focusses on the man in the story and not on the woman, and his characterisation of Penelope preserves intact the commentators' moral points. Penelope is very much the 'trewe wif' who, although she may lament over her husband's *lachesse*, still loves him and remains faithful to him (see IV 178-85). Penelope's letter to Ulysses is loosely based on *Heroides* I: Ulysses' tardiness in returning to his wife is described well in Ovid's text.[24] Gower omits all Ovid's references to the Trojan War.[25] What remain are Penelope's complaint about her husband's tardiness (which Gower needed to point his moral about Sloth) and her protestation of fidelity, which Gower would have found emphasised in his commentary. There is no disjunction between the commentators' moral and Gower's moral. Indeed, Ulysses' sloth appears all the more reprehensible because he is slow in returning to so good a wife.

For the Ovid-commentators, Phyllis exemplified foolish love or infatuation. When Demephon did not return to her, because of intemperate love she hanged herself:

de stulto habens exemplum per Phillidem, quae Demophonti reditum ut suis disponeret concessit, quae expectare non valens ex amoris intemperantia se laqueo suspendit...[26]

Her example is set before us to dissuade women from shamefully clinging to men:

Intentio vero est Ovidii in hac epistola reprehendere mulieres uiris turpiter adherentes sicut Phillis.[27]

Phyllis loved a stranger, and such a love is foolish:

Intentio autoris in hac epistola est dissuadere nos a stulto amore. Intentio mittentis, id est Phillidis, est reuocare Demomphontem ad suum amorem, cui multa beneficia contulerat. Iste Demophon fuit filius Tesei... Transiens per Troiam a Phillide regina Tracum hospitatus est. Que cum maritum non haberet eum adamauit et cum eo illegitime concubuit. Vnde illa reprehenditur, nam bone fame uacare deberet sed ignoto se et sua credidit. Vnde maximum malum sibi contigit.[28]

Gower tells the story of Phyllis and Demephon in Book IV of the *Confessio* (731-878), where it functions as a 'gret ensample' of forgetfulness, an aspect of Sloth. Once again, Gower re-directs the story by expanding that part of it which was not the concern of the commentators, and preserves intact their moral points. The fact that Phyllis's love is foolish makes Demephon the more reprehensible. When he fails to return to her, her love grows beyond the bonds of moderation:

> Hire love encresceth and his lasseth,
> For him sche lefte slep and mete...
> (IV 782-3)

She sends Demephon a letter (this is loosely based on *Heroides* II) to protest that

> sche is overcome
> With strengthe of love in such a wise,
> That sche noght longe mai suffise
> To liven out of his presence;
> And putte upon his conscience
> The trowthe which he hath behote,
> Wherof sche loveth him so hote,
> Sche seith, that if he lengere lette
> Of such a day as sche him sette,
> Sche scholde sterven in his Slowthe...
> (IV 788-97)

Gower tells how Phyllis places a lantern high in a tower, in the hope that it might attract back Demephon's ship. In the morning, after a night spent in vain waiting, she loses all remnants of self-control:

> Doun fro the Tour sche gan to renne
> Into an Herber all hire one,
> Wher many a wonder woful mone
> Sche made, that no lif it wiste,
> As sche which all hire joie miste,

> That now sche swouneth, now sche pleigneth,
> And al hire face sche destreigneth
> With teres...
>
> (IV 832-9)

Then she hangs herself, a detail which Gower took from a commentary on the *Heroides,* since it is not in Ovid's Latin.[29] Ovid brings out the pathos of her situation,[30] whereas Gower, although certainly aware of the pathos, clearly shares the belief of the commentators that hers was a foolish love.

Gower's treatment of the story of Phyllis is also unlike Chaucer's treatment – a point of some substance, as it illuminates a basic difference between the *Legend* and the *Confessio.* Although Chaucer took from the commentators certain details which are not in Ovid's Latin,[31] he did not subscribe to the scholastic belief that Phyllis was a foolish lover. Being concerned to portray her as one of love's martyrs, Chaucer studiously avoided making her appear foolish.[32] Instead he contrasts the faithlessness of Demephon with the honour of Phyllis, who emerges as a 'trewe lovere' and a woman greatly wronged. Judicious pruning of Phyllis's letter as given in the *Heroides* contributes to this effect:

> But al hire letter wryten I ne may
> By order, for it were to me a charge;
> Hire letter was ryght long and therto large.
> But here and ther in rym I have it layd,
> There as me thoughte that she wel hath sayd.
>
> (2513-17)

Her inordinate fasting and weeping, her vigil in the tower, and her intemperate behaviour on the beach are all omitted. Concerning the motivation for her suicide, all Chaucer says is that she 'so harde and sore abought' Demephon's faithlessness that 'She for dispeyr fordide hyreself'. For Chaucer, the story does not pertain to ethics as the commentators understood the term, but to what might be called 'the ethics of love'. Above, it was argued that in his prologues to the *Legend* (F 466-74; G 456-64) Chaucer appealed to the *utilitas* proper to love-poetry. This may now be taken a stage further with the suggestion that he deliberately adapted the traditional explanation of such *utilitas* for his own avowed purpose, the furtherance of 'trouthe *in love*'.

At the end of his story of Phyllis, Chaucer indicates its exemplary aspect:

> Be war, ye wemen, of youre subtyl fo,
> Syn yit this day men may ensaumple se;
> And trusteth, as in love, no man but me.
>
> (2559-61)

The point of this joke depends on our understanding of how he has broken with the commentators' method of using this Ovidian story, and others like it, to exemplify aspects of morality. Chaucer was concerned to exemplify

goode women, maydenes and wyves,
That were trewe in lovynge al her lyves...
(474-5)

– and therefore he consistently ignored the criticism of his heroines which he found
in the Ovid-commentaries. By contrast, while Gower's concern 'seems to be with a
lover's faults and failings, we are never allowed to forget that these reflect vices
common to all mankind'.[33] Indeed, in the *Confessio* there is no distinction between
lovers' virtues and Christian virtues, between lovers' sins and real sins: Gower
manifests his conviction that virtue is virtue and sin is sin. The ideals of *fyn amors*
are related to the moral perspective found in the 'Mediaeval Ovid'. Gower uses the
figures of lover and lovers' priest, but transcends the values they represent. In the
Legend, the 'lawe' of love is afforded (perhaps for ironic purposes?)[34] a validity
independent of the traditional moral code: in the *Confessio*, Amans and Confessor
ultimately serve not the God of Love but the God of mediaeval Christianity. In
sum, Gower worked within the terms of reference provided by the 'Mediaeval
Ovid', whereas Chaucer refused those terms. Hence it seems unfair to establish
Chaucer's *Legend* as a standard against which to measure Gower's *Confessio* and
find it wanting.

The dangers of establishing Chaucer as a standard are particularly marked in the
case of his attitude to stories about incest. Commentaries on the *Heroides* explain
that Ovid described love which was *incastus* in order that his readers should
recognise and avoid it, stories of this kind being justified as part of the *Heroides*-
paradigm of diverse *exempla*. Thus, it would appear that Gower's attitude to the
story of Canace was more typical than was Chaucer's. What is unusual is not
Gower's use of stories about incest but the strong reaction to them expressed in the
Introduction to the Man of Law's Tale.

How then did the commentators describe Canace's relationship with her brother
Machareus? In what may be called the 'mainstream' commentaries on the *Heroides*
(as far as England is concerned) the terms *incestus* and *illicitus* are practically
synonymous:

> agit Ovidius de amore secundum amoris omnes species, que est legitimus amor, scilicet
> coniugium, stultus scilicet fornicatio, illicitus scilicet incestus. Legitimum commendat in
> Penelope, arguit in Phillide stultum, illicitum dampnat in Phedra et in Canace.[35]

In such a context the term *incestus* seems to mean 'unchaste' in a general sense.
What concerned the commentators was that their *incestae* had had illicit love-
affairs: hence Helen of Troy could be included in this group because she had broken
with her 'legal man' Menelaus.[36] Canace was usually described simply as an
exemplum of illicit love. The fact that the commentators did not emphasise the
consanguineous aspect of the affair may have influenced Gower's choice of the
story of Apollonius, and not the story of Canace, as his *exemplum* of incest.[37]

Gower's handling of the story of Canace is quite consistent with his treatment of the stories of Penelope and Phyllis. He expands that part of the story which did not interest commentators on the *Heroides*, and makes their description of Canace the basis of his characterisation of her (III 143-336). For the commentators and for Gower, Canace's love was *illicitus* and Gower explains precisely what that means through his distinction between the 'lawes of nature' and 'lawe positif'. Canace offended against the latter, which was established by men acting in accordance with right reason.[38] Because her love was not unnatural, and because the wrath of her father was so terrible, Gower can tell her tale with a degree of sympathy.

The stories discussed above are by no means the most important stories in the *Confessio Amantis*, and they are certainly not Gower's best, but our comparison of the attitudes to these stories held by Gower and by the scholastic commentators has served to illuminate Gower's conception of the good lover as indistinguishable from the good man. More light may be cast on Gower's application of this principle by discussing the second aspect of his widening of the moral perspective provided by the 'Mediaeval Ovid', namely the way in which the *exempla amantum* are related to the *casus virorum illustrium* described in Book VII.

The political facet of the *Confessio Amantis* was so important to Gower that he drew attention to it in the Latin passage which provides a summary of his major works:

> Tercius iste liber qui ob reuerenciam strenuissimi: domini sui domini Henrici de Lancastria ... Anglico sermone conficitur, secundum Danielis propheciam super huius mundi regnorum mutacione a tempore regis Nabugodnosor vsque nunc tempora distinguit. Tractat eciam secundum Aristotelem super hiis quibus rex Alexander tam in sui regimen quam aliter eius disciplina edoctus fuit. Principalis tamen huius operis materia super amorem et infatuatas amantum passiones fundamentum habet.[39]

Gower's *principalis materia* falls within the subject-area of ethics; his other material falls within the subject-area of politics, which, according to Aristotle, embraces the subject-area of ethics (or *vice-versa*). As T. A. Sinclair puts it,

> For Aristotle, as for Plato, the subject of political philosophy, or politikè, embraced the whole of human behaviour, the conduct of the individual equally with the behaviour of the group. Ethics was, therefore, a part of politics; we might also say that politics was a part of ethics.[40]

Although there is no evidence that Gower knew Aristotle's *Politics* or any of the mediaeval commentaries on it,[41] he was certainly aware of this belief in the link between politics and ethics. In Book VII of the *Confessio* is found a scheme of the division of the sciences which Gower took from Brunetto Latini's *Tresor*.[42] Brunetto was 'exceptionally well acquainted' with Aristotle's works, and his division of the sciences into the theoretical, the rhetorical and the practical is 'in effect the same as Aristotle's classification of knowledge as Theoretical, Poetical and Practical'.[43] His division of practical philosophy into ethics, economics and politics is also derived from Aristotle. Gower put his own slant on what he took from the *Tresor:* 'ethique', 'iconomique' and 'policie' are considered as aspects of 'a kinges regiment' (see VII 1649-83).

Book VII of the *Confessio* contains a veritable *de regimine principum*, a little treatise on the proper methods of ruling a country. Both the English text of Book VII and its Latin commentary ostentatiously refer to Aristotle as the great authority on politics, although Gower's information concerning Aristotle's views seems to be limited to the account found in Brunetto's *Tresor* and to the pseudo-Aristotelian *Secreta Secretorum* (supposed to have been written by Aristotle for the instruction of King Alexander),[44] which Gower accepted as genuine. From these sources Gower derived much of the 'policie' with which he sought to balance the love-lore which was his *principalis materia:*

> To every man behoveth lore,
> Bot to noman belongeth more
> Than to a king, which hath to lede
> The people; for of his kinghede
> He mai hem both save and spille.
> And for it stant upon his wille,
> It sit him wel to ben avised,
> And the vertus whiche are assissed
> Unto a kinges Regiment,
> To take in his entendement:
> Wherof to tellen, as thei stonde,
> Hierafterward nou woll I fonde.
> (1711-22).

Pagan and Christian *auctoritates* on politics are grouped together. King Solomon is juxtaposed with King Alexander, the sage Daniel with the sage Aristotle.

Although ethics and politics were closely related in the classification of the sciences which Gower took from Brunetto Latini, Gower had a considerable technical problem in assimilating the *materia* of 'policie' to the *principalis materia* of love. He met this challenge with considerable wit and skill, as may be shown by an examination of the adroit way in which he manoeuvred from love in Book VI to 'policie' in Book VII and back again to love in Book VIII.

In Book VI, Confessor offers Amans several *exempla* which warn against the use of sorcery by lovers, the final major *exemplum* being the tale of how the young Alexander pushed the magician Nectanabus to his death. In telling this tale reference is made to Aristotle's tuition of Alexander (2274, 2411-3). The curiosity of Amans having been aroused, he asks Confessor to explain the teachings of Aristotle. Confessor praises this commendable impulse on the part of his pupil, while protesting that, as a servant of Venus, he cannot really be expected to teach 'wisdom'. His convolution is humorous rather than awkward (VI 2420-6). These lines echo Book I 35-41, where it is stated that love and wisdom often seem to be at variance:

> ... love is maister wher he wile,
> Ther can no lif make other skile;
> For wher as evere him lest to sette,

> Ther is no myht which him may lette.
> Bot what schal fallen atte laste,
> The sothe can no wisdom caste,
> Bot as it falleth upon chance...

But here, at the end of Book VI, the apparent variance of love and wisdom is a problem for Gower's Confessor and not for Gower. Confessor admits that even he is interested in wisdom, and promises to explain 'some part thereof',

> For wisdom is at every throwe
> Above alle other thing to knowe
> In loves cause and elleswhere
> (VII 15-17)

This attitude was shared by the mediaeval commentators on Ovid, who placed love in the full context of Christian *scientia*. Ovid may be the expert on love, but if one wants to know about politics recourse must be had to Aristotle.

Thus, in Book VII itself, Gower recounts 'tales wise of Philosophres' about the 'policie' of kings. These are organised according to the five political virtues (truth, liberality, justice, wisdom and charity), a division probably suggested to Gower by the *Secreta Secretorum* – he may have thought he was following Aristotle. Constant reference is made to Solomon and Aristotle, respectively the main Scriptural authority and the main pagan authority on politics.

At the end of Book VII, Amans explains to Confessor that while he has enjoyed all these 'politic' tales his 'herte is elleswhere': he is in pain because of love and is anxious to be shriven.

> Forthi, my goode fader diere,
> Lef al and speke of my matiere
> Touchende of love, as we begonne...
> (5421-3)

Yet Gower's return to his *principalis materia* is anything but abrupt. His discussion at the end of Book VII of the political virtue of chastity provides the occasion for commendation of chastity in marriage. Chastity, it is claimed, is of special importance for a king, but marriage is a natural and sacred bond which no man should break (VII 4215-25). This affirmation of 'honeste love' reads as an amplification and embellishment of the views of the Ovid-commentators. In the context of Books VII and VIII, it reiterates the connection between politics and ethics by reminding us that those virtues necessary for 'a kinges Regiment' are necessary for the moral 'Regiment' of any man. The way has been prepared perfectly for the celebration of the laws of marriage with which Book VIII begins (1-189). Was there anything incongruous about a priest of Venus extolling the virtue of chastity and attacking the sin of incest, the main topic of Book VIII? Not to those mediaeval readers who believed that Ovid had taught *de iusto amore* and had reprehended love which was foolish or wicked.

Knowledge of scholastic literary theory also provides us with new insight into a major issue which has puzzled critics, namely the relationship between Gower's *prologus* and the rest of the *Confessio Amantis*. The *prologus* and Book I 1-92 may be regarded as an 'extrinsic' prologue and an 'intrinsic' prologue respectively, Gower's models being the prologues used in mediaeval commentaries on Scriptural works which pertained to ethics, the Sapiential Books of the Old Testament.

This raises the general question of the relevance of theological literary theory to ME literature, a topic which I have discussed at length elsewhere.[45] Suffice it to say here that Scriptural commentaries such as those produced in the early fourteenth century by 'classicising friars' like Robert Holcot, John Lathbury and Thomas Ringstead, were among the 'best-sellers' of their day.[46] While poets like Gower and Chaucer were not trained theologians, they were very much aware of the major theological issues of their day. The theology of someone like Holcot would certainly have been congenial to Gower and Chaucer, particularly what he had to say about predestination and about the virtues of the 'good pagan'.[47] Quite apart from the theology, these 'classicising' commentaries were of interest to vernacular poets because they contained many extracts from pagan writers, both philosophers and poets.[48] For these and other reasons, there is nothing incongruous in assuming that Gower was familiar with the format and mode of procedure characteristic of commentaries on Scripture.

The differences between the 'extrinsic' and 'intrinsic' kinds of scholastic prologue may now be considered. In xii c. commentaries on *auctores*, the heading *extrinsecus* introduced a discussion of the place in the scheme of human knowledge occupied by the art or science relevant to one's text, while the heading *intrinsecus* introduced a discussion of the text itself. Thus the gloss of an anonymous xii c. grammarian proceeds as follows:

> Extrinsecus autem docteur quando ipsius artis naturam inquirendo docemus quid sit ipsa ars, quid genus eius, que materia, que partes, que species, quod instrumentum, quis artifex, quod officium, quis finis, quare vocetur, quo ordine ipsa sit docenda et discenda...
>
> Intrinsecus autem eam considerantibus primo perspiciendum est que sit auctoris intentio in hoc opere, que sibi utilitas, que cause suscepti laboris sive operis, quis ordo, ad ultimum quis titulus.[49]

In the thirteenth century, Aristotelian science fostered a new kind of 'extrinsic' prologue in which the branch of philosophy relevant to a given text was related to the Aristotelian hierarchy of the sciences. This would be followed by an 'intrinsic' prologue in which *intentio* and *modus procedendi* were discussed. Sometimes the 'extrinsic' prologue was elaborated on the structure of the four causes (efficient cause, formal cause, material cause and final cause); sometimes the four causes appeared instead in the 'intrinsic' prologue.[50]

By the fourteenth century, there were many possible permutations. The *Postilla litteralis* of Nicholas of Lyre, O.F.M. (*c.* 1270-1340) begins with an Aristotelian 'extrinsic' prologue which discusses *sapientia* and *scientia*, the hierarchy of the sciences, and the corresponding hierarchy of the books which teach the various sciences.[51] Lyre states that the philosophers' knowledge pertains only to this present life, whereas sacred Scripture directs us to that blissful afterlife of which the philosophers are ignorant. A science can be said to be more eminent than another in two ways. According to Aristotle's *De Anima*, these are, the greater nobility of one subject as opposed to another, and the greater certainty of one *modus procedendi* as opposed to another. Sacred Scripture, the basis of theology, clearly excels all other knowledge on both these counts. The Bible has for its subject God, the sum of nobility. The Bible also excels in mode of procedure, because in theology the first principles from which one proceeds are immutable truths. Theology, the science which seeks the highest wisdom, is most properly called *sapientia*. The *sapientia* of catholics and saints, which is Holy Writ, is to be distinguished from the lesser *sapientia* of the philosophers. What may manifestly be concluded from Scripture is to be accepted as true; what is repugnant to it is simply false. Then Lyre moves to an 'intrinsic' prologue, in which he describes his personal purpose and his *modus procedendi* in writing the commentary.[52] He has provided us with parallel discussions of the *intentio* and *modus* of the divine *auctor*, God, and the human writer, himself.

Whereas Lyre, in this general introduction to his complete *Postilla*, was concerned with *sapientia* as theological truth, commentators on the Sapiential Books were concerned with the *sapientia* of the philosophers. Solomon (traditionally regarded as the *auctor* of all the Sapiential Books) was held to be a *sapiens* in such philosophical disciplines as politics and ethics, and in the commentaries this wisdom was related to an Aristotelian definition of *sapientia*. For example, in the 'extrinsic' prologue to his very popular commentary on the Book of Wisdom, Robert Holcot, O.P. (died *c.* 1349) explains how all the human arts and sciences contribute to God's glory.[53] Holcot lists the four virtuous dispositions which God, the divine *auctor*, requires in his audience. The first is simplicity of heart. A man cannot serve two masters. Therefore, as Matthew iv 10 says, 'praise the Lord God and seek Him alone'. The second virtue is humble judgement. *Sapientia* puffs up, if charity does not assist. Thirdly, the divine *auctor* requires in a listener the virtue of accurate reporting: what is said without fiction must be repeated and communicated without malice (Wisdom vii 13). Solomon and Seneca agree on this point. As Seneca puts it, wisdom is a noble possession of the soul which enables its owner to scorn greed, and when it is distributed it grows and increases. Holcot adds that it is the office of the *sapiens* to instruct the less wise and courteously to support the uninformed: perhaps he had in mind the catch-phrase which Thomas Aquinas had derived from Aristotle, *sapientis est ordinare* ('it is the function of the wise man to order').[54] Fourthly, the listener must practise what he hears in the proper fashion. Once again, *auctoritates* from both pagan and Scriptural sources are quoted to prove the point. Holcot then moves on to state the supremacy of sacred Scripture over philosophical wisdom. Having done this, he feels free to concentrate on philosophical wisdom.

Holcot's 'intrinsic' prologue focusses on the Book of Wisdom itself:

> Circa librum istum, qui liber Sapientiae nuncupatur, sunt in principio tria notanda. Primo est de eius nomine, secundum de eius autore, tertium de eius fine.[55]

The *nomen libri* is 'Wisdom', and this means many things to many men. For the peripatetics, *sapientia* was an intellectual and speculative power, the most noble of the intellectual virtues. Thus, Aristotle says that the *sapiens* seeks to know things in their causes and in certitude. Certain theologians, Holcot continues, take wisdom as a supernatural or infused gift, by which a man may gain knowledge of things human and divine. Yet another opinion is held by the Stoics and by moral philosophers such as Socrates, Seneca and Boethius, who regard wisdom as a collection of intellectual and moral virtues, and thus the *sapiens* is a kind of virtuoso philosopher. It is concluded that this must be the view of Solomon also, because his book does not treat of one moral or intellectual virtue in particular, but of philosophical virtue in general. Holcot then proceeds to his second 'intrinsic' heading.[56] There are various opinions concerning the authorship of Wisdom: was Solomon the author, or was it Philo Judaeus? Solomon is eventually identified as the principal author of Wisdom, and Philo as its editor. Concerning the third 'extrinsic' heading (*finis*), Holcot explains that Solomon's end or ultimate objective was the encouragement of a certain disposition in men. The first aspect of this disposition concerns civil government. Cicero is quoted on the bestial life of men before the establishment of good laws. The Orpheus myth as recounted by Boethius points the same moral. Wisdom is the basis of any good state, hence Plato claimed that philosophers should be kings and kings philosophers. The second aspect of Solomon's intended disposition concerns the expulsion of one's enemies and the fortification of one's cities. Because old men are wise, the great Alexander had no general in his army under the age of sixty years; they seemed to be senators rather than soldiers. Aristotle and Solomon agree that sapience is better than strength, and that a prudent man is greater than a powerful man. The third and final aspect of the recommended disposition concerns correction. Proverbs xxix 15 states that reproof and the rod teach wisdom: a child left to himself will bring his mother to shame.

Holcot's prologues have been discussed at some length in order to make clear the extent to which, by the early fourteenth century, commentaries on the Sapiential Books had become repositories of Scriptural and pagan *auctoritates* on such common subjects as ethics and politics. Both Aristotle and Solomon had used their natural reason; they were philosophers and not theologians.[57] Moreover, they were interested in the same things (at least, according to the commentators). The juxtaposition of Solomon and Aristotle in late-mediaeval exegesis is more understandable if one remembers that Aristotle was considered to possess a considerable authority in many of those matters raised by Solomon. Hence there was increasing recourse to secular *auctoritates* on commentaries on the Sapiential Books, what Miss Smalley has called a 'secularization of sources'.[58] The assumed justification for this seems to have been that the Sapiential Books discussed pagan beliefs which had to be clarified from pagan sources, and that they taught natural science, ethics and politics, subjects in which pagan writers were held to have considerable expertise.[59] Solomon was supported by the pagan philosophers (as our analysis of Holcot's prologues has shown) and indeed by the pagan poets, including Ovid.[60] These *auctores* could 'come together' because it was believed that they operated on a similar plane. Ovid's works were supposed to pertain to ethics –

> Utilitas permaxima est, quoniam perlecto hoc libro, et pudice castitatem observare studeant, et impudice et inceste castitati adhereant ... Ethice supponitur quia tractat de moribus in docendo bonos mores et reprehendo malos.[61]

– and so were the Sapiential Books, as this example from Hugh of St Cher's commentary on Ecclesiasticus makes clear:

> Intentio auctoris est nos instruere de virtutibus et exemplis Sanctorum informare: vt eos imitando, cum ipsis mereamur vitam aeternam ... Huius libri vtilitas est virtutum cognitio ... Supponitur autem liber iste totaliter morali philosophie: quia totus est de moribus sive virtutibus.[62]

Here we find the rationale for two types of assimilation undertaken by Gower. First, in Book VII pagan and Scriptural *auctoritates* on common subjects (natural philosophy, politics, ethics) are assimilated. Gower's ostentatious use of Aristotle as a source of philosophical wisdom throughout Book VII has already been mentioned. The expertise of Solomon is consulted also, for in Solomon one may see the thing most necessary for a worthy king, namely wisdom:

> In Salomon a man mai see
> What thing of most necessite
> Unto a worthi king belongeth.
> What he his kingdom underfongeth,
> God bad him chese what he wolde,
> And seide him that he have scholde
> What he wolde axe, as of o thing.
> And he, which was a newe king,
> Forth therupon his bone preide
> To god, and in this wise he seide:
> 'O king, be whom that I schal regne,
> Yif me wisdom, that I my regne,
> Forth with thi poeple which I have,
> To thin honour mai kepe and save'.
>
> (VII 3891-904)

Commentaries on the Sapiential Books were read as repositories of philosophical wisdom, and it is tempting to speculate that Gower's practice in Book VII was influenced by such commentaries.

Secondly, politics (the main *pars philosophiae* of the *prologus*, Book VII and the epilogue) are assimilated to ethics (the main *pars philosophiae* of the rest of the *Confessio*). The beginning of the *Confessio* resembles a commentary on a Sapiential Book, which first treats of the 'extrinsic' aspects of the book in the context of a discussion of wisdom in general, and then moves on to discuss the book itself under such 'intrinsic' headings as *intentio auctoris, nomen, materia* and *utilitas*. Gower's *prologus* is an 'extrinsic' prologue about *sapientia;* the treatise which follows is about *amor:*

> For this prologue is so assised
> That it to wisdom al belongeth ...
> What the prologue is so despended,
> This bok schal afterward ben ended
> Of love ...
> *(Prologus 66-75)*

Gower links *sapientia* and *amor* through the donnish joke that love 'many a wys man hath put under'. Hence it seems fitting that a *prologus* on wisdom should be followed by a treatise on love. Gower's declared intention is 'in som part' to advise 'the wyse man': hence the *prologus* warns of the ways in which the Church, the commons and the earthly rulers have ceased to follow wisdom. Gower admits that only God has the wisdom necessary for full understanding of worldly fortune:

> ...this prologue is so assised
> That it to wisdom al belongeth;
> What wysman that it underfongeth,
> He schal drawe into remembrance
> The fortune of this worldes chance,
> The which noman in his persone
> Mai knowe, bot the god al one.
> *(Prologus 66-72)*

This point is echoed at the end of the *prologus:*

> And now nomore,
> As forto speke of this matiere,
> Which non bot only god may stiere.
> (1086-8)

In his 'intrinsic' prologue (Book I 1-92) Gower proceeds to explain precisely what is within his compass:

> I may noght strecche up to the hevene
> Min hand, ne setten al in evene
> This world, which evere is in balance:
> It stant noght in my suffisance
> So grete thinges to compasse,
> Bot I mot lete it overpasse
> And treten upon othre thinges.

173

> Forthi the Stile of my writinges
> Fro this day forth I thenke change
> And speke of thing is noght so strange,
> Which every kinde hath upon honde,
> And whereupon the world mot stonde,
> And hath don sithen it began,
> And schal whil ther is any man;
> And that is love, of which I mene
> To trete, as after schal be sene.
>
> (I 1-16)

Thus Gower admits that he cannot solve all the problems which he canvassed in the *prologus*. A human *auctor* cannot reorganise the present world in accordance with those principles of order which the divine *auctor*, God, followed in His creation, but he can impose an appropriate order on his own creation, his treatise on love. The way in which Gower explains what is within his compass parallels the way in which a commentator like Holcot would move from *sapientia* in general to the particular branch of *sapientia* proper to the text, from the *causa causarum*, God, to the *causae* of the text.

The form of Gower's 'intrinsic' prologue is made absolutely clear by the Latin commentary, which employs the usual 'intrinsic' headings:

> Postquam in Prologo tractatum hactenus existit, qualiter hodierne condicionis diuisio caritatis dileccionem superauit, *intendit auctor* ad presens suum libellum, cuius *nomen* Confessio Amantis nuncupatur, componere de illo amore, a quo non solum humanum genus, sed eciam cuncta animancia naturaliter subiciuntur. Et quia nonnulli amantes ultra quam expedit desiderii passionibus crebro stimulantur, *materia libri* per totum super hiis specialius diffunditur [italics mine].[63]

The heading *modus agendi* is not mentioned in the Latin commentary, but it is discussed in the English text. Gower proposes to teach wisdom through *exempla* – just as, according to the commentators, both Ovid and Solomon had done:

> ... in good feith this wolde I rede,
> That every man ensample take
> Of wisdom which him is betake,
> And that he wot of good aprise
> To teche it forth, for such emprise
> Is forto preise; and therfore I
> Woll wryte and schewe al openly
> How love and I togedre mette,
> Wherof the world ensample fette
> Mai after this, whan I am go,
> Of thilke unsely jolif wo ...
>
> (I 78-88)

The *utilitas* of the work is indicated in the epilogue: obviously Gower wanted to leave his reader with an assurance about the moral perspective in which his *principalis materia* had been placed. After Venus takes her leave (VIII 2941-6) he proceeds to pray for the state of England, to warn of the evil of the disunity of the land, and to summarise the duties of a king. We have returned to the concerns of the *prologus* and the *de regimine principum* of Book VII. Gower is reminding us that his work contains some unambiguous 'lore'. Then he stresses the fact that he also has examined his 'lust' from a moral standpoint. Part of the 'intrinsic' prologue (I 21-8) is echoed in the statement that love can encourage a man to act contrary to reason and prohibit him from acting wisely (see VIII 3143-51).

Gower is not saying that *amor* and 'vertu moral' are incompatible – quite the contrary. He has taken pains to teach *de iusto amore,* to praise chaste married love and to condemn vicious love. Some kinds of love can be irrational and unwise; by contrast, charity, the divine love, is wholly consonant with wisdom (see VIII 3162-72). The poet is not retracting his concern with *amor* (as C. S. Lewis suggested)[64] but is merely accepting that *amor* is limited, that *caritas* is intrinsically superior to *amor.* In the body of his text he wrote not as a theologian but as a philosopher, as a *sapiens* in the subject-areas of ethics and politics. These disciplines, as parts of practical philosophy, are intrinsically inferior to the 'higher science' of theology. In sum, Gower had to provide for his *Confessio* what mediaeval scholars had provided for the works of Ovid and Solomon, a clear statement of its moral *utilitas.*

The didactic aspect of the *Confessio* is emphasised not only in the *prologus,* Book VII and the epilogue but also throughout the Latin commentary. This commentary is in such complete sympathy with the moral *intentio* professed in the English text that we need not doubt that Gower himself provided it. Here I wish to discuss only one aspect of this commentary, the way in which it describes Gower's use of *personae* in the *Confessio.* This may have been influenced by the common scholastic method of analysing *personae,* good examples of which are provided by expositions of Solomon's use of *personae* in the Sapiential Books. For example, in his very popular commentary on Ecclesiastes, St Bonaventure tackled the problem of Solomon's stance in that work.[65] Only the work of a good author has authority: if Solomon was a wicked man, can his work have any authority? It is explained that Ecclesiastes was written not by a sinner but by a penitent man looking back over his sins and regretting them. Sometimes he speaks in his own person, sometimes in the persons of others (*in persona aliorum*). When, for example, he speaks in the person of the foolish man, he does not approve of this foolishness but abhors it; when he speaks as a wise man his words are directly conducive to correct behaviour. Moreover, Solomon was careful to spell out his good intention at the end of Ecclesiastes. The reader must appreciate the work in its entirety; if he does so, he will find that his author has been entirely consistent.

Similarly, the commentary on the *Confessio Amantis* is determined to prove that Gower is a good author. A clear distinction is made between what Gower says in his own person (the *sapiens* of the *prologus* and epilogue) and what he says in the persons of those who are subject to love (including Amans and Confessor). The commentary accompanying the 'intrinsic' prologue tells us that the author is going to 'feign himself' to be a lover and to speak *in persona aliorum:*

> Hic quasi in persona aliorum, quos amor alligat, fingens se auctor esse Amantem, varias eorum passiones variis huius libri distinccionibus per singula scribere proponit.[66]

Similarly, at the end of the treatise the commentary heralds the return of the author in his own person:

> Hic in fine recapitulat super hoc quod in principio libri primi promisit se in amoris causa specialius tractaturum. Concludit enim quod omnis amoris delectacio extra caritatem nichil est. Qui autem manet in caritate, in deo manet.[67]

In claiming that the pleasure of every kind of love except charity amounts to nothing, the commentary goes farther than the English text which (as has been suggested above) recognises the limitations of earthly love and the vices which its abuse can bring, but certainly does not condemn it outright. The commentary seems anxious to assure the reader that, although Amans and Confessor are the servants of love, John Gower is interested in both love and wisdom; that while the work is mainly about love, love has been placed in the context of wisdom. In short, the Latin commentary is an integral part of Gower's work. When read with the English text, it emphasises the singleness of the writer's purpose and the unity of his materials.

Our main conclusions may now be summarised as follows. Gower's *Confessio Amantis* seems to work by assimilation of materials which, although they may appear heterogeneous to the modern reader, would have been regarded as quite compatible by the learned mediaeval reader. Diverse *exempla amantum* are brought together: some commend chaste love while others warn of unchaste love, thus teaching a quite consistent morality. Moreover, pagan and Christian materials on common subjects are combined, Gower's justification being the widespread belief that 'the clerk Ovide' and 'Salomon' shared many assumptions about subject-areas and modes of scientific procedure. Finally, the *materia* of 'policie' is assimilated to the *principalis materia* of love: this is acceptable because Gower believed that his *exempla amantum* pertained to ethics, and deliberately widened his moral perspective to include politics. Thus, the work of 'moral Gower' reflects the strong moral bias of the literary theory of his day.

ACKNOWLEDGEMENTS

I am grateful to the following institutions for permission to print brief extracts from MSS: The Bodleian Library, Oxford; Balliol College, Oxford; the Bern Burgerbibliothek.

NOTES

[1] See, for example, the criticisms by Nevill Coghill *The Poet Chaucer* 2nd edn. (Oxford 1967) p. 86, and D. Pearsall 'Gower's Narrative Art' *PMLA* LXXXI (1966) 477.

[2] C. S. Lewis *The Allegory of Love* (Oxford 1936) p. 199. However, I cannot accept Lewis's suggestion that 'the key to Gower's solution ... is to be found in Andreas [Capellanus]'.

[3] For the argument that late-mediaeval exegesis contains much viable literary theory see A. J. Minnis 'Discussions of "Authorial Role" and "Literary Form" in Late-Medieval Scriptural Exegesis' *Beiträge zur Geschichte der deutschen Sprache und Literatur* XCIX (1977) 37-65, hereafter referred to as '"Authorial Role" and "Literary Form"'.

[4] A full account of Gower's literary roles is provided in my thesis 'Medieval Discussion of the Role of the Author: a preliminary survey, with particular reference to Chaucer and Gower' (unpubl. Ph.D. thesis, Queen's University of Belfast 1976).

[5] Book VII of the *Confessio* is often dismissed as a mere digression: *e.g.*, Lewis describes it as a digression 'on a large scale' about 'a general scheme of education' (*op. cit.* pp. 213-14).

[6] See N. Callan 'Thyn Owne Book: a note on Chaucer, Gower and Ovid' *RES* XXII (1946) 272; J. B. Dwyer 'Gower's *Mirour* and its French Sources' *SP* XLVIII (1951) 491-3; M. Wickert *Studien zu John Gower* (Cologne 1953) p. 181 n. 17; R. Hazelton '*The Manciple's Tale:* Parody and Critique' *JEGP* LXII (1963) 23; J. Wimsatt 'The Sources of Chaucer's "Seys and Alcyone"' *MÆ* XXXVI (1967) 239 n. 24.

[7] The difficulty of establishing precisely which source provided a particular detail is manifest in modern attempts to establish Chaucer's debt to the 'Mediaeval Ovid': see J. L. Lowes 'Chaucer and the *Ovide moralisé*' *PMLA* XXXIII (1918) 302-25; S. B. Meech 'Chaucer and the *Ovide moralisé*: a further study' *PMLA* XLVI (1931) 182-204; 'Chaucer and an Italian Translation of the *Heroides*' *PMLA* XLV (1930) 110-28. More recently, Miss M. C. Edwards has shown that the argument for Chaucer's use of an Italian translation of the *Heroides* (as argued by Meech) must depend on verbal echoes alone: the details which Meech cites as proof could also have been obtained from a commentary on the *Heroides*. See M. C. Edwards 'A Study of Six Characters in Chaucer's *Legend of Good Women* with reference to medieval scholia on Ovid's *Heroides*' (unpubl. B. Litt. thesis, Oxford 1970) p. 113. A similar problem exists in establishing precisely which sources Gower used for his Ovidiana: see C. Mainzer 'Gower's use of the "Mediaeval Ovid"' *MÆ* XLI (1972) 215-16, 221, 223.

[8] Mainzer 'Gower's use of the "Mediaeval Ovid"' pp. 215-22.

[9] *Ibid.* p. 215.

[10] *Ibid.* p. 223.

[11] From Bern, Burgerbibliothek MS 411 (xii c. - from Orléans?) *cit.* Edwards *op. cit.* p. 28. Edwards (p. 41) argues that this commentary belongs to a class of text known in xiv c. England. For her grouping of commentaries into classes of text, see pp. 27, 41. For the class of text which Chaucer may have known, see p. 114.

[12] *Republic* X 604-7, in *Ancient Literary Criticism: the Principal Texts in New Translations* ed. D. A. Russell and M. Winterbottom (Oxford 1972) pp. 72-4.

[13] For discussion, see A. J. Minnis 'Literary Theory in Theologians' Discussions of *Formae Tractandi*' *New Literary History* XI (1979) 133-45.

[14] This view is described more fully in the second chapter of my book *Medieval Theory of Authorship: Scholastic Literary Attitudes in the Later Middle Ages* (London, 1984; 2nd edn. Aldershot, 1988).

[15] *PL* CXVI 196C. A. Wilmart thought this commentary was by Anselm of Laon, a suggestion which has found little support. For a recent discussion see V. I. J. Flint 'Some Notes on the Early Twelfth Century Commentaries on the Psalms' *Réch. théol. anc. et med.* XXXVIII (1971) 80-8.

[16] E. Vinaver ed. *The Works of Sir Thomas Malory* 2nd edn. (Oxford 1971) p. xv.

[17] See, e.g., G. R. Owst *Literature and Pulpit in Medieval England* 2nd edn. (Oxford 1966) p. 208; J. H. Fisher *John Gower, Moral Philosopher and Friend of Chaucer* (London 1965) p. 139.

[18] The most comprehensive study is M. C. Edwards *op. cit.* All my Chaucer references are to F. N. Robinson ed. *The Works of Geoffrey Chaucer* 2nd edn. (Oxford 1957).

[19] For full discussion of late-mediaeval notions of *forma* see '"Authorial Role" and "Literal Sense"' pp. 41, 52-64.

[20] *Heroides* XI, in *Ovid: Heroides and Amores* ed. G. Showerman (Loeb 1947) pp. 133-41.

[21] Printed from Cod. Vat. Lat. 2792 by F. Ghisalberti 'Medieval Biographies of Ovid' *Journal of the*

Warburg and Courtauld Institutes IX (1946) 44. For the argument that this commentary belongs to a class of text known in xiv c. England, see M. C. Edwards *op. cit.* p. 41.

[22] See the extracts from *accessus* quoted on pp. 207, 214.

[23] G. C. Macaulay ed. *The English Works of John Gower* EETS ES 81-2 (Oxford 1900-1) I 321-5. All Gower references are to this edition.

[24] *Heroides* I 1-2, 57-8, 81-114, in *ed. cit.* pp. 10, 14, 16-18.

[25] Cf. Macaulay's note on ll. 147ff., in *English Works* I 502.

[26] From Munich Clm 1947, printed by R. B. C. Huygens *Accessus ad auctores; Bernard d'Utrecht; Conrad d'Hirsau* (Leiden 1970) p. 31. The *scholia* on the *Heroides* printed by Huygens must be treated with caution in the context of English literature: two of the MSS containing them were produced in the Bavarian monastery of Tegernsee. Edwards claims that these *scholia* did not form part of the 'mainstream' of mediaeval commentary on the *Heroides: op. cit.* pp. 41-2.

[27] Oxford, Balliol College MS 143 fol. 4ʳ. This MS did not reach England until the mid-fifteenth century, but its commentary seems to belong to a class of text present in xiv c. England: see Edwards *op. cit.* p. 27.

[28] Oxford, Bodleian Library MS Canon. Class. Lat. 1 fol. 2ʳ.

[29] See C. Mainzer *op. cit.* p. 223. *E.g.,* it occurs in Bern, Burgerbibliothek MS 411; Oxford, Balliol College MS 143; Florence, Laurenziana MS Plut. 36. 28; Munich, Clm 818: see Edwards *op. cit.* pp. 95-6.

[30] See *Heroides* II 9-42, 91-102, 131-144, in *ed. cit.* pp. 20-2, 26-8, 30.

[31] S. B. Meech argues that these details are from Filippo's Italian translation of the *Heroides: op. cit.* pp. 119ff.

[32] Edwards believes that Chaucer shares the commentators' attitude to Phyllis, but I cannot accept her argument that Chaucer wants us to see how Phyllis 'compounds sin with sin' (*op. cit.* p. 105). All Edwards's evidence from Ovid-commentaries rather indicates the considerable contrast between Chaucer's attitude to Phyllis and the commentators' attitude. Chaucer appears to be deliberately avoiding the moral tone of the commentators – and here he differs from Gower.

[33] J. A. W. Bennett 'Gower's "Honeste Love"', in *Patterns of Love and Courtesy* ed. J. Lawlor (London 1966) p. 110. As Professor Bennett was the first critic to appreciate how Gower treats *amor* in a moral way, his study provided the basis for subsequent discussions of the unity of the *Confessio Amantis.*

[34] For the argument that the *Legend* is really a satire against women, see H. C. Goddard 'Chaucer's *Legend of Good Women' JEGP* VII (1908) 87-129; VIII (1909) 47-111. This argument was refuted by J. L. Lowes 'Is Chaucer's *Legend of Good Women* a travesty?' *ibid.* pp. 513-69.

[35] From Paris, BN MS Lat. 7994, *cit.* Ghisalberti *op. cit.* p. 46. According to Edwards, this commentary belongs to a class of text which existed in xiv c. England: *op. cit.* p. 41.

[36] 'incesti habet exemplum per Helenam, quae Paridi nupsit legitimo viro suo sumpta Menelao': Huygens *op. cit.* p. 31.

[37] For the mediaeval popularity of the story of Apollonius, see P. Goolden ed. *The Old English Apollonius of Tyre* (Oxford 1958); J. Raith *Die alt- und mittelenglischen Apollonius-Bruchstücke* (Munich 1956).

[38] Cf. R. A. Peck *Confessio Amantis: John Gower* (New York 1968) p. xxiii. For a fuller discussion of the problem see H. A. Kelly *Love and Marriage in the Age of Chaucer* (Cornell 1975) pp. 136-46.

[39] *English Works* II p. 480.

[40] *Aristotle: The Politics* transl. T. A. Sinclair (Harmondsworth 1962) p. 21.

[41] The *Politics,* although it had been translated by William of Moerbeke c. 1260 and commented on by Albertus Magnus and St Thomas Aquinas, had little influence on xiii c. scholars. Miss Smalley was unable to find an exact quotation from it in a xiii c. Bible-commentary: see 'Some Latin commentaries on the Sapiential Books in the late thirteenth and early fourteenth centuries' *Arch. d'hist. doct. et litt. du moyen age* XVIII (1950) 121. In the fourteenth century the *Politics* became more important. Exegetes undertook the task of harmonising its teaching with the Scriptures: Smalley p. 121. Nicole Oresme (d. 1382) translated it into French: see A. D. Menut ed. *Maistre N. Oresme, Le Livre de Politiques* Trans. American Philosophical Soc. n.s. 60 (1970). However, there is nothing about politics in the *Confessio* which Gower could not have taken from Brunetto's *Tresor* and the pseudo-Aristotelian *Secreta Secretorum:* cf. *English Works* II 522.

[42] *English Works* II 522.

[43] *English Works* II 521-2.

⁴⁴ For the significance of the *Secreta Secretorum* and its numerous translations see M. A. Manzalaoui 'The *Secreta secretorum* in English Thought and Literature from the Fourteenth Century to the Seventeenth Century, with a preliminary survey of the origins of the *Secreta*' (unpubl. D. Phil. thesis, Oxford 1954).

⁴⁵ See my article 'The Influence of Academic Prologues on the Prologues and Literary Attitudes of Late-Medieval English Writers', forthcoming in *Mediaeval Studies.*

⁴⁶ See B. Smalley *English Friars and Antiquity in the Early Fourteenth Century* (Oxford 1960) pp. 141-2, 214-15, 222-3.

⁴⁷ For Holcot's views on these subjects, see *ibid.* pp. 185-93; also H. Oberman '"Facientibus quod in se est Deus non denegat gratiam": Robert Holcot O.P. and the beginnings of Luther's theology' *Harvard Theological Review* LV (1962) 317-42 (especially pp. 317-30). Chaucer's interest in such subjects is manifested by his translation of Boethius, *Troilus and Criseyde, The Knight's Tale, etc.* For a summary of Gower's views on predestination see *Confessio Amantis, prologus* 529-84; for his interest in 'olde Philosophres wise', see Book VII.

⁴⁸ *E.g.*, Robert Henryson took the *moralitas* of his *Orpheus and Eurydice* from the Boethius-commentary composed by Nicholas Trevet, perhaps the best classical scholar among the 'classicising friars': see Henryson's own statement in H. H. Wood ed. *The Poems and Fables* 2nd edn. (Edinburgh 1958) p. 142. Chaucer seems to have made use of Trevet's commentary in translating Boethius: see K. O. Petersen 'Chaucer and Trivet' *PMLA* XVIII (1903) 173-93. In his *La Male Regle*, Thomas Hoccleve takes the story of Ulysses and the Mermaids from Holcot's Wisdom-commentary: see Hoccleve's own statement in F. J. Furnivall and I. Gollancz edd. *The Minor Poems* EETS ES 61 and 73 (Oxford repr. 1970) 33. Chaucer seems to have known Holcot's Wisdom-commentary: see R. A. Pratt 'Some Latin Sources of the Nonnes Preest on Dreams' *Speculum* LII (1977) 538-70.

⁴⁹ Printed by R. W. Hunt 'The Introductions to the "Artes" in the Twelfth Century', in *Studia medievalia in honorem R. M. Martin* (Bruges 1948) pp. 100-1.

⁵⁰ For discussion of the 'four causes' in a literary context, see *ibid.* pp. 107-10. See further '"Authorial Role" and "Literary Form"' pp. 40-1.

⁵¹ See the *Generalis prologus* printed in *Biblia sacra cum Glossa ordinaria et Postilla Nicolai Lyrani* (Lugduni 1589) I (unfoliated).

⁵² *Prologus specialis de intentione auctoris et modo procedendi*, printed *Biblia sacra* I.

⁵³ R. *Holkoth in librum Sapientiae* (Basel 1586) pp. 1-6.

⁵⁴ See *S. Thomae Aquinatis in Metaphysicam Aristotelis commentaria* 3rd edn. (Marietti 1935) pp. 14-15. Cf. the beginning of Aquinas's commentary on the *Ethics (St. Thomas Aquinas: Commentary on the Nicomachean Ethics* transl. C. I. Litzinger (Chicago 1964), I 6).

⁵⁵ Holcot *In lib. Sap.* p. 6. Holcot followed a similar procedure in his commentary on Ecclesiasticus: a general discussion of *sapientia* precedes a discussion of *auctor* and *divisio libri.* See Holcot *super librum Ecclesiastici* (Venice 1509) fols. 2ʳ-4ʳ. Another example of this procedure occurs in the prolegomena to the Lamentations-commentary of John Lathbury (d. 1362), printed *Latteburius in threnos Ieremiae* (Oxford 1482) (unfoliated).

⁵⁶ Holcot *op. cit.* pp. 6-9.

⁵⁷ See B. Smalley 'Some thirteenth-century commentaries on the Sapiential Books' *Dominican Studies* III (1950) 267-8. For the use of natural reason by 'the philosophers' see M.-D. Chénu 'Les "Philosophes" dans la philosophie chrétienne médiévale' *Revue des sciences phil. et théol.* XXVI (1937) 28-31, and *Introduction à l'étude de S. Thomas d'Aquin* 2nd edn., Univ. de Montreal, Pub. de l'Inst. d'Étud. Méd. 11 (Montreal and Paris 1954) p. 116. In the early fourteenth century, discussion of pagan reason revolved around the thorny issue of what could be known *ex puris naturalibus* (in purely natural conditions, without the aid of divine grace): see Oberman *op. cit.* pp. 317-30; *Archbishop Thomas Bradwardine: a fourteenth-century Augustinian* (Utrecht 1958) pp. 35-42, 47, 142, 149-55, etc; *The Harvest of Medieval Theology* (Michigan 1967) pp. 45-50, 128-9, 138-9, 156, 211; P. Vignaux *Justification et prédestination au XIVe siècle* Bibl. de l'École des Hautes Études, sciences relig. 48 (Paris 1934) pp. 115-27.

⁵⁸ Smalley 'Some Latin commentaries' p. 116 (note 41).

⁵⁹ Smalley 'Some Latin commentaries' pp. 103, 114; 'Some thirteenth century commentaries' pp. 267-8. The notion that pagan beliefs had to be clarified from pagan sources is manifest in the early-xiv c. commentaries on Augustine's *De Civitate Dei:* see Smalley *English Friars and Antiquity* pp. 62-3, 104-8, 129-31.

⁶⁰ For discussion of the use of Ovid made by the 'classicising friars', see Smalley *English Friars and Antiquity* pp. 102, 106, 152, 155-6, 189, 226. For a general survey, see S. Viarre *La survie d'Ovide dans la littérature scientifique des XIIe et XIIIe siècles* (Poitiers 1966).

⁶¹ Printed by Ghisalberti *op. cit.* pp. 44-5.

⁶² *Hugonis Cardinalis Postilla* (Paris 1530-45) III fol. 153ʳ.

⁶³ *English Works* I 35-6. Gower's method of using 'extrinsic' and 'intrinsic' prologues along with a Latin commentary may be contrasted with the practice of Thomas Usk in his *Testament of Love*. In his general prologue, Usk treats of the 'extrinsic' and 'intrinsic' aspects of his book together:

> Wherof Aristotle, in the boke *de Animalibus*, saith to natural philosophers: 'it is a greet lyking in love of knowinge their creatour; and also in knowinge of causes in kyndely thinges'. Considred, forsoth, the formes of kyndly thinges and the shap, a greet kindely love me shulde have to the werkman that hem made. The crafte of a werkman is shewed in the werke. Herfore, truly, the philosophers, with a lyvely studie, many noble thinges right precious and worthy to memory writen; and by a greet swetande travayle to us leften of causes of the propertees in natures of thinges ... And bycause this book shal be of love, and the pryme causes of steringe in that doinge, with passions and diseses for wantinge of desyre, I wil that this book be cleped THE TESTAMENT OF LOVE.

(*Chaucerian and other pieces* ed. W. W. Skeat (Oxford 1897) p. 3). In his prologue to Book II, Usk discusses the final cause in general and the final cause of his book in particular: see p. 49.

⁶⁴ Lewis *op. cit.* p. 218.

⁶⁵ *S. Bonaventurae Opera omnia* (Quaracchi 1882-1902) VI 8.

⁶⁶ *English Works* I 37.

⁶⁷ *Ibid.* II 474-5.

NATURAL LAW AND
JOHN GOWER'S *CONFESSIO AMANTIS*

KURT OLSSON

John Gower's frequent use of the concept of natural law in the *Confessio Amantis* provides a rich example of the adaptation of legal topoi to the literary concerns of writers in late medieval England. In his sources Gower finds various, sometimes opposed ideas about the *jus naturae*, and in the ambiguity of the term and the multiple meanings assigned to it he finds a means to organize material he has gathered for this vast encyclopedic work. That the poet knew so much about so complex a subject perhaps will not surprise us, for his knowledge of law has been a common topic in writings about him from the Renaissance to the present. But the range of his knowledge of this concept has never been adequately shown. Recent critics, though they note the importance of natural law in the *Confessio*, commonly assume that the term meant only one or two things to Gower. Such is not the case. In order to enlarge our sense of what the concept for him includes, in the first part of this inquiry I shall identify five separate meanings of the *jus naturae* that he inherited from others and introduced in his poem.

There is value in seeing the scope of Gower's knowledge of natural law, for it offers one more proof of his gift as an encyclopedic poet. But there are other reasons for examining his treatment of the subject. Gower is not content merely to collect and present ideas he has found in legal texts. He also seeks to unify them in a full, coherent statement, and this, though complicating his task, also makes the outcome more noteworthy. Some of his ideas were, even when isolated, a source of controversy in medieval legal history; when combined, they often gave rise to extended debate and increasingly complex and intricate arguments. Gower restates the problem of the *jus naturae* in the *Confessio*, and despite the range of meanings he introduces, he seeks simplicity of argument as well as richness. His fiction demands simplicity especially because its main character, the pupil Amans, is a slow and reluctant learner. But the fiction also allows Gower to enrich his statement about *jus naturale* because the education that fiction recounts is both intensive and extensive.

In the frame narrative, we may recall, a frustrated Amans asks Venus to bestow on him "som wele" in his amorous suit, but the goddess insists that he first confess his sins to her priest, Genius. Through the ensuing dialogue, which occupies virtually all eight books of the poem, Genius defines the sins, tells illustrative tales, offers Amans "lore" on a wide variety of subjects, and hears the confession. On certain topics in the priest's instruction, more is offered than Amans seems to need, but on other subjects less is said than seems appropriate in a compendium of narrative and lore. The *Confessio* is not merely a fiction about a confession, not merely a collection of tales and ideas. Its various elements coalesce in the poet's sustained argument involving *jus naturale*. Little by little Genius ties together the various meanings of the *jus naturae* he has introduced, and, as slowly as Amans seems to require, he adopts in his statement other terms and concepts with equally impressive medieval ancestries: his many references to charity, grace, Fortune, and "honeste" (*honestum* or *honestas*), to name but a few of these concepts, add clarity and depth to his argument concerning the *jus naturae*. Thus, in looking at Gower particularly, we may see how the concept of natural law can affect the shaping of a long medieval poem, and how a poem can enrich the history of a major concept. After introducing the five meanings Gower assigns to the *jus naturae*, I shall describe in a second part of this paper some of the basic features of the argument of the *Confessio*.

1. The *jus naturae* as the law of animal nature. As defined by the Roman jurist Ulpian and codified by Justinian in the *Corpus iuris civilis*,

Natural law is what nature has taught all animals, for this law is not proper to the human race, but to all living beings. . . . From it descends the union of male and female, which we call marriage; from it the begetting and rearing of offspring.[1]

Natural law in this sense governs or affects every aspect of sentient life, and in the course of his poem Gower will note the extent of its influence. His first concern, however, is with sexual desire or the love that "every kinde hath upon honde" (I.11).[2] In a marginal gloss he announces this as the theme of his work and uses terms reminiscent of Ulpian to describe it: "The author intends in his present book, called the *Confessio Amantis*, to write concerning that love by which not only the human race, but also animals of whatever kind are naturally subjected."[3]

Among late medieval poets Gower is certainly not unique in applying the law of animal nature to love—Jean de Meun, for example, had done so in the *Roman de la Rose* [4]—but Gower goes beyond such writers in exploring issues raised by glossators, decretists, and theologians who comment on Ulpian's definition. One such issue was the controversy generated by

182

Ulpian's statement that "hinc descendit maris atque feminae coniugatio, quam nos matrimonium appellamus." How can marriage be judged a part of the *jus naturae* when the latter is what Nature has taught all animals? Gower, like writers before him who also take Ulpian's idea seriously, answers this question by a refinement. Near the end of the poem he is concerned with *conjugatio*, sexual desire, and marriage when he writes,

> The Madle is mad for the femele,
> Bot where as on desireth fele,
> That nedeth noght be weie of kinde.
>
> (7.4215–17)

In the large context of this passage—a section of the work explaining chastity—the poet resolves the specific problem of whether "habere plures est contra naturam" by making a distinction between nature as animal nature and nature as reason. Reason identifies what is fitting or "honeste" for mankind: it promotes married love and teaches a man to perceive his wife as "to him wel more honeste / Than other thing which is unknowe" (7.4224–25). The term "honeste" is basic to the developing argument of the *Confessio*. As J. A. W. Bennett has shown, Gower frequently applies it to love in marriage.[5] In a large context, however, the poet uses it to reinforce his distinction between the laws of sentient and rational nature. Thus, sexual love is a "lawe of kinde"—a law of animal nature—that must be modified to become "honeste" for mankind. This idea had been anticipated in medieval legal tradition: "Natural law of this kind has been modified through the order of distinguished and worthy [honesti] custom, namely that only certain persons, and only under the lofty celebration of marriage, may be joined." [6]

Given his knowledge of that tradition, Gower could have altered Ulpian's definition by championing "reson" and "love honeste" early in the *Confessio*. But he did not. What is unusual about his treatment of natural law is that he devotes so much space to exploring nuances of Ulpian's sense of the term. And in the fiction, what compels him to dwell on a love common to all nature instead of one proper to mankind is Amans, who seems to follow the laws of nature "al at large." Thus, on the matter of *procreatio*, for Ulpian simply a law of animal nature, Amans seems to take a firm "theological" stand, introducing a Biblical text to challenge the priest's defense of virginity:

> god to man be weie of kinde
> Hath set the world to multeplie;
> And who that wol him justefie,
> It is ynouh to do the lawe.
>
> (5.6422–25)

In legal writings the divine command—"crescite et multiplicamini"—can be treated with considerable sophistication as a law of nature, but in poetry it is often humorously misinterpreted by characters who embody *sensualitas*.[7] Such is the case in the *Confessio*: the "lawe" has little to do with Amans' specific love; it has much to do with an attitude based in animal "kinde." Gower's own stance is markedly different from that of his persona. Again it is revealed late in the poem when, through the priest Genius, he expressly accommodates natural law to reason and a generic moral probity (*honestum*), as well as to the special honesty of marriage and chastity. Genius praises Apollonius of Tyre because

> he hath ferst his love founded
> Honesteliche as forto wedde,
> Honesteliche his love he spedde
> And hadde children with his wif.
>
> 8. 1994–97

Bennett, recalling the priest's "original role, in the *Roman* [*de la Rose*], as sponsor of reproduction," does not find it surprising "that Genius should link 'honest' marriage with child-bearing."[8] To the extent that Gower's priest is modeled on the Genius of the *Roman*, however, it is indeed surprising that he should celebrate honest marriage at all. In fact, the connection he makes is more adequately explained by a medieval theory of natural law that accommodates both reason and "honesty": "Procreation can be taken in two ways: according as it is an act delighting in touch, or according to the effect, namely offspring. If in the second way, . . . then it will be through reason welcoming it on account of the honor ["honestatem"] of marriage, and it will be according to natural law so defined."[9] This idea anticipates Gower's own view. In the fiction, however, Amans cannot distinguish between the two senses of procreation. In Book 5 he comically admits his desire for a "lusti touch"—*actus delectans in tactu*—and such desire, for him, is the law. Kind love is a compulsion, and he is content to follow where it leads. He certainly is not yet prepared to modify "kinde" into something "honeste."

Amans' sense that he is constrained to love by nature is a focal concern of the confession, and the priest frequently agrees that it is not in Amans' power to reject the *leges naturae*:

> kinde assaileth the corage
> With love and doth him forto bowe,
> That he no reson can allowe,
> Bot halt the lawes of nature.
>
> (3.154–57)

184

But this is a controversial point. Henry Kelly, in commenting on a like statement of it (3.342–59), contends that "Gower has once again let his confessor run away with himself" and suggests, following a marginal gloss in another context, that "Genius is not speaking the truth but merely the opinion of lovers." [10] The matter, unfortunately, is not so simple, for though this indeed might be the opinion of lovers, it is not therefore necessarily false or handled by Gower ironically. Whether a person "may . . . fordon the lawe of kynde" [11] is a question that late medieval poets often take seriously. In the *Roman de la Rose*, for example, Raison, without a trace of irony or humor, makes the same point as Gower's priest: natural love is irresistible in the sense that Nature forces creatures—"ausinc li home com les bestes"—to it. [12] And this power in nature was also a concern for writers other than the poets. According to some legal authorities, for example, the law of animal nature, a *motus sensualitatis*, is an instinct that, in its first impulses, is involuntary: "primi motus non sunt in nostra potestate." [13] On grounds such as these Genius is justified in excusing or showing compassion toward those who love "be weie of kinde."

But neither Gower nor his priest in the fiction is content merely to exonerate the impulses of animalic "kinde." The poet sees in man a twofold nature, a nature divided according to a principle made popular by Peter Lombard: "What may not be in common with the beasts pertains to reason; what you find in this common with the beasts, however, pertains to sensuality." [14] Gower sees those things described by the term *sensualitas*—a term he replaces with "kinde" or the "lawe of kinde"—as more ambiguous than writers like Peter would have them. A suggestion about that ambiguity that might help us in reading the *Confessio* is provided by William of Auxerre. William separates sensuality into two kinds. The first he identifies as "brute sensuality or what is moved through the manner of nature: it is irrational, and it is not subject to free will." The second he describes as

human sensuality, that is, the inferior part of the concupiscible power. The human concupiscible power indeed has two parts, the superior by which it desires eternal things, and the inferior by which it desires temporal things. And according to each part it is moved voluntarily, and therefore in it is sin and in it are the first impulses by which, in an improper manner, we desire temporal things prior to the judgment of reason. [15]

In contrast to Peter Lombard, William therefore argues that sensuality in us "non est communis cum brutis."

Genius in fact takes a double stance toward Amans that reflects ideas represented by these two writers. On the one hand, he recognizes that "kinde" may cancel choice and the judgment of reason, and in this sense Amans' love "be weie of kinde" or his sensuality is of the sort identified by Peter Lombard: it involves "quod [est] commune cum beluis." On the other hand, the priest, late in the confession especially, insists on the lover's powers of reason and choice, even in matters of love. In this sense, Amans' sensuality is of the second type identified by William: it is human sensuality, and therefore it is subject to free will. Occasionally in one statement, Genius reveals the paradox in his position, in Amans' sensuality, and finally in the animalic "lawe of kinde" itself:

> love is of so gret a miht,
> His lawe mai noman refuse,
> So miht thou thee the betre excuse.
> And natheles thou schalt be lerned
> That will scholde evere be governed
> Of reson more than of kinde.
>
> (3.1194–99)

2. The *jus naturae* as an instinct leading to charity. The "lawe of kinde" is sometimes an impulse to be tolerated or condemned, but it also can become, in Genius' view, a source of good. In a second meaning, it is a social instinct that is extended first to those related by blood—as in the *educatio* of offspring—and then to other members of the same species. Ulpian did not elaborate on this instinct as a law of animal nature, but some of his commentators did. One such author is the decretist Huguccio:

Natural law is called an instinct and order of nature by which like are propagated from like, by which like rejoice in like, by which they agree among themselves, by which they nurture their offspring, desire peace, avoid injuries, and do the other things which must be done according to sensuality, that is, natural appetite: this law seems to be nothing other than sensuality. Concerning it one learned in the law has said: natural law is what nature has taught all animals.[16]

Gower also sees this instinct as a common law that is not distinctive to mankind. He might argue, for example, that "Men schal noght finde upon his liche / A beste forto take his preie" (3.2588–89) in order to show that a "lawe of kinde" as well as reason should keep man from injuring others. In other contexts he might find in nature a principle to guide us to such virtues as gratitude and pity. "Kinde" in these contexts complements but is not identified with reason. Gower ultimately subscribes to the ancient and medieval commonplace that man is uniquely a social animal because he is endowed with powers of reason and speech, but in evolving this second meaning of natural law, he does not stress these differentiae of man. His emphasis rather falls on a law, common to sentient "kinde," that like is naturally drawn to its like and by nature is inclined to support, nurture, and protect it. Thus in the poem a number of virtues—compassion, trust, patience, and benevolence—are implicitly or explicitly presented as originating in a basic recognition of and sensitivity to a nature shared.

The poet also uses topoi concerning things naturally "set to the comune" or beings naturally like to promote that affection he describes in the Prologue:

> Forthi good is, whil a man may,
> Echon to sette pes with other
> And loven as his oghne brother.
> (P. 1048–50)

Gower's statement about how such love is generated out of the "lawe of kinde" develops gradually over the course of the entire *Confessio*, but many of the ideas involved had been briefly catalogued by Alain de Lille:

> Consult nature: she will teach you to love your neighbor as yourself. For indeed, she has made all things common and has made a single origin for all things, because 'All mankind descends from a like beginning.' If you deny to another what you wish done to yourself, you attack nature and weaken a common law.
>
> Impose on no one what you yourself cannot endure; offer those things to others that you wish offered to you. How can you despise your nature in another, who embrace the same thing in yourself? Every animal loves its like, so every man ought to love his neighbor. All flesh is joined to its like company.[17]

Alain's assertion, "If you deny to another what you wish done to yourself, you attack nature," is drawn from a topos also familiar to Gower. Indeed, Genius' single most important statement about the "lawe of kinde" in its second, expanded meaning is taken from it:

> he that made lawe of kinde
> Wolde every man to lawe binde,
> And bad a man, such as he wolde
> Toward himself, riht such he scholde
> Toward an other don also.
> (2.3275–79)

This divine command appeared frequently in medieval interpretations of the *jus naturae*, sometimes as a gloss on Romans 2:14: "the gentiles, who have no law, do by nature what the law prescribes."[18] When Gower introduces it, he is interested in how the emperor Constantine, before his conversion, is moved to pity, and the very context of this passage is therefore reminiscent of the text in Romans. Much later in the poem the association of this law with the *gentes* is confirmed by Gower's version of a tale he found in the *Secretum Secretorum*, where a pagan—a *magus orientalis* in the original—states his creed:

> be the lawe which I use
> I schal noght in mi feith refuse
> To loven alle men aliche,
>
> ---
>
> So schal I live in unite
> With every man in his degre.
> For riht as to miself I wolde,
> Riht so toward alle othre I scholde
> Be gracious and debonaire.
>
> (7.3223–25*, 3229–33*)

The "lawe of kinde" described in the tale of Constantine is therefore not restricted to those who accept a "newe lawe" of "Cristes lore," but applies to all mankind.

Gower is also interested in how this law guides man to charity, and there is precedent for the connection he sees. Some medieval writers argue, in fact, that natural law is nothing other than charity. Peter Abelard associates the two terms, and he introduces as a link between them the divine command that also appears in Gower's narrative:

The words of natural law are those that commend the love of God and neighbor, such as these: 'What you do not wish done to you, do not do to another' (Tob. 4:16); and: 'What you wish men would do to you, do also to them' (Matt. 7:12).[19]

The tale of Constantine is an exemplum of this virtue: after the emperor enacts the law, "ferforth he was overcome / With charite" (3301–02), and "Thurgh charite thus he despendeth / His good" (3311–12).

But there is something about the natural goodness of Constantine that causes uneasiness, forcing us to ask whether Gower at this point in the poem meant by charity what a writer like Abelard meant. The emperor's *caritas* lacks some of the qualities we have come to associate with the theological virtue, and even as the virtue of a pagan, it cannot be identified with that love of God which Langland perceived in the Saracens:

Hit may be that Sarrasyns hauen · a suche manere charite,
Louye, as by lawe of kynde · oure lord god al-myghty.[20]

In Gower's poem it would appear that the "charite" treated in Book 2 as a specific antidote for envy is distinct from the higher charity mentioned in the Prologue and expounded in later books. By the conclusion of the work we have a much clearer sense that love "confermed of charite" is the end of human action and desire, and that charity is, in fact, "the vertu sovereine." Moreover, we have a clearer sense that man's charitable deeds reflect a fullness of his nature, including the clear judgment of his "reson."

The outcome of the tale of Constantine provides the most important evidence that we have not yet achieved this higher love. Although the emperor is virtuous, Genius proceeds to expose the "venym" of the famous donation: the gift betrays Constantine's confusion over goods, "of temporal, / Which medleth with the spirital" (3491–92). This confusion has its origin in natural law itself, as we shall discover when we advance to a third sense of the term, developed by Gower during his treatment of avarice in Book 5 of the poem.

3. The *jus naturae* as primitive nature. At the outset of Book 5, Gower describes the world shortly after its creation:

> Ferst whan the hyhe god began
> This world, and that the kinde of man
> Was falle into no gret encress,
> For worldes good tho was no press,
> Bot al was set to the comune.
>
> (5.1–5)

Because of avarice, however,

> werre cam on every side,
> Which alle love leide aside
> And of comun his propre made.
>
> (13–15)

As his source for this discussion contrasting a primitive state of nature when all goods were shared with a subsequent state marked by greed, violence, and division, Gower could have used any of a number of authors who developed the topos of the golden age. He could have found this commonplace in ancient writers, of course, or in writers such as Boethius or Jean de Meun:

riche estoient tuit egaument
et s'entramoient loiaument.
Ausinc pesiblement vivoient,
car naturelment s'entramoient,
les simple genz de bone vie.[21]

The idea of natural love among those equally rich—an idea also implied in the second meaning of the *jus naturae*—underlies Gower's statement in the opening distich of Book 5: "Obstat auaricia nature legibus."

In connecting the notion of all things possessed in common with the concept of *jus naturale*, Gower follows writers who explore the literary topos of the golden age, but he also draws upon others who share his interest in natural law. This larger tradition included the Fathers, Isidore and medieval grammarians, Gratian and the decretists, and later theologians.[22] Some of these authors, while explaining "omnium quaedam communis possessio," raise serious questions about natural law itself: either it is prescriptive and unchangeable, or it is merely descriptive of an original "state of nature." Thus, following the familiar distinction between nature *ante peccatum*—that time, to use the words of Chaucer's Parson, "er that synne bigan, whan natureel lawe was in his right poynt in paradys" [23]— and nature *post peccatum*, an author could argue that a law ordering the common possession of all things belonged to instituted nature, but it was necessarily replaced in a fallen world by laws of acquisition and restitution.[24]

Gower, in presenting the *jus naturae*, often seems to imply that it is an immutable good even in a postlapsarian world, a world "out of reule and mesure." He sometimes treats it in its second meaning as a remedy for *natura lapsa* without accounting for the fact that it has itself been vitiated by mankind. In Book 5, however, he explores this problem through an excursus which implies as background a commonplace division of man's history into three periods. As briefly stated by Hugh of St. Victor, "There are three periods through which the course of the present world runs. The first is the period of natural law; the second the period of written law; the third the period of grace. The first age extends from Adam to Moses." [25] In this framework, natural law was seen as the first remedy for original sin. The written law was then given, as one author expresses it, "to repair natural law, corrupted through sin." [26]

Gower incorporates this history in his review of the world's religions. His account begins with the worship of the pagan gods, an appropriate topic in Book 5 because avarice "est simulacrorum servitus." [27] Such idolatry is concentrated in a first period, a time after the flood when "al was torned to likinge / After the fleissh" (1616–17) and when men "the

190

high god ne knewe, / Bot maden othre goddes newe" (1621–22). The second period begins with Abraham, who "fond out the rihte weie," proceeds through Moses, to whom God "yaf the lawe," and ends with the "baptesme of the newe lawe, / Of which Crist lord is and felawe" (1779–80), which begins the third period.

All three periods are relevant in the evolving argument of the *Confessio*, but the first period is especially appropriate in showing the weakness of natural law and the inability of man naturally to recover "thastat of Innocence." The first age is a time of worshiping nature—the stars, the elements, various beasts—and it is marked by a shifting of "thonour / Which due is to the creatour / . . . to the creature" (777–79). This age passes in a confusion over goods—which are little and which great, which are proper and which common. In a perverse way, all things are "set to the comune," and because of this, the first age provides an important lesson for Gower's contemporaries, who live at a time, as Genius remarks, when avarice has become the chief vice.[28] But this natural or fleshly age also provides a lesson for Amans because its confusion over goods is most memorably exemplified in those who serve Venus.

Rather startlingly, Genius in Book 5 attacks the goddess he serves, but there is good reason for this attack in the stance he here takes toward natural law. If in one perspective Venus, or the natural love she sponsors, might be thought generous and kind, now, in another perspective, she or that love appears prodigal, lacking in "mesure," and foolish. The goddess is condemned for committing incest with her lecherous son, for teaching "That wommen scholde here bodi selle" (1431), and for making love common:

> Sche made comun that desport,
> And sette a lawe of such a port,
> That every womman mihte take
> What man hire liste, and noght forsake
> To ben als comun as sche wolde.[29]
>
> (5.1425–29)

As good as natural law in its second meaning may be, it must be enlarged to accommodate man's proper nature, a capacity to separate good and evil, to identify virtue as a mean, to weigh goods according to their worth, and to distinguish between mere possession and love. Amans is unquestionably "kinde": he can even be said to act towards his lady as he would have her act toward him. But his love lacks measure, and it is, at last, a kind of avarice. His confusion over goods is exemplified in his comical admission of sacrilege: he ogles at his mistress in church—"al mi contemplacion / . . . / Is only set on hire ymage" (7126–28)—and he tries to lead her when "sche wolde gon offre" in order to "winne . . . therby / A lusti touch, a good word eke" (7140, 7146–47). This humorous confession of idolatry, especially because it is preceded by Genius' excursus on a primitive law of nature and on man's enduring confusion about the value of things, points a need not only for grace, but for discrimination and a higher natural law than the "kinde" Amans represents. And as the historical excursus in Book 5 points the way to that law—a law of "reson"—a cosmological excursus in Book 7 takes the reader to its threshold.

4. The *jus naturae* as cosmic order. In Book 7, where Gower treats the education of Alexander in its three parts of Theorique, Rhetorique, and Practique, we are introduced to images of *justitia naturalis* in the created universe. Gower does not, in this book, introduce the goddess Nature, present a myth of creation, use formulae such as *natura naturans* and *natura id est deus*, or address the large cosmological issues that engaged the attention of writers on nature during centuries immediately preceding his own. He writes literally about God as the first cause "Of which that every creature / Hath his beinge and his nature" (7.89–90), but he devotes much less space to theology than to those sciences that help explain the interdependence of physical things in the universe. His argument about that universe rests on a definition of the *jus naturae* originating in writers such as William of Auxerre, Hugh of St. Cher, and Roland of Cremona: this is the law which is present

in the concord of all things; Plato treats such natural justice in the *Timaeus:* one element cannot be without another; whence, as Augustine says, the judgment of divine liberality is that a creature, of whatever kind, is compelled to offer itself.[30]

A number of assumptions underlie Gower's implied use of this definition. In the Prologue of the *Confessio* the poet introduces the principle that whatever is, exists so long as it is one, and there he explores its negative implication: Sin is "moder of divisioun," and because of the sin that "ferst began in Paradis," man suffers division in his "complexioun," his body and soul, his language, and his relationship with other men and with nature (P.849–1052). Book 7 develops an idea of man the microcosm reunified in himself, and it does so, first, by observing unity in the macrocosm. A view of the interdependence of all things in the larger universe becomes a means of identifying what the whole man should be.

The concord of all things, in contrast to that love based on the likeness of specific natures, assumes unlikeness. Each creature has a proper nature that allows it to contribute to the whole, and yet, because of its natural limitation, that creature is dependent on others whose nature differs from its own. But this interdependence implies an element of determinism in the universe. Not only is each creature bound or ruled by its own nature, but, because it is assigned a place in the larger universe, it is also to some extent restricted by what surrounds it.[31] For Gower, the external powers which especially affect men are the "constellacion" and Fortune, and in Book 7 these are treated, respectively, in the sections devoted to Theorique and Practique.

In evolving the section on Theorique, Gower selects from his primary source—the *Trésor* of Brunetto Latini—those passages that serve to emphasize man's limitation according to "kinde."[32] Because all things are interdependent, man does not seem to be the cause of what he does. He is directed by the planets, natural things in his world, his place of origin, the elements, his complexion. This idea of the "grete world" affecting the "litel" also relates to a premise of earlier books of the poem: it would seem to reinforce Amans' sense that he is not free, that he is driven by "kinde" and natural love to do what he does. Now the coercion of "kinde"— Amans' sensuality—appears all the more unavoidable because of the powers in the external, physical world that also influence him.

But Book 7 ascends through powers. Genius also shows how man is distinct from the beasts with which he shares the "lawes of nature":

> Alle othre bestes that men finde
> Thei serve unto here oghne kinde,
> Bot to reson the Soule serveth.
>
> 515–17

And this leads the priest finally to a consideration of Rhetorique and Practique. Man is unique because of his power of speech, a power "noghwhere elles sene / Of kinde with non other beste" (1514–15). But though in one sense man by this faculty is able to transcend physical nature and its influence because language is more powerful than "alle erthli thinges" (1547–49), in another sense he is not necessarily freed by language from the bondage of his own sensuality or indeed from the potentially harmful effects of rhetoric itself, since language can be used "to evele or goode." For Genius, what is essential for man is the highest art—Practique—an art "Which stant in disposicion / Of mannes free eleccion" (45–46). And in dealing with the practical art, Gower articulates the *jus naturae* in its fifth sense—the law of "reson"—a law that provides a wholly new outlook on sensuality or the "lawe or kinde": the latter now becomes an instinct or appetite that is distinctive to man in the sense that he possesses the reason and free will to accept or reject its impulses.

5. The *jus naturae* as natural reason, the judgment of reason, free will, or the power to choose good over evil.[33] This sense of the *jus naturae* is discussed in a variety of contexts in medieval legal tradition, but the most relevant inquiries for our purposes are those that comment on Ulpian's law of animal nature even while they examine man's proper nature. Some writers who identify the law of nature with reason or powers unique to man do so by reducing Ulpian's law to the status of mere *sensualitas* or natural appetite: thus, for one author, "Certainly the beasts copulate, but they are moved by the appetite of natural impulse alone, not by natural law." [34] Other writers preserve a sense of a "law" of animal nature, but at the same time argue that this law is altered in mankind by *ratio naturalis*.[35] The two groups differ in their terminology and often in the ideas their terminology implies, but their common field of interest encourages dialogue between them, and it is against the background of such dialogue that Gower occasionally uses "kinde" to refer alternatively to natural appetite and reason:

> It sit a man be weie of kinde
> To love, bot it is noght kinde
> A man for love his wit to lese.
>
> (7.4297–99)

But the difference between the groups is also important to Gower's poem. The poet prefers the distinction between an *animalic* law of nature and reason to the distinction between a *rational* law of nature and sensuality. He applies the former distinction to his treatment of marriage, for example, and thus follows a tradition of glossators who make the same distinction when they argue that marriage is ordained not by the law of nature but by reason.[36] More largely, Gower is inclined to see the good (and not merely the danger) in what others might identify as sensuality, and he can perceive more by working through the sometimes more neutral and sometimes more positive terms or concepts of "kinde" and the "lawe of kinde." This is not to disregard what we have already observed: the poet knows the limitation of the "lawe of kinde," especially in its first meaning. This law would be wholly restrictive and inviolable—a law in the narrowest sense—were it not for reason. Reason offers choices, and its laws provide a means of liberation from the constraints of "kinde." Gower's use of the distinction between an animalic law of nature and reason nevertheless gives his argument point and direction. His emphasis shifts from what binds to what frees man, and this means, at last, that the law of animal nature must be modified in the human species:

194

> For god the lawes hath assissed
> Als wel to reson as to kinde,
> Bot he the bestes wolde binde
> Only to lawes of nature,
> Bot to the mannes creature
> God yaf him reson forth withal,
> Wherof that he nature schal
> Upon the causes modefie,
> That he schal do no lecherie,
> And yit he schal hise lustes have.
> (7.5372–81)

"Reson" obviously applies to the issue of greatest concern to Amans: if love can overturn the heart from "reson in to lawe of kynde" (8.3146), reason in its turn can order love, letting man have his pleasure, yet keeping him from lechery. But it is also clear in the last books of the poem that Gower is concerned with more than Amans' pleasure and the insight of conscience that might regulate it. The laws of "reson" influence all human behavior, and in referring to them in various contexts near the end of the poem, the poet seeks to show how man is guided in his proper nature to a happiness unknown to the "bestes."

The richness of Gower's allusions to the law of nature illustrates the extent of his encyclopedic knowledge, and it is a temptation to argue that his treatment of the *jus naturae* can explain all things in the *Confessio*. But it cannot. It cannot explain all the nuances of Gower's varied assortment of tales and excursus, all the details of the confessional dialogue, or all facets of the "vices dedly" that Genius introduces. But his treatment, nevertheless, can illumine elements in the structure of the poem that have hitherto eluded the most determined critics. It can begin to explain the rationale for the work—the large contours of the priest's argument, his varied stances, the placement of specific excursus, and the occasionally unusual choice of topics to govern the dialogue within particular books.

It is natural to assume that an inquiry into the whole of the *Confessio* should begin with its major topics, the seven capital vices. As means of discovery, they will obviously help Genius perceive the nature and extent of Amans' guilt. They will show why the lover is divided in himself, why he cannot his "wittes gete." But Genius' insights into the lover's condition are isolated, discrete perceptions framed by the species of the vices; they are not unified in a single, coherent view of Amans' inner "querele" or his history as a lover. And that, I think, is because a psychology of moral sickness, though important, is ultimately less important to the priest than Amans' cure. Through the topoi of the vices, the priest comes to present an ideal of the remade man, *homo renovatus*, and the unity of his argument

195

and the poem rests not so much on the sins as on a psychology of regeneration.

Genius does not wholly succeed in "remaking" Amans, for the lover
recovers his wits only through acts of "grace" by Cupid and Venus, but
nevertheless the priest prepares Amans for conversion, and later his teaching sustains "Gower," the sometime lover:

> Homward a softe pas y wente,
> Wher that with al myn hol entente
> Uppon the point that y am schryve
> I thenke bidde whil y live.
>
> (8.2967–70)

To the end of presenting the psychology of a man made whole, Genius
defines specific remedial virtues such as humility, mercy, and largess; he
champions virtue in tales illustrating the vices—in good characters who
are the victims of misdeeds of others. But most importantly, he proceeds
in stages of the confession to identity and expound higher and higher
capacities in man, and he uses his various meanings of natural law to
sharpen his auditor's perception of what man, ideally, can become.

With the exception of Book 7, each of the eight books of the *Confessio*
treats one of the deadly sins. The sins introduced in Books 1, 2, and 3 are
the most unnatural of the seven—pride is "unkynde" (1.2565), envy "hath
kinde put aweie" (2.3140), and wrath does "to kinde no plesance" (3.8)—
and the person who succumbs to them variously shows his contempt for
natural "lawes." Nature encourages "felaschipe," but he is self-centered
and, much like a figure later introduced, "Unto non other man is frend, /
Bot al toward himself al one" (5.5492–93). Men are made equal and
"franchised" by a common nature (2.3263), but he scorns natural equality.[37] In nature malice is unknown (3.386–87), but he acts maliciously,
exhibiting ill-will or practicing deceit. Nature "in hir lawe" commends
peace (3.2264), but he, given to impatience and wrath, injures others.

In opposition to his exemplars of these sins, Genius introduces characters in Books 1–3 who are guided by the "lawe of kinde," characters who
by nature display good-will toward others and seek their company. In
nature, like perceives and is attracted to like. Obviously, such kindness is
first manifested in the family, where it is based as much on instinct as on a
formal recognition of connection by blood. In Gower's version of the
legend of Constance, for example, the priest offers as a foil to the monstrous unkindness—the hatred, envy, and "bacbitinge"—of the tale's two
wicked mothers, the goodness of Alle, a king drawn by natural affection to
the child he has not yet recognized as his son:

> The king was moeved in his thoght
> Of that he seth, and knoweth it noght;
> This child he loveth kindely,
> And yit he wot no cause why.
>
> (2.1379–82)

On the basis of a perceived resemblance, Alle loves instinctively.

Genius returns to scenes such as these elsewhere in the *Confessio* to illumine the *jus naturae* in its second meaning: among those closest in nature we should see the greatest accord. But far more important to the priest's statement about this law is man's natural capacity to extend such love to the rest of mankind. Every man "in the balance / Of kinde [is] formed to be liche" (2.3244–45), and each should be moved by "kinde" to respond to that likeness—a shared humanity—in others. Such a response is the origin of virtue in a number of Genius' exemplars in the early books, including that of the king in Book 1 who leaps out of his carriage to embrace two very old pilgrims, and who then explains his action:

> I beheld tofore my sihte
> In hem that were of so gret age
> Min oghne deth thurgh here ymage,
> Which god hath set be lawe of kynde,
> Wherof I mai no bote finde.
>
> (1.2228–32)

Such natural humility is also displayed by the emperor Constantine, for this exemplar is led to perform his acts of "charite" partly out of a recognition that "Mai non eschuie that fortune / Which kinde hath in hire lawe set" (2.3250–51). But his virtue, like that of others who observe the "lawe of kinde," also grows out of the related natural impulse "to loven alle men aliche." Genius notes a similar impulse in exemplars of compassion, trust, patience, generosity, and mercy, and he thereby shows that such virtues are interconnected "be weie of kinde." In building a case for their common origin in the *jus naturae*, Genius makes it apparent that he hopes to do more in these early books than merely identify separate remedies for the malicious sins. In Books 1–3, he reveals how men are led by nature to gather in peaceful "compaignie," establish relationships of good-will and trust, and practice not only one but many related virtues that directly benefit others.

The priest does not limit his perception of the good in "kinde" to the first three books. The *jus naturae* in its second meaning forbids treachery, malice, and violence wherever they occur, and in the later books scenes of such unkindness are common enough. Nevertheless. Genius also makes it

197

increasingly apparent that "kinde" as a law is insufficient for man. The last sins introduced in the confession are the most difficult to moderate by "kinde" because they are in us by nature. Although a measure of what is needed to satisfy physical wants has been established in "kinde," [38] it is incapable of keeping man from loving temporal or corporal goods too much, indeed from injuring others to obtain them. What is worse, in a world of immoderate loves, "kinde" is only partially successful in teaching man benevolence. By nature man should be inclined to graciousness, trust, and a liberality modeled on the "fre largesse" of Nature herself, but as Genius points out in his excursus on religion in Book 5, this is a fallen world where man's longings "after the fleissh" often lead to mistrust and deception. To the extent that a nature remains innocent, it becomes prey to those who are "unkinde." Earlier in the poem one exemplar might well assert to another:

> For hou so this fortune falle,
> Yit stant mi trust aboven alle,
> For the mercy which I now finde,
> That thou wolt after this be kinde.
>
> (3.2703–06)

But in Book 5 the priest enlarges on what he only hints at earlier, that those who are "kinde" are vulnerable either to their own sensuality or to the unkindness of others.

The poet finally sees man released from the bondage of vitiated nature by grace, but in the last three confessional books—Books 5, 6, and 8—he also focuses our attention on "reson" (the *jus naturae* in its fifth meaning) as a key element in man's regeneration. Genius suggests in many places, and not only near the end of the confession, that "reson" must complement "kinde" as a law for the human species. In the later books, however, he stresses the effects of reason in tempering man's sensual appetite, and given the nature of avarice, gluttony, and lechery—the last three sins—it is only appropriate that he should do so. By these sins man not only falls prey to fleshly desire, but also loses what his proper nature should provide: through avarice, he rejects "the stiere / Of resonable governance" (5.2226–27); through gluttony, he forgets "Or he be man, or he be beste" (6.47); and through lechery, he finally descends to the likeness of a beast, indulging his appetite as a "Stalon in the Fennes" (8.160). Reason and its "lawes" clearly supply natural remedies for these sins.

Genius also sees other powers in reason. As in Books 1, 2, and 3 he discovered a good in the "lawe of kinde" independent of its power to offset the sins of malice, so in Books 5, 6, and 8, he identifies a good in "reson" independent of its power to remedy the sins of "nature." Not only through these later books, but through Books 4 and 7 as well, he hopes to show what man can achieve by "reson" once he is freed from the worst elements in his sensual "kinde." This prospect appears in the last three confessional books; it is offered in its greatest breadth in Book 7, a book devoted in its entirety to Alexander's education in Philosophie; but it begins to appear in Book 4.

Book 4, the middle confessional book, provides a significant transition in Genius' argument. Whereas in the course of treating the seven vices, the confessor gradually shifts his emphasis from remedies grounded in a "lawe of kinde" to remedies grounded in "reson," in handling sloth in Book 4, he applies both laws to Amans' condition and offers as his judgment what seems to be, at first glance, a contradiction. On the one hand, he commends Amans' busyness as a lover: he is not one of the slothful who deny their amorous nature (the *jus naturae* in its first meaning). On the other hand, the priest suggests that in another way Amans is slow: drawn to his mistress by "kinde," he neglects great goods, loving them too little. These are goods that "reson" can identify, and the priest, now starting to describe them, initiates a phase of his argument that leads eventually into Book 7.

First Genius repeats his earlier claim that all men are equal at birth:

> Of mannes berthe the mesure,
> It is so comun to nature,
> That it yifth every man aliche.
> (4.2231–33)

But now the priest is also interested in what distinguishes men, and that, he notes, is a function of labor: virtue makes man "gentil," and "studie" makes him wise. In a digression on inventors, Genius introduces the founders of "mechanical" arts such as cookery, wool-making, and hunting, as well as the founders of portraiture, music, and the science of physiognomy. He devotes most of this excursus, however, to the inventors of alchemy and the verbal arts. These two regions of human knowing represent fields more fully expounded in the later description of Alexander's education: the introduction of the "craft" of alchemy, "wrought be weie of kinde" (4.2508), anticipates the emphasis on corporeal things in Theorique, and the introduction of the verbal arts obviously foreshadows the later treatment of Rhetorique. What is conspicuous by its absence is a counterpart to Practique: instead of showing how inventors apply reason to deeds, as they have applied it to "kinde" and words, Genius introduces as his sole instance of the practical art the *ars amatoria*, specifically the "remedies" described by Ovid; Amans, who still has much to learn, will read Ovid's books "if thei mihte spede / Mi love" (2675–76). In Book 7, this practical art will be displaced by another which is more clearly grounded in the law of "reson" and which, to use Ciceronian terms adopted by Genius, is more profitable because more honest.

Elsewhere in Book 4, however, Genius begins to separate loves by the criterion of honesty, which for him means something quite unlike that introduced in a courtly "ars honeste amandi." The tale of Rosiphelee, one of the best in the entire collection, reveals the unkindness of a woman who defies love, but this story is followed by the tale of Jephthah's daughter, a woman who scorns marriage. This juxtaposition of tales allows Genius to contrast marriage—"ilke feste, / Wherof the love is al honeste" (1483–84)—with love of "paramours" or love by "Cupides lawe," which is full "Of janglinge and of fals Envie, / Fulofte medlid with disese" (1474–75). In Book 4, more largely, charity (a sidenote identifies it: "Nota de amore caritatis") takes on its fuller meaning as a love that

> above alle othre is hed,
> Which hath the vertus forto lede,
> Of al that unto mannes dede
> Belongeth.
>
> (2326–29)

Amans' labor, according to which, he tells us, "I serve, I bowe, I loke, I loute" (1169), contrasts with deeds issuing from this higher love, and his repeated failure leads him to the final point of sloth, Tristesce.

Book 4 is important not only because it begins to reveal what "reson" can discover, but because its defense of reason is juxtaposed with a defense of sensual "kinde": the conflict between these two positions gives rise to a key question about Genius' treatment of Amans that must be answered before the confession ends. Although the priest here commends "reson" and charity, he also tells Amans not to yield to despair by giving up his suit too quickly: the lover cannot know "what chance schal betyde" (1779) or when "love his grace wol . . . sende" (3504). How can Genius attack "Cupides lawe" when he also defends it by encouraging Amans to place his trust in chance or the grace of Love? To be sure, he here has the dual obligation of keeping Amans from despair and at the same time showing him that in "reson," charity, and grace—even the grace of Love—he may discover his escape from "kinde" and the ill-fate he finds so difficult to bear. But the problem is a deeper one: it originates in the *jus naturae*, and in the *jus naturae* Genius finds its solution.

As a servant of Venus, Genius accepts Amans' love as natural because it follows the *jus naturae* in its first sense. As a priest inclined to virtue and reason, however, he judges that same love in Amans to be unnatural because it violates the *jus naturae* in its fifth sense. So long as we assume a logic of exclusion, this is a contradiction: Genius cannot have it both ways. But the logic of his argument is inclusive. Even after he has finished presenting his case for "reson," Genius still judges the law of animal nature to be a good in the human species provided it is adapted to and ordered by higher laws. Late in the poem the priest rejects Amans' *claim* of kindness because the lover identifies nature exclusively with sensual appetite and pleasure and thus divorces it from the *jus naturae* in all its other senses. It is not Genius' intent to reject "kinde" love itself, but to enlarge Amans' perception of it. By gradually adding new meanings to "nature," he shows that such love can be something more than the mere observance of "Cupides lawe," and in enlarging the concept of natural law to its fullest meaning, he shows how love "be weie of kinde" can become most natural for man.

This instruction in love follows the pattern of the confession as a whole, where the priest, we have noted, bases remedies for the principal vices on progressively larger and more complex senses of nature. In that process of transforming perception, he often lifts terms to higher meanings, and this is what he does with those words of encouragement he utters in Book 4. In later books the priest still consoles Amans: "Mi Sone, bot abyd thin ende, / Per cas al mai to goode wende" (5.4565–66), he states in Book 5, and in his encouragement, he mixes terms of chance or Fortune with terms of grace: "Of time which thou hast despended, / It mai with grace been amended" (5.7813–14), and a few lines later, he finds an analogy in the sudden change from "Wynter wast and bare" to summer:

> And soudeinliche ayein his floures
> The Somer hapneth and is riche:
> And so per cas thi graces liche.
>
> (7830–32)

Amans is likely to think of sudden change as success in love's cause, but the confessor perceives change differently, and this becomes more and more apparent as the argument proceeds. In Book 6, while sustaining Amans' hope, he shifts his focus from the grace of Fortune and the deities of love to grace of another kind. Cupid the "blinde Boteler" has given Amans a drink: it will remain bitter, Genius tells the lover, "til god the sende / Such grace that thou miht amende" (6.389–90).[39]

If Amans is to be fit for this divine gift of amendment, he must understand more clearly the extent of his bondage to "kinde," the heavens,

Fortune, and the apparent whims of his mistress and Venus; obviously, he must also reperceive the extent of his own power to choose. Genius' treatment in the last books, roughly analogous to that applied by Boethius' physician in the *Consolation*, involves turning his patient's attention to an internal source of freedom.

In Book 6 the confessor still suggests that Amans is destined to a specific natural love, the premise being that "ther is no wyht / That mai withstonde loves miht" (6.317–18). By Book 8, however, he will insist that Amans has a choice and will urge him to leave love that is a "Sinne" and "Tak love where it mai noght faile" (8.2086). That final insistence on Amans' freedom is justified by the perception offered in Book 7, a perception of man restored to his own nature and rightly placed in the universe. As the topics of this didascalic book shift from Theorique to Practique, from natural destiny (the *jus naturae* in its fourth meaning) to practical "reson" and the points of kingship, so too does Genius' perspective on Amans' bondage to "kinde." The introduction of Practique which is based upon "mannes free eleccion" follows in its distinction from "kinde" and natural destiny treated under Theorique that distinction between human sensuality and brute sensuality that concerned medieval writers such as William of Auxerre. In the full perspective on man's nature that Book 7 offers, Genius can now show that the "lawe of kinde" or sensuality in man, because it is subject to reason and free will, is distinct from that nature in the "bestes." This distinction is more important than the fact that all sentient beings commonly endure an external "fortune" and a natural destiny. Man, unlike the beast, can order his love of temporal goods, and this power becomes a focal concern in the priest's discussion of Practique and the five essential virtues of a king.

Gower's choice of those virtues or "pointz" has vexed scholars. The group of five has no strict counterpart in the *Secretum Secretorum* or any other treatise *de regimine principum*.[40] But Gower did have a source. Having advanced beyond animalic "kinde" as well as the "constellacion" that so strongly influences it, he seeks a way to treat those things that seem to bind or inhibit man's power to choose or act, things that seem to represent a natural destiny, but which, in fact, are irresistible because man has failed by reason to recognize them as things he has chosen for himself. Gower found what he sought, I believe, not only in other storehouses of tales or other "kinges bokes," but in the *Consolation of Philosophy*. The five points of Policie, not in some absolute sense, but in the sense in which Gower defines and embodies them in exposition and narrative, are devised as remedies for the human desire for the five great *temporalia*, the gifts of Fortune. As each virtue, supported by the others, displaces a gift— Truth-power, Largess-fame, Justice-wealth, Pity-office, Chastity-sensual pleasure—so the virtues together order man's lower nature and become interdependent strengths in the remade man which liberate him from the compulsions of "kinde."

Man is *homo renovatus* when he achieves the five virtues, but the last temporal good (the pleasure of the senses) and the last virtue (Chastete) present a special problem. Man cannot achieve felicity if he practices four of the virtues but lacks the fifth; chastity is an especially difficult virtue to maintain, however, because man is natural or fleshly and "schal hise lustes have." In a passage of Book 5 that appears in only some manuscripts of the *Confessio*, Genius observes:

> Out of his flessh a man to live
> Gregoire hath this ensample yive,
> And seith it schal rather be told
> Lich to an Angel manyfold,
> Than to the lif of mannes kinde.
> Ther is no reson forto finde,
> Bot only thurgh the grace above,
> In flessh withoute flesshly love,
> A man to live chaste hiere.
>
> (5.6395*–6403*)

In all manuscripts of the poem, however, Gower makes the same point while discussing chastity in Book 7:

> And natheles, bot it be grace
> Above alle othre in special
> Is non that chaste mai ben all.
>
> (4242–44)

The human dilemma—that man cannot live "out of his flessh"—will make grace a necessity, especially for Amans, an exemplar of "flesshly love." And Genius, by juxtaposing the topics of incest and "love honeste" in Book 8, will prepare for the intervention of grace by taking his argument to its limit—to a perception of what "reson" finally demands of the lover.

The reader turning to Book 8 expecting a collection of stories and sayings about lechery, much as he had found six of the earlier books to treat the six other vices, will be surprised to find that the poet here deals exclusively with incest, tells few stories, and seems to limit his argument to a history and defense of laws of consanguinity. Nowhere, not even at the end of Book 7, where he presents chastity as the virtue counterposed to lust, does Gower justify his choice of incest as the chief exemplary species of the last of the "vices dedly." The relevance of his choice becomes apparent, however, in the setting of medieval legal thought. His argument grows out of a view of history and the *primordia nature* that had appeared, rather more starkly, among the Schoolmen:

All that is contrary to natural law always is and has been culpable; but the union of brother and sister has not always been culpable, as, for instance, in the beginning; therefore it is not according to natural law that brother and sister are excepted.[41]

The final book of the *Confessio* begins with an account of creation—"The myhti god, which unbegunne / Stant of himself and hath begunne / Alle othre thinges" (8.1–3)—and in this the poem seems imitative of another, more famous medieval work of confession. But the account quickly becomes a history involving perspectives on the issue of *cognatio* or blood relationship and marriage; these perspectives are ordered first by the *primordia nature* and later by the *racionis arbitrium* and *ecclesie legum imposicio*.[42] In the earliest times, Genius argues,

> it was no Sinne
> The Soster forto take hire brother,
> Whan that ther was of chois non other.
>
> (68–70)

This argument, as it progresses, focuses the concerns of the poem in a rather remarkable way. The terms of man's earliest history, we recall from Book 5, are fixed in Amans' head: when the priest defends virginity, the lover observes that he understands better the divine command to increase and multiply. In Book 8, incest represents an analogous issue. Just as some legal authorities observe that the command "crescite et multiplicamini" was a natural law especially appropriate before the earth was replenished,[43] so Genius notes that incest was permissible until the time of Abraham, when "The nede tho was overrunne, / For ther was poeple ynouh in londe" (100–01). But just because incest was permissible once or because it is encouraged in nature, that does not mean that "nou aday" we are permitted to follow those "That taken wher thei take may" (152). Again, this excursus into history is important to Gower because it identifies a psychological issue. By natural law like things are drawn together. Clearly there can be no greater likeness in nature than likeness by blood, and incest therefore manifests physically that natural law "quo similia similibus gaudent." History gives Gower a further insight into this law. It is obviously no longer the case that the incestuous can claim "ther was of chois non other": the only justification for that claim is brute appetite.

Incest is an especially powerful exemplary species of lechery in the priest's argument because it reveals what it is like for man to live without choice, as a "beste" limited to momentary sensual pleasure with those who live in closest proximity:

> For love, which is unbesein
> Of alle reson, as men sein,
> Thurgh sotie and thurgh nycete,
> Of his voluptuosite
> He spareth no condicion
> Of ken ne yit religion,
> Bot as a cock among the Hennes
> Or as a Stalon in the Fennes,
> Which goth amonges al the Stod,
> Riht so can he nomore good,
> Bot takth what thing comth next to honde.
>
> (153–63)

Honest love stands in opposition in this bestial appetite. Gower's use of the term "honeste" in an argument where he is concerned as well with issues of primordial nature, marriage, incest, and nature multiplied, has a clear precedent in legal tradition.[44] But two senses of "honeste," not often distinguished in the *honestum* or *honestas* of legal texts, have been introduced by Gower in the poem, and both senses apply to his discussion of honest love.

In one sense, "honeste" is derived from the *honestas* that became, in ancient and medieval treatises on the cardinal virtues, a species of temperance. Thus in Book 7 the *honestas* of chastity is set against *voluptas:* "honesty, attending to the impulses of unchasteness, more especially preserves the cleanness of body and soul." [45] Honest love can mean chaste love, and consequently, when the priest contrasts honest love and incest, as in the powerful, concluding tale of the *Confessio*—the tale of Apollonius of Tyre—his implied statement about the latter reflects a traditional idea: those related by blood are to be kept from union "either for the seemliness of nature or for the increase of chastity." [46]

In another, much larger sense, Gower perceives "honesty" as the genus of all virtue. It is the moral good unique to the human species; the "honesty" of chastity and other virtues are but aspects of it. Honesty in this generic sense—Gower's "honeste" as upright and "honestete" as moral probity—may be identified with the *honestum* that Cicero defined as moral worth "commended in and for itself, apart from any profit or reward." [47] For Cicero, men are capable of this good—they can do things which are proper, right, and "honest"—because nature has endowed them with reason. Gower, similarly, sees something as honest when it is suited to man's proper nature, to "reson" and not merely to "kinde." Genius uses the term in this larger sense in earlier passages of the poem (see, for example, 3.2596–98), and he also uses it in this sense in Book 8. He insists that

> love and reson wolde acorde.
> For elles, if that thou descorde,
> And take lust as doth a beste,
> Thi love mai noght ben honeste.
>
> (8.2023–26)

Undoubtedly, "honeste" here still carries the meaning of shamefast or chaste, but it also conveys a meaning of reasonable. Obviously, what is needed to ensure that "love and reson wolde acorde" is a power of discrimination, reason itself. Reason identifies what is "honeste," and what is honest is consistent with "reson."

In the last books of the poem, as the "lawe of kinde" is limited to its most restricted sense—the brute appetite so vividly exemplified by incest—the law of "reson" expands to encompass all human knowledge and virtue. The discussion of "love honeste" in Book 8 is anticipated in the preceding book, but there Genius also refers to a much larger field for "reson" and "honestete." Alexander is taught

> *Noght only upon chastete,*
> *But upon alle honestete;*
> Wherof a king himself mai taste,
> Hou trewe, hou large, hou joust, hou chaste
> Him oghte of reson forto be,
> Forth with the vertu of Pite,
> Thurgh which he mai gret thonk deserve
> Toward his godd.
>
> (7.5387–94) [emphasis added]

This larger meaning of honesty, introduced early in the *Confessio* and elaborated at its close, reflects a rich medieval literature dealing with the Ciceronian terms *honestum* and *utile* and sometimes also a third term—*delectabile*. It is appropriate for the final judgment of Amans' love that all three terms should have appeared in medieval works on confession. Among the questions a priest is to ask in the confessional, one involves the end sought by the sinning, and in the Statutes of Coventry, the possible answers are explored:

Why: because of what end. One is accustomed to distinguish a three-fold end: the profitable, the honest, and the delightful. Many commit sins because of expediency, many because of pleasure; no one can commit a sin because of honesty.[48]

This test of ends applies to all actions, and it is in this framework that Genius finally comes to judge Amans' limited desire by the standard of honesty. We have been told earlier in the poem that "love honeste in sondri weie / Profiteth" (4.2297–98) and that marriage "should be moderated by the rule of honest pleasure." [49] Now, in Book 8, the concluding argument about Amans' case concentrates not only on honest love, but on "lust" and "profit." It is clear that Amans, though he seeks "lust," gains little pleasure from his quarrel, and in Book 8 the priest shows him what he already fears, that his love is useless: in the lover's sin, Genius says, "I not what profit myhte availe" (8.2091). And by presenting a new end—an honest one—to Amans, the confessor takes his treatment of the *jus naturae* to its limit, for "honestete" is the all-encompassing end of the highest natural law he knows, the law of "reson."

Genius has done his job admirably: by his argument he has restored the power of reason in his pupil, and he has taught him about the most profitable love, a love that cannot fail (8.2070–2148). To be sure, he has not changed him in the most important sense, as Amans himself knows:

> Mi resoun understod him wel,
> And knew it was soth everydel
> That he hath seid, bot noght forthi
> Mi will hath nothing set therby.
>
> (2191–94)

Nevertheless, he has prepared him for a dream, a dream in which Cupid, by his grace, removes the lancegay from his heart. When Amans wakens from that dream, he sees himself transformed: "I was mad sobre and hol ynowh" (2869).

In the largest sense, then, the fiction of the *Confessio* traces the psychological recovery of Amans. And we have seen how terms associated with the *jus naturae* have been modified and expanded in the course of the argument conducing to that change. The "lawe of kinde" as sensual appetite shifts from something irresistible to something chosen. Natural law as the attraction between beings naturally like expands to virtuous fellowship and "charite." Charity becomes less a *motus naturae* and more a *motus gratiae* through which man achieves the fullness of his proper nature. Grace means less the compliance of the mistress and more that divine gift which makes man's amendment possible. Reason extends beyond the "insihte of conscience" that judges sexual desire to an "honestete" that not only ensures chaste love, but also guides man in all his choices and actions.

How then, in summary, might we describe the role of natural law in Amans' recovery? The lover's health is restored by a process involving the application of the "lawe of kinde," reason, and grace to his condition. In a general sense, the model—the rationale—for this process is suggested by Hugh Ripelin of Strassburg when he identifies three things that incite us to good works. Hugh's statement is relevant not as a direct source for Gower's developing argument, but as a useful brief description of the elements in the law of nature, reason, and grace that the poet ultimately celebrates:

Three things incite us to good works, namely the law of nature, which is written in the heart of man, saying: 'Whatever you wish men to do to you do also to them,' etc. Reason, which calls these things delightful, profitable, and honest. Grace, which says that God is to be served because he is supremely good; that one's neighbor is to be succored, because he is a son of God, an image of God, and a partner in beatitude. Grace is not given to him, who does not make himself fit for grace.[50]

Grace, for Amans, is a necessity, and natural law—including both "kinde" and "reson"—has been the primary means of making Amans fit to receive it. Moreover, natural law has been a primary reference point in teaching Amans how to act, once he is empowered to act freely: from it he learns what natural love *in corde hominis* should be, and from it he learns how honesty, profit, and delight can be united meaningfully in human experience. In a work so devoted to remaking the man, however, it is proper also that we be shown the limitation of nature and reason and that we be asked to shift our attention at last to a higher power. And thus, as the tale of Amans ends with a gift given to him, so Gower, the former lover, ends his poem by praying for a gift for his readers and himself, a gift that transcends natural law and encyclopedic knowledge about it:

> Bot thilke love which that is
> Withinne a mannes herte affermed,
> And stant of charite conformed,

> The hyhe god such love ous sende
> Forthwith the remenant of grace;
> So that above in thilke place
> Wher resteth love and alle pes,
> Oure joie mai ben endeles.
>
> (8.3162–64, 3168–72)

NOTES

1. "Ius naturale est, quod natura omnia animalia docuit. nam ius istud non humani generis proprium est, sed omnium animalium. . . . hinc descendit maris atque feminae coniugatio, quam nos matrimonium appellamus, hinc liberorum procreatio et educatio." *Inst.* 1.2, ed. P. Krueger (Berlin, 1872), p. 3; cf. *Dig.* 1.1.1.3.

2. Quotations of Gower's works are from the edition of G. C. Macaulay, 4 vols. (Oxford, 1899–1902).

3. ". . . intendit auctor ad presens suum libellum, cuius nomen Confessio Amantis nuncupatur, componere de illo amore, a quo non solum humanum genus, sed eciam cuncta animancia naturaliter subiciuntur." *Works*, 2:35.

4. Guillaume de Lorris and Jean de Meun, *Le Roman de la Rose*, 5733–36, ed. Félix Lecoy (Paris, 1974), 1:176.

5. "Gower's 'Honest Love,'" in *Patterns of Love and Courtesy*, ed. John Lawlor (London, 1966), pp. 107–21.

6. "Lex huiusmodi naturalis modificata est per ordinem discreti et honesti moris, scilicet ut non nisi tales persone et sub tanta celebritate coniugii iungerentur." Rufinus, *Summa Decretorum*, ed. Heinrich Singer (Paderborn, 1902), p. 7.

7. Most notably Chaucer's Wife of Bath, *Canterbury Tales*, 3.26–29, ed. F. N. Robinson, *The Works of Geoffrey Chaucer*, 2nd ed. (Boston, 1957), p. 76.

8. Bennett, pp. 117–18.

9. "Procreatio potest duobus modis accipi: prout est actus delectans in tactu; uel secundum effectum, scilicet prolis. Si secundo modo, . . . tunc erit per rationem excipientem ipsam per honestatem nuptiarum et erit de iure naturali sic dicto." Albertus Magnus, *Summa de bono*, in the selection edited by Odon Lottin, *Le droit naturel chez Saint Thomas d'Aquin et ses prédécesseurs*, 2nd ed. (Bruges, 1931), p. 43.

10. *Love and Marriage in the Age of Chaucer* (Ithaca and London, 1975), p. 144.

11. Chaucer, *Troilus and Criseyde*, 1.238 (*ed. cit.*, p. 392).

12. *Roman*, 5745–54 (*ed. cit.*, 1:177)

13. Azo, *Summa Institutionum* 1.2, ed. F. W. Maitland, *Select Passages from the Works of Bracton and Azo*, Selden Society, 8 (1895), 32, 34; repeated by Bracton, *De Legibus et Consuetudinibus Angliae*, more recently edited by George E. Woodbine (Cambridge, Mass., 1968), 2:26.

14. "Quod non sit commune cum bestiis, ad rationem pertinet: quod autem in ea reperis commune cum beluis, ad sensualitatem pertinet." *Sententiae in IV libris distinctae* 2. dist. 24. cap. 5.2, 3rd ed. (Quaracchi, 1971), 1:454; cf. Augustine, *De Trinitate* 12.12.17 (*PL* 42:1007); Alain de Lille, *De planctu Naturae* (*PL* 210:443) and *Distinctiones dictionum theologicalium*, "ratio" (*PL* 210:922).

15. ". . . sensualitas brutalis vel que mouetur per modum nature: et est irrationabilis, nec subest libero arbitrio. . . . sensualitas humana que est inferior pars vis concupiscibilis. Uis enim concupiscibilis humana habet duas partes, superiorem qua concupiscit eterna, et inferiorem qua concupiscit temporalia. Et secundum vtramque partem mouetur voluntarie, et ideo in ea est

peccatum et in ea sunt primi motus quibus indebito modo concupiscimus temporalia ante iudicium rationis." *Summa aurea in quattuor libros sententiarum* (Paris, 1500–01; reprt. Frankfurt-Main, 1964), fol. 131ra.

16. "Dicitur ius naturale instinctus et ordo nature quo similia de similibus propagantur, quo similia similibus gaudent, quo inter se conueniunt, quo partus nutriunt, quietem appetunt, molestias fugiunt et cetera faciunt que secundum sensualitatem id est naturalem appetitum habent fieri: hoc ius nil aliud uidetur esse quam sensualitas. De hoc iure dicitur a legisperito: ius naturale est quod natura omnia animalia docuit." *Summa Decretorum* (Lottin, p. 109).

17. "Consule naturam, illa te docebit diligere proximum tuum sicut te ipsum. Ipsa etenim fecit omnia communia, unum fecit omnibus ortum, quia *Omne genus hominum simili descendit ab ortu.* Si alii negas quod tibi vis fieri naturam impugnas, jus commune enervas.

"Nulli imponas quod ipse pati non possis; haec exhibe aliis, quae tibi optas exhiberi. Quomodo in alio tuam potes aspernari naturam, qui in te ipso eamdem amplecteris? Omne animal sibi simile diligit, sic omni homo diligere deberet proximum suum. Omnis caro conjungitur ad sui similem societatem." *Summa de arte praedicatoria* (*PL* 210:154).

18. See Alain de Lille, *Distinctiones*, "natura" (*PL* 210:871); Peter Lombard, *In Epistolam ad Romanos* (*PL* 191:1345); for other views of the connection between God's command and the *jus naturae*, see *Sententie Anselmi*, ed. F. Bliemetzrieder, *Anselms von Laon Systematische Sentenzen* (Münster, 1919), p. 79; Hugh of St. Victor, *De sacramentis* 1.11.7 (*PL* 176:347–48); Gratian, *Concordia discordantium canonum*, ed. A. Friedberg, 2nd ed. (Leipzig, 1879), 1. dist.1.

19. "Verba autem legis naturalis illa sunt, quae Dei et proximi charitatem commendant, sicuti ista: *Quod tibi fieri non vis, alteri ne feceris* (*Tob.* IV, 16); et: *Quod vultis ut faciant vobis homines et vos facite illis* (*Matth.* VII, 12)." *Expositio in Epist. Pauli ad Rom.* 1 (*PL* 178:814).

20. *The Vision of William Concerning Piers the Plowman*, C.18.151–52, ed. W. W. Skeat (Oxford, 1886), 1:463.

21. *Roman de la Rose*, 9491–95 (*ed. cit.*, 2:39); see also *Consolation of Philosophy*, 2. m.5; Chaucer, "The Former Age" (*ed. cit.*, p. 534 and note, p. 859).

22. See, for example, Ambrose, *De officiis* 1.28.132 (*PL* 16:62); Isidore, *Etymologiae* 5.4; Gratian, 1. dist.8, pt.1, C.1; Johannes Teutonicus, *Glossa ordinaria* (Lottin, p. 23); William of Ockham, *Dialogus* 2.3.6.

23. *Canterbury Tales*, 10.920 (*ed. cit.*, p. 258).

24. See, for example, John of la Rochelle's contribution to the *Summa fratris Alexandri* 248 (Quaracchi, 1948), 4.2:350.

25. "Tria enim sunt tempora per quae praesentis saeculi spatium decurrit. Primum est tempus naturalis legis; secundum tempus scriptae legis; tertium tempus gratiae. Primum ab Adam usque ad Moysen." *De sacramentis* 1.8.11 (*PL* 176:312); see also Anselm, *Sententie diuine pagine* 5, and *Sententie Anselmi* (ed. Bliemetzrieder, pp. 35, 78–79).

26. ". . . ut legem naturalem per peccatum corruptam repararet." *Ysagoge in theologiam* 2, ed. Artur Landgraf, *Écrits théologiques de l'école d'Abelard* (Louvain, 1934), p. 132; see also *Summa sententiarum* 4.2 (*PL* 176:120).

27. See Macaulay's note on 5.1952 (*Works*, 2:519).

28. 5.7610; see Lester K. Little, "Pride Goes Before Avarice: Social Change and the Vices in Latin Christendom," *American Historical Review*, 76 (1971), 16–49.

29. Cf. *Roman de la Rose*, 13845–68 (*ed. cit.*, 2:171–72).

30. ". . . in concordia omnium rerum; et de tali iustitia naturali agit Plato in Thimeo: unum elementum non potest esse sine alio: unde, ut dicit Augustinus, iudicium divine largitatis est quod quelibet creatura compellitur dare seipsam." William of Auxerre, *Summa aurea* (Lottin, pp. 33–34); for Roland of Cremona and Hugh of St. Cher, see also Lottin, pp. 115–16.

31. The assumptions underlying Gower's sense of universal harmony are topoi quite variously formulated in writers such as Boethius, *Consolation*, 3. pr.11; John of Salisbury, *Metalogicon* 1.1, ed. Clemens C. I. Webb (Oxford, 1929), p. 6; and Chalcidius, *Timaeus a Calcidio translatus commentarioque instructus*, ed. J. H. Waszink, *Plato Latinus*, ed. R. Klibansky (London, 1975), 4:206.

32. In concentrating on bodily or "erthli" things in his treatment of Theorique, Genius describes what the elemental order of the universe contributes to the human constitution, and how the planets, the signs of the zodiac, and the stars bear special influence over geographical place, the human complexions, time, and other physical things. In *Li Livres dou Tresor*, Brunetto Latini likewise devotes little space to theology and writes extensively on the world of nature while discussing the theoretical arts, and he shirks none of the things the English poet considers—the complexions, the heavens, the *mapamounde*. But Brunetto incorporates more: he traces the history of mankind through its ages, describes great men of the past, writes at length on natural history, and even introduces architecture as a theoretical art. Because Gower is concerned in treating Theorique with topics that contribute to a clear image of how nature "determines" the course of human affairs, he avoids Brunetto's catalogue of beasts, for example, and shifts his emphasis to Astronomie, reminding us that without it, "All othre science is in vein / Toward the scole of erthli thinges" (628–29).

33. These meanings are conveniently catalogued by the decretists. Among the six meanings of *jus naturale* listed in the *Summa Lipsiensis*, for example, one may discover three of the above possibilities; see Lottin, p. 108.

34. "Pecora quidem coeunt, non tamen iure naturali, sed solo naturalis motus appetitu mouentur." Simon of Bisignano, in the selection edited by Lottin, pp. 106–07.

35. See Azo, *ed. cit.*, p. 34; Accursius, *In Institutiones* 1.2 (Venice, 1499), fol. 3vb; *Summa Vindobonensis*, ed. J. B. Palmerius (Bonn, 1913–14), p. 6; *Summa Institutionum 'Iustiniani est in hoc opere,'* ed. Pierre Legendre (Frankfurt-Main, 1973), p. 27; on the tendency of the civilians to accept Ulpian's definition and of the decretists to prefer those meanings where the law of nature is identified with reason, see the post-glossator Cinus of Pistoia, *In Digesti Veteris libros*, 1.1.1.

36. See, for example, Johannes Faber: "Non videtur quod sit de instinctu naturae matrimonium: sed coniunctio corporum sic quia natura adeo prona est ad

fornicationem, sicut ad matrimonium. . . . Ratio enim naturalis sic dictat, quod liberi per utrumque parentem, simul educari debeant, et erudiri, et ideo ne parentes incerti sint, ratio naturalis, et necessaria, dictat matrimonium." *In Institutiones commentarii* 1.2 (Lyon, 1557, reprt. Frankfurt-Main, 1969), 6v; W. Onclin cites other instances of this position in Accursius, Jacobus de Arena, and Albericus de Rosate, in "Le droit naturel selon les Romanistes des XIIe et XIIIe siècles," *Miscellanea Moralia in Honorem Arthur Janssen* (Louvain, 1949), pp. 336–37; see also Ennio Cortese, *La Norma Giuridica* (Milan, 1962–64), pt. 1:69–71.

37. One guilty of presumption, for example, "Nec sibi consimilem quem putat esse parem." *Works*, 2:86.

38. See, for example, 5.121–24, 6.1152–58, and 7.4215–17.

39. For a brief discussion of the development of the concept of grace in later books of the *Confessio*, see Patrick J. Gallacher, *Love, the Word, and Mercury* (Albuquerque, 1975), pp. 60–63.

40. Allan Gilbert, for example, found no source, though he suggested that "such a conception as Gower's five points . . . would probably have been derived from some treatise rather than devised by the poet himself." "Notes on the Influence of the *Secretum Secretorum*," *Speculum*, 3 (1928), 85–86.

41. "Omne quod est contra legem naturalem semper est et fuit culpabile; sed non semper fuit culpabilis coitus fratris cum sorore, sicut in principio; ergo non ex lege naturali est quod excipiatur [sic] frater et soror." John of la Rochelle, *Summa fratris Alexandri* 254 (ed. cit., 4.2: 359).

42. These terms are taken from Gower's marginal gloss at 8.1 (*Works*, 3:386).

43. See Philip the Chancellor, *Summa de bono*, and John of la Rochelle, *Summa de preceptis*, in the selections edited by Lottin, pp. 112–13, 120.

44. ". . . lex naturalis quoddam dictat quia debitum, quoddam vero quia decens et honestum. Lex ergo naturalis a matrimonio excepit fratrem et sororem, non quia debitum, sed quia honestum et decens, maxime in natura multiplicata, quia lex etiam, licet hoc in statu naturae non mulitiplicatae concederet, non tamen in statu naturae multiplicatae." John of la Rochelle, *Summa fratris Alexandri* 254 (ed. cit., 4.2:360).

45. ". . . honestas impudicicie motus obtemperans tam corporis quam anime mundiciam specialius preseruat." *Works*, 3:353.

46. ". . . sive ad decorem naturae, sive ad pudicitiae argumentum [sic]." Hugh of St. Victor, *De sacramentis* 2.11.4 (*PL* 176:483).

47. *De finibus* 2.14.45, trans. H. Rackham, Loeb Classical Library (New York, 1914), p. 133.

48. "Cur: propter quem finem. Solet autem triplex distingui finis, utile, honestum, delectabile. Multi committunt peccata propter utilitatem, multi propter delectationem; nullus potest committere peccatum propter honestatem." "Statutes of Bishop Alexander of Stavensby for the Diocese of Coventry and Lichfield (1229–37)," ed. F. M. Powicke and C. R. Cheney, *Councils and Synods* (Oxford, 1964), 2.1:224.

49. ". . . honeste delectacionis regimine moderari debet." *Works*, 3:382.

50. "Ad opera bona tria nos incitant, scilicet lex naturae, quae scripta est in corde hominis, dicens: *Quaecumque vultis ut faciant vobis homines, et vos facite illis*, etc. Ratio, quae dicit ea esse delectabilia, utilia et honesta. Gratia, quae dicit serviendum esse Deo, quia summe bonus: subveniendum proximo, quia Dei filius, quia imago Dei, quia in beatitudine socius. Gratia non datur ei, qui se non habilitat ad gratiam." *Compendium theologicae veritatis* 5.2, in Albertus Magnus, *Opera Omnia*, ed. A. Borgnet (Paris, 1890–98), 34:154.

I am grateful to Professor Siegfried Wenzel and the editorial board of *Medievalia et Humanistica* for reading this essay and offering many helpful suggestions; I also wish to thank the National Endowment for the Humanities and the University of Idaho Research Council for their financial support of this project.

SUGGESTIONS FOR FURTHER READING

1. Bibliographies

Robert F. Yeager. *John Gower Materials: A Bibliography Through 1979*. New York: Garland, 1981.

Albert E. Hartung, ed. *A Manual of the Writings in Middle English: 1050–1500*, Vol. 7. New Haven, Connecticut: Connecticut Academy of Arts and Sciences, 1986. [Contains a survey and a detailed bibliography of Gower studies by John H. Fisher, R. Wayne Hamm, Peter G. Beidler, and Robert F. Yeager, complete through approximately 1985.]

Peter Nicholson. *An Annotated Index to the Commentary on Gower's Confessio Amantis*. Binghamton, New York: Medieval & Renaissance Texts & Studies, 1989. [Includes a detailed survey of twentieth-century commentary on the poem.]

2. Book-length studies

William George Dodd. *Courtly Love in Chaucer and Gower*. Harvard Studies in English, vol. 1. Boston: Ginn, 1913. [An early attempt to assess the relation between love and morality in the *Confessio*.]

Maria Wickert. *Studien zu John Gower*. Köln: Üniversitäts-Verlag, 1951. Trans. Robert J. Meindl, *Studies in John Gower*. Washington, D.C.: University Press of America, 1981. [Mostly on the *Vox Clamantis*, but contains an important chapter on "Gower's Narrative Technique."]

John H. Fisher. *John Gower: Moral Philosopher and Friend of Chaucer*. New York: New York University Press, 1964. [Essential study of Gower's reputation, his biography, his literary career, and his relationship to Chaucer.]

Götz Schmitz. *The Middel Weie: Stil- und Aufbauformen in John Gowers "Confessio Amantis"*. Studien zur Englischen Literatur, Band 11. Bonn: Bouvier, 1974. [The study from which Schmitz' essay above is an excerpt.]

Patrick J. Gallacher. *Love, the Word, and Mercury: A Reading of John Gower's Confessio Amantis*. Albuquerque, New Mexico: University of New Mexico Press, 1975. [A study of the various manifestations of speech and "The Word" in the poem.]

Russell A. Peck. *Kingship and Common Profit in Gower's Confessio Amantis*. Carbondale, Illinois: Southern Illinois University Press, 1978. [Finds a correspondence between Gower's political themes and the plot involving the education of Amans.]

Alexandra Hennessey Olsen. *"Betwene Ernest and Game": The Literary Artistry of the* Confessio Amantis. New York: Peter Lang, 1990. [An attempt to apply modern linguistic and structuralist techniques to the study of Gower's poem.]

R.F. Yeager. *John Gower's Poetic: The Search for a New Arion.* Publications of the John Gower Society, II. Cambridge: D.S. Brewer, 1990. [A wide-ranging study of the structure and language of Gower's major works.]

3. *Essays and Articles*

W.P. Ker. "John Gower, Poet." *Quarterly Review*, 197 (1903), 437–58.

Peter Fison. "The Poet in John Gower." *Essays in Criticism*, 8 (1958), 16–26.

John McNally. "The Penitential and Courtly Traditions in Gower's *Confessio Amantis*." In *Studies in Medieval Culture*, ed. John R. Sommerfeldt. [Kalamazoo, Michigan]: Medieval Institute, Western Michigan University, 1964. Pp. 74–94.

Donald G. Schueler. "Some Comments on the Structure of John Gower's *Confessio Amantis*." In *Explorations of Literature*, ed. Rima Drell Reck. Baton Rouge, Louisiana: Louisiana State University Press, 1966. Pp. 15–24.

——. "Gower's Characterization of Genius in the *Confessio Amantis*." *MLQ*, 33 (1972), 240–56.

Paul M. Clogan. "From Complaint to Satire: The Art of the *Confessio Amantis*." *Medievalia et Humanistica*, n.s. 4 (1973), 217–22.

Anthony E. Farnham. "The Art of High Prosaic Seriousness: John Gower as Didactic Raconteur." In *The Learned and the Lewed: Studies in Chaucer and Medieval Literature*, ed. Larry D. Benson. Harvard English Studies, 5. Cambridge, Massachusetts: Harvard University Press, 1974. Pp. 161–73.

Thomas J. Hatton. "The Role of Venus and Genius in John Gower's *Confessio Amantis*: A Reconsideration." *Greyfriar*, 16 (1975), 29–40.

Kurt O. Olsson. "Rhetoric, John Gower, and the Late Medieval *Exemplum*." *Medievalia et Humanistica*, n.s. 8 (1977), 185–200.

Michael D. Cherniss. "The Allegorical Figures in Gower's *Confessio Amantis*." *Res Publica Litterarum*, 1 (1978), 7–20.

Paul Strohm. "Form and Social Statement in *Confessio Amantis* and *The Canterbury Tales*." *Studies in the Age of Chaucer*, 1 (1979), 17–40.

Rosemary Woolf. "Moral Chaucer and Kindly Gower." In *J.R.R. Tolkien, Scholar and Storyteller*, ed. M. Salu and R.T. Farrell. Ithaca, New York: Cornell University Press, 1979. Pp. 221–45.

Marie Collins. "Love, Nature and Law in the Poetry of Gower and Chaucer." In *Court and Poet*, ed. Glyn S. Burgess. ARCA, no. 5. Liverpool: Cairns, 1981. Pp. 113–28.

R.F. Yeager. "John Gower and the Exemplum Form: Tale Models in the *Confessio Amantis*." *Mediaevalia*, 8 (1982), 307–35.

A.J. Minnis, ed. *Gower's Confessio Amantis: Responses and Reassessments.* Cambridge: D.S. Brewer, 1983. [Contents: J.A. Burrow, "The Portrayal of Amans in *Confessio Amantis*"; Christopher Ricks, "Metamorphosis in Other Words"; Alastair Minnis, " 'Moral Gower' and Medieval Literary Theory"; Paul Miller, "John Gower, Satiric Poet"; Charles Runacres, "Art and Ethics in the *Exempla* of *Confessio Amantis*"; Elizabeth Porter, "Gower's Ethical Microcosm and Political Macrocosm"; Jeremy Griffiths, "*Confessio Amantis*: The Poem and Its Pictures"; and Derek Pearsall, "The Gower Tradition."]

Judith Davis Shaw. "*Lust* and *Lore* in Gower and Chaucer." *Chaucer Review*, 19 (1984), 110–22.

Olga C.M. Fischer. "Gower's *Tale of Florent* and Chaucer's *Wife of Bath's Tale*: A Stylistic Comparison." *English Studies*, 66 (1985), 205–25.

David Hiscoe. "The Ovidian Comic Strategy of Gower's *Confessio Amantis*." *PQ*, 64 (1985), 367–85.

Peter Nicholson. "The 'Confession' in Gower's *Confessio Amantis*." *Studia Neophilologica*, 58 (1986), 193–204.

Winthrop Wetherbee. "Genius and Interpretation in the 'Confessio Amantis'." *Magister Regis: Studies in Honor of Robert Earl Kaske*, ed. Arthur Groos. New York: Fordham University Press, 1986. Pp. 241–60.

Kathryn Lynch. "John Gower's Fourteenth-Century Philosophical Vision." In *The High Medieval Dream Vision: Poetry, Philosophy, and Literary Form*. Stanford: Stanford University Press, 1988. Pp. 163–98.

James Simpson. "Ironic Incongruence in the Prologue and Book I of Gower's *Confessio Amantis*." *Neophilologus*, 72 (1988), 617–32.

Hugh White. "Division and Failure in Gower's *Confessio Amantis*." *Neophilologus*, 72 (1988), 600–16.

R.F. Yeager, ed. *John Gower: Recent Readings*. Studies in Medieval Culture, vol. 26. Kalamazoo: Western Michigan University, 1989. [Thirteen essays, all but one on the *Confessio Amantis*, originally read at the annual meetings of the John Gower Society at the International Congress of Medieval Studies in Kalamazoo between 1983 and 1988.]